Connecting People with Jobs

Towards Better Social and Employment Security in Korea

OECD
BETTER POLICIES FOR BETTER LIVES

Please cite this publication as:
OECD (2018), *Towards Better Social and Employment Security in Korea*, Connecting People with Jobs, OECD Publishing, Paris.
http://dx.doi.org/10.1787/9789264288256-en

ISBN 978-92-64-28824-9 (print)
ISBN 978-92-64-28825-6 (PDF)

Series: Connecting People with Jobs
ISSN 2616-4132 (print)
ISSN 2616-4140 (online)

Photo credits: Cover Sergio77/Shutterstock.com.

Corrigenda to OECD publications may be found on line at: *www.oecd.org/about/publishing/corrigenda.htm*.

Foreword

Giving people better opportunities to participate in the labour market improves well-being and strengthens economic growth. Better labour market and social protection policies help countries to cope with rapid population ageing by mobilising potential labour resources more fully. Many OECD countries achieved record employment levels prior to the global financial crisis, but in all countries employment rates differ markedly across population groups. High unemployment, weak labour market attachment of some groups in society, and frequently unstable, poor-quality employment reflects a range of barriers to working or moving up the jobs ladder. In many countries the crisis has accentuated long-standing structural problems that are causing these disadvantages. It is a major challenge for policy makers in the coming years to address these problems and make OECD labour markets and, thus, OECD economies more inclusive.

Therefore, the OECD Employment, Labour and Social Affairs Committee is carrying out a set of reviews of labour market and social protection policies to encourage greater labour market participation and better employment among all groups in society with a special focus on the most disadvantaged, who face the greatest barriers and disincentives to finding good work. This includes a series of country studies, *Connecting People with Jobs*, which provide an assessment of how well activation policies help all groups to move into productive and rewarding jobs and a number of policy recommendations that could improve the situation.

This report on Korea is the fourth country study published in this series. It has a special focus on low-income jobseekers and low-income workers and policies geared towards closing the considerable gaps these groups are facing around income and employment support. The report was prepared by Hyeongso Ha, Christopher Prinz (project leader) and Marko Stermšek, economists in OECD's Skills and Employability Division. Statistical assistance was provided by Sylvie Cimper and Agnès Puymoyen and editorial assistance by Lucy Hulett and Katerina Kodlova. Comments were provided by Mark Keese, Veerle Miranda, Mark Pearson and Stefano Scarpetta. The report benefited greatly from discussions with experts and government officials during an OECD mission to Korea in late 2016, and comments on a draft version provided by several Korean ministries and stakeholders.

Table of contents

Tables

Figures

Boxes

Acronyms and abbreviations

ALMP(s)	Active Labour Market Programme(s)
AW	Average wage (full-time)
BIEN	Basic Income Earth Network
BLSP	Basic Livelihood Support Programme
CHF	Swiss francs
EAPS	Economically Active Population Survey
EI	Employment Insurance
EITC	Earned Income Tax Credit
ERA	Early Reemployment Allowance
ESPP	Employment Support Package Programme
EU	European Union
EUR	Euros
GDP	Gross domestic product
IACI	Industrial Accident Compensation Insurance
ISSA	International Social Security Association
KDI	Korea Development Institute
KLI	Korea Labour Institute
KOMWEL	Korea Worker Compensation and Welfare Service
KRW	Korean won
MISSOC	Mutual Information System on Social Protection
MOEL	Ministry of Employment and Labour
MW	Minimum wage
NEET	Not in employment nor in education or training
NOK	Norwegian kroner
NRR(s)	Net replacement rate(s)
PES	Public employment service
PPP	Purchasing power parity
SME(s)	Small and medium-sized enterprises
SRP	Self-Reliance Programme
SSA	Social Security Administration (United States)
USD	United States dollars

Executive summary

The government of Korea is determined to find ways to close considerable gaps in the country's social protection system and ensure adequate employment and income support for low-income jobseekers and the working poor. Current gaps are the combined result of a system that excludes some people outright and allows others to go undocumented and, therefore, without social protection coverage. This situation contributes to considerable inequality and poverty, reinforces widespread labour market duality and leads to poorer job outcomes alongside lower, less-inclusive economic growth.

Korea has gone through remarkable economic development over the past 40 years, rapidly catching up with the level of well-being in the average OECD country, and witnessing a fast social transformation. The labour market, however, has not kept pace with the development and continues to show a number of peculiarities that distinguish it from most other OECD countries. Most noteworthy are Korea's very high shares of self-employment and non-regular employment, especially among older workers, and employment in small businesses with short lifetimes that, in turn, result in very low job tenure for the average worker.

Over the past two decades, Korea has introduced and continuously improved a rather comprehensive welfare state with a strong focus on activation and employment. Nevertheless, features of Korea's labour market, which include a high degree of duality and a high level of informality, make it difficult for some measures to reach workers and jobseekers. As a result, Korea's Employment Insurance measure, for example, effectively covers only about half of the workforce. Half of those not covered are non-salaried workers while the other half includes workers who are formally excluded and those not enrolled although they should be. The latter mostly concerns dependent self-employed workers and undocumented workers employed in micro-businesses.

Many incremental welfare reforms, especially in the past ten years, have improved the situation. Important reforms include the possibility for self-employed people to opt into *Employment Insurance*; an effort to customise *Basic Livelihood Security Programme* payments to claimants' needs; the introduction and expansion of the *Employment Success Package Programme*, which provides targeted employment support and training as well as some income support to people not entitled to other benefits; and the introduction of an *Earned Income Tax Credit* to benefit the working poor with a recent expansion to self-employed people. These were important steps although the share of low-income jobseekers and low-wage workers not covered or supported by any measure remains stubbornly high. More could be done to extend welfare measures to them.

This report concludes that Korea is now at a critical stage of development. Significant additional action will be needed to diminish the ongoing gaps and make income and employment supports more effective and inclusive. Without additional steps, Korea will fail to realise the social and labour market outcomes it aspires to achieve.

Korea's social protection system is especially weak for workers facing health problems; an issue that receives limited attention in the public debate. Sick workers gain no statutory income support during the entire time they are sick, although those eligible for Employment Insurance benefits may defer their entitlement until they are well enough to look for work. Access to support for sickness in Korea requires cutting the employment relationship, burdening many of them with unnecessarily long periods out of work.

Moving forward, Korea must continue and accelerate the reforms of its labour market and social protection institutions to expand the reach of its social and employment support. Building upon recent changes, future reforms should strengthen the enforcement of existing legislation; further expand existing measures; and bring in new measures as necessary; while ensuring in all cases that strong activation and positive employment outcomes remain a key focus.

Concretely, the OECD recommends to policy makers in Korea to:

- Boost Employment Insurance coverage by making it mandatory for self-employed workers and expand income support to workers leaving their job voluntarily (with a benefit sanction replacing the current disqualification penalty).
- Better enforce Employment Insurance rules by i) expanding the resources of the relevant monitoring authorities to observe and sanction offending employers, and ii) promoting and rigorously applying the arbitration procedure through which non-insured workers can claim Employment Insurance entitlements.
- Improve the situation of workers with health problems by introducing i) a degree of statutory employer liability for all workers, and ii) a cash sickness benefit, matched by a strong focus on rehabilitation and return to work.
- Maximise the impact of the effective Employment Success Package Programme by increasing its number of participants and improving the quality of services, especially among private providers.
- Ease access to the Basic Livelihood Security Programme including by gradually phasing-out the family support obligation and improving its effectiveness for conditional benefit claimants.
- Boost support for the working poor through the Earned Income Tax Credit by further increasing both the number of people covered and the size of the credit, in harmony with other measures, including the minimum wage.

The effect of any such actions will be stronger if Korea also makes further efforts to address widespread labour market duality and eliminate incentives to hire workers on non-regular employment contracts or to engage dependent self-employed workers.

Assessment and recommendations

A strong economy but a fragmented labour market

Korea has gone through remarkable economic development over the past 40 years. Korea's export-led, manufacturing-driven growth strategy has yielded faster economic growth than virtually anywhere else in the world, rapidly diminishing the gap between Korea and the OECD average in GDP per capita terms. Parallel to its rapid economic transformation, Korea has witnessed a considerable social transformation towards becoming one of the world's most highly educated societies alongside rapid population ageing as a result of low fertility and rising life expectancy.

The labour market, however, has not kept pace with this fast development. Many Koreans struggle with jobs of poor quality and low social protection. A strong focus on labour market flexibility has served larger companies and export-oriented industries well. However, such gains have been distributed unevenly between the individuals employed in such companies and those affiliated with them through outsourcing and subcontracting. Labour regulations and agreements are geared towards protecting permanent jobs but often fail to provide for those in less regular employment situations.

The Korean labour market has a number of characteristics that distinguish it from those in most other OECD countries: a) a high share of workers employed in small and micro-businesses, especially in low-productivity services; b) a high share of self-employment (more than 20% of the workforce); c) a short average survival rate of small businesses (with only around half of them surviving for more than four years); and d) short job tenure for the average worker (with one in three workers having less than one year of job tenure, and one in two among those in small firms – the highest share in the OECD).

These labour market characteristics are related to the deep segmentation in Korea between regular and non-regular jobs and explain the high prevalence of labour market "outsiders" who have not benefited to the same degree from the country's fast economic growth. This has led to considerable disparities among certain groups of non-regular workers, own-account workers and those not able to work long hours, especially sick or disabled people. In addition, female labour force participation is low and women are highly over-represented in poorly-paid non-regular jobs, leaving Korea with one of the biggest gender wage and gender employment gaps in the developed world.

To fulfil Korea's growth potential, these labour market problems will have to be addressed and both job quality and social protection improved. In particular, the situation of own-account workers and employees of small businesses will have to be tackled as they face low wages, short job tenure and weak social protection. People who lose their regular job often become trapped in such forms of employment. Changing this situation will require concerted action by the government and social partners on various policy fronts some of which – such as the situation of redundant workers or that of older workers – have been addressed by other OECD reports.

This report looks in more depth at the policies and institutions that contribute to better and more widespread social protection, labour market inclusion and job quality in Korea. In particular it looks at the effectiveness of four government programmes:

- The *Employment Insurance* (EI) programme, which provides contributory unemployment benefits for eligible jobseekers who lose their job involuntarily;
- The *Basic Livelihood Security Programme* (BLSP), which provides means-tested, non-contributory social assistance for people living below the poverty line;
- The *Employment Success Package Programme* (ESPP), which is a form of employability support with a non-contributory benefit component (means-tested for some but not for others); and
- The *Earned Income Tax Credit* (EITC), which provides in-work support for both salaried and non-salaried workers who earn a low income.

In addition, the report looks at the situation of Koreans struggling with health problems and temporary work incapacity, a group that often falls between the cracks. This is an issue that receives too little attention in policy circles and in the public debate.

Social protection reforms have generated strong momentum

Headline labour market statistics in Korea highlight many positive trends. Employment rates are on an increasing path and have reached the OECD average of 66% of the working-age population. The unemployment rate, at just over 3.5%, is among the lowest for an OECD country while long-term unemployment – a big problem in many OECD countries – is virtually non-existent. These positive outcomes, however, must be seen against the background of a system that provides relatively limited protection to those without a job. For many in Korea, unemployment entails no entitlement to income or employment support. Under such circumstances, jobseekers are compelled to accept any available job as quickly as possible, which contributes to the enduring existence of poor-quality jobs and the persistent fragmentation of the labour market.

Survey data suggest that the share of workers in Korea who benefit from social support when they lose or choose to change a job is much lower than in other OECD countries – lower than 10%, compared with around 20% in Australia and the United Sates and over 30% in Canada, for example. Data also suggest that Korea's social protection measures do much less to lift people out of relative income poverty. Moreover, the data show that people with health problems fare particularly badly. All of these findings are related directly to the limited accessibility and scope of public income support in Korea.

Korean policy makers have not been idle. Continuous reforms enacted during the past decade have sought to introduce both a broader safety net and more effective employment support for jobseekers while improving the effective coverage and enhancing the support available for both low-income workers and jobseekers. These reforms have mostly focused on: a) offering EI to a wider group within the labour force; b) better customising BLSP entitlements to beneficiaries' needs; c) introducing targeted ESPP for low-income jobseekers and vulnerable groups; and d) introducing and gradually expanding in-work support through EITC, the statutory minimum wage and other measures.

Reforms have been successful in offering better support to ever more Koreans: EI, BLSP, ESPP and EITC caseloads have increased continuously in the past decade. Nevertheless, the principal ongoing issue social and labour market programmes in Korea encounter are their limited take-up and coverage. Combined together, Korea's four main working-age benefits (EI, BLSP, ESPP and EITC) were received by almost 4 million individuals in 2015 – equivalent to around 10% of the working-age population. While this represents important gains made, the overall number still appears somewhat low considering that more than 13 million Koreans of this age are inactive or unemployed while another 7 million are employed but earning less than a full-time statutory minimum wage.

Despite strong progress, therefore, each of the four main measures has further to go:

- EI eligibility criteria have expanded several times since the measure was introduced in 1995. In principle, EI now covers virtually all employees (including non-regular and daily workers) on a compulsory basis while self-employed persons (employers and own-account workers) can choose to opt in. In practice, however, only 53% of the entire labour force in Korea is entitled to EI. The rest include three principal groups: self-employed people who almost never choose to insure; a large group of workers who should be insured but go undocumented and miss out on coverage (especially among small enterprises); and those legally not entitled to support, including contributing family workers.
- BLSP today covers around 3.2% of the population, following major changes in 2015 to expand coverage and better customise payments to households' needs. However, the family support obligation – a unique Korean feature that implies the earnings and assets of a claimant's children and parents are also taken into account in determining entitlement – continues to exclude an estimated half of all potential beneficiaries.
- ESPP was introduced in 2009 to help jobseekers who are not entitled to EI and not receiving BLSP but facing considerable disadvantages, especially in the form of low income. The eligibility criteria have since been expanded to include not only low-income jobseekers but other disadvantaged groups, elderly jobseekers earning below the median wage and youth. The fast-increasing number of ESPP participants currently encompasses about 300 000 per year although there is still potential to expand the programme to a multiple of this.
- EITC was introduced in 2008 to benefit low-income workers and their families. Entitlement now covers regular and non-regular workers as well as, since 2015, self-employed persons. Currently about six in ten EITC recipients are non-permanent employees while around 25% more are self-employed. With a total number of over 900 000 recipients, EITC coverage may still be considered low relative to Korea's 7 million workers earning below 50% of the average wage. EITC's low income threshold and low take-up rates, especially among the self-employed, contribute to this shortcoming.

Improving social protection

Korea has made significant progress over the past 25 years to develop and expand its social safety net. In doing so, it took many of the experiences from other OECD countries on board and successfully avoided many of their mistakes. Most importantly, Korea managed to maintain strong work incentives while keeping dependence on social benefits low. This was achieved by introducing, as part of each new measure, a strong focus on activating jobseekers alongside relevant employment services. It was also achieved, to some extent, by setting benefit levels relatively low and keeping entitlement criteria strict. In combination with a low tax on income from labour, this means that work generally pays in Korea while waiting on a benefit is neither attractive nor easy to achieve.

Strong activation measures are in place for jobseekers entitled to EI; they have clear job-search obligations and are closely monitored by Employment Centres. Under BLSP, the link between social transfers and activation has also been strengthened over the years and seems stronger in Korea than in many other OECD countries. BLSP recipients with work capacity (as assessed by the pension insurance authority on request of a local welfare office) receive a *conditional* payment and must get in touch with their local Employment Centre for case-managed counselling including, if necessary, support to address financial and social problems and potential participation in ESPP.

Despite a strong activation framework and rising beneficiary rates, Korea's approach can be improved. *First*, much of the spending on active labour market measures goes to direct job creation programmes. This leaves little funding for other measures. Direct job creation programmes were shown to do little to help jobseekers into private-sector employment and have been downsized considerably or even abolished in most other OECD countries. *Second*, total spending on social benefits is low relative to other OECD countries. Despite continuous expansion of the welfare state by expanding programmes and introducing new ones, total public social spending in Korea is only half the level of the average OECD country and just one-third of the level of most European countries including France and Italy. For those covered by the measures in place in Korea available support may be sufficient but many workers and jobseekers do not receive any support.

Korea is now at a critical crossroads. If it wants to strengthen its safety net and improve job quality for a larger part of the working-age population, significant additional action will be needed. Critical choices will have to be made on what programmes or measures to expand without damaging the strong work incentives currently in place. Experience from many OECD countries has shown that it can be difficult to find the right balance between entitlements and obligations, especially for low-income groups. Moreover, future projections suggest that public social spending will increase rapidly in the coming decades in line with Korea's changing demographic realities and because the system will gradually mature. This makes it important that better outcomes are achieved for the monies currently spent and new action is funded in a sustainable way.

Continuing EI, BLSP, ESPP and EITC reforms

Korea must continue and maybe accelerate incremental reform of its labour market and social protection institutions to expand the reach of its social and employment support. Blind spots in social protection coverage exist, to some extent, in every OECD country as a result of the coverage conditions they impose. However, the impact of these blind spots on overall unemployment protection is greater in Korea than elsewhere since the excluded groups represent a much larger share of the total labour force.

Boosting EI coverage

Key issues for Korea's EI include the low voluntary registration of self-employed persons, low registration and effective coverage of those working in small businesses and the exclusion of contributing family workers and other groups of non-regular workers.

Fuller EI coverage is important in Korea because: a) those who receive EI benefits are well supported in their job search by the Employment Centres; b) their efforts are closely monitored, with weekly counselling meetings; c) special support is offered for those who have low employability or lack motivation; and d) benefit deferrals are available for jobseekers in case of temporary work incapacity due to sickness. All this contributes to better job matches and better social and economic outcomes.

A number of OECD countries manage to extend employment insurance coverage to some of the workers currently legally omitted or effectively excluded in Korea. These countries' examples light the way for broader coverage in Korea under EI. Workers who leave their jobs voluntarily, for example, gain unemployment benefit coverage in many OECD countries, though typically with a period of benefit suspension. Korea is relatively strict in this regard, disqualifying most jobseekers deemed to be voluntarily unemployed.

Self-employed persons may opt in for EI coverage on a voluntary basis, though this approach has not resulted in significant coverage rates in Korea nor elsewhere. Several OECD countries therefore have mandatory EI registration for self-employed workers, sometimes excluding those with very low income or employers with a certain number of employees. Greece and Slovenia are two countries that have switched from voluntary to mandatory coverage for self-employed persons. Mandatory coverage would be especially important for the many rarely insured dependent self-employed workers in Korea, whose income is concentrated on one client and who are hardly different from salaried workers. Mandatory coverage for as many of the labour force as possible has the great advantage that more people would be brought in contact with the Employment Centre and offered employment services, thus, be helped into better jobs and better careers.

With further expansion of EI, attention should be paid to maintaining its high efficiency. Where broader EI coverage results in higher EI revenues, scaling up may be possible without a change in premium rates – provided the new groups face a similar average risk of unemployment. An expansion of the system to cover voluntary unemployment to some degree, however, might require a premium increase.

Enforcing EI regulations

A relatively high rate of undocumented work in Korea has resulted in low EI coverage among a group of employees who, by all rights, ought to be covered. Some 4 million employees were excluded from EI coverage in this way in 2016 – about 23% of all employees in the private sector aged below 65 – most of them in smaller enterprises.

The situation of workers in this "effective blind spot" can only be improved through better enforcement of EI regulations and stricter monitoring of employers' responsibility to enrol their workers in social insurance. This may require stricter penalties for those who flout the rules. It may also require tightening the reporting requirements of employers for non-regular workers and harmonising them across all types of workers.

Stricter enforcement of existing EI rules may also require boosting the resources of the tax authorities and the labour inspectorate to monitor enterprises to ensure all workers and labour costs are properly documented. Korea's labour inspectorate currently has very limited resources to fulfil such a monitoring role. Employers are rarely sanctioned for not registering their workers while the penalties involved are too low to be considered a real deterrent. Recent research has shown that 80% of informal employees in Korea are accounted for by non-compliance with existing labour standards and laws while only 20% can be attributed to actual exclusions observed within the law.

Maybe surprisingly, most workers in Korea are covered by *Industrial Accident Compensation Insurance* (IACI): More than 17.5 million workers are IACI-insured while only 12.5 million are EI-insured. The recent shift in responsibility for EI registration, as of January 2017, to the Korea Workers' Compensation and Welfare Service – which is now responsible for both EI and IACI registrations – should help in expanding EI coverage to all those workers who should rightly be affiliated under both measures.

Stricter enforcement of EI legislation would not only secure fair coverage for those who should be entitled but also ensure fair competition among employers. Reneging on EI contributions by neglecting to document workers, after all, offers an unfair competitive advantage that can add pressure on otherwise lawful employers to do the same.

In this regard, more could be achieved through one key feature of EI (already in place since its inception in 1995) that enables undocumented workers to claim the entitlements they should have been due. Undocumented workers for whom EI contributions have not been made but who are otherwise entitled to its support (by having lost their job involuntarily; and fulfilled at least 180 days of work within an 18-month period) can request a "confirmation of insured status" from their local Employment Centre. If their claim is assessed as valid, such jobseekers pay the EI and national pension contributions they should ordinarily have paid during their undocumented employment (for up to a maximum of three years) in exchange for entitlement to EI benefits. Under such circumstances, the employer (or employers) who hired but neglected to document such workers are mandated to pay the corresponding part of their EI and national pension contributions (also up to three years) plus a one-off fine of KRW 30 000 per worker.

If promoted and applied more rigorously, this procedure has considerable potential to boost employers' compliance with their formal obligations under EI. Currently, every year only up to about 1 000 workers benefit from this regulation. This number could increase very significantly if more workers knew of the procedure. The compliance of employers could also be strengthened if the cost they could encounter was higher: by, for example, mandating them to pay *all* of the unpaid insurance contributions (including the employees' part) under such circumstances or imposing a more meaningful fine. Expanding EI entitlement to voluntarily jobseekers, as proposed above, would further increase the effectiveness of this procedure to punish wrongful employers.

Using EI funds more effectively

The *Social Insurance Premium Subsidy Programme* covers part of the EI contribution of low-income workers in small companies and their employers. Such subsidies are funded through general government expenditure and paid on a permanent basis. They provide an added incentive for small employers to register their workers formally and comply with their social insurance obligations. The programme has contributed to some increase in EI coverage although the associated deadweight costs are large. Targeting the subsidy more closely and phasing it out after some time could improve the programme's effectiveness. More rapid phase-out periods could apply to higher earners or to larger enterprises.

The significant deadweight cost associated with the premium subsidy programme would become less of an issue if the confirmation-of-insured-status procedure was strengthened under EI. The message to employers would then become very clear: registering workers for EI is obligatory and will be monitored closely; small companies and low-paid workers will be supported through subsidies; but those who continue to neglect to document their workers will incur significant costs, ex post and irrespective of the reasons for job loss, through a swift, effective, well-publicised arbitration process.

The *Early Re-employment Allowance* (ERA) enables EI beneficiaries returning to work before their benefits are exhausted to receive a lump-sum payment, calculated as a share of their remaining EI entitlement. Given the relatively low EI benefit payment duration and the near inexistence of long-term unemployment in Korea, this measure is costly and not very effective as suggested by past evaluations. For instance, ERA is used mostly by men in their 30s and 40s who find new employment easily. It may be more effective to invest these funds into closer monitoring of small and medium-sized enterprises to make sure they document workers and their wages and comply by EI rules. Abolition of ERA is currently being considered and a bill is pending at the national assembly.

There is also a need for the Korean government to act on the EI benefit structure and payment level. At the time of its introduction, EI payments replaced 50% of jobseekers' previous wages, with minimum and maximum payment levels set at around 20% and 80% of the average wage, respectively. Over time, this margin has narrowed (because the floor is linked to the minimum wage and the ceiling changed discretionarily) turning EI into a virtually flat-rate payment of KRW 46 584-50 000 per day for all beneficiaries. This shift has changed the nature of the system. Compared with other OECD countries' floor and ceiling amounts, the EI benefit floor in particular emerges as strikingly high.

Looking ahead, Korea has several options:

- *To turn EI into a genuine flat-rate payment*: If fixed at 90% of the minimum wage, this would be the highest-value flat-rate unemployment benefit in the OECD. At 50% of the average wage, the benefit would be similar to the average payment in many countries with contributory unemployment benefit measures and still relatively high for low-wage earners. If the planned minimum wage increase materialises, the payment would be higher than the benefit ceiling in most of the other OECD countries (relative to their average wage).
- *To re-establish EI's original insurance rationale*: This would require delinking the EI floor from the minimum wage and raising the floor and the ceiling in the future in line with the average wage. To re-establish the situation back in 1995, the benefit floor would have to be lowered to around 33% of the current minimum wage and the ceiling set to roughly 150% of its current level.
- *To introduce a stronger insurance element than is currently the case but keep the link between the EI benefit floor and the minimum wage*: Such a solution could include one or several of the following elements: a) lowering the benefit floor back to 70% of the minimum wage, as was the case when EI was introduced, or lower than this; b) rising the formula replacement rate from its current 50% of previous gross earnings to something closer to 80%; and c) rising the benefit ceiling to a fixed multiple of the floor.

The government could also consider delivering EI benefits in five instalments per week as is done in Finland and Sweden, for example, instead of in seven as is currently the case. This would effectively spread the payments out over a longer period but offer EI more flexibility to maintain the current daily benefit minimum and maximum levels. This reduction could offset the large predicted increase in the benefit floor (in line with the forthcoming increase of the minimum wage) while increasing the potential duration EI can be claimed for – which is rather short by international standards – by an equivalent amount, thus potentially leaving premium rates unchanged.

It is a political choice which of these different routes to follow. Each way comes with different economic and social implications and might entail different degrees of public acceptance. For example, high benefit floors or high flat-rate payments can weaken the work incentives of low-income groups considerably. Genuine or effectively flat-rate payments, like those made today, weaken the insurance principle and put in question the financing structure; such type of EI payment is normally better funded from taxes than insurance premiums. And increases in the benefit ceiling or the aspired replacement rate will most likely require a corresponding increase in the premium rate.

Expanding access to BLSP

Recent BLSP reform has addressed many of the measure's previous weaknesses through smoother taper rates and the use of different income thresholds for the measure's four main components (living benefit, medical benefit, housing benefit, education benefit). BLSP benefits are now better customised to individual needs; eligibility has been broadened; and work incentives have been improved.

Probably the biggest remaining bottleneck for broader coverage under BLSP is the family support obligation: a rule – specific to BLSP – by which not only the income of the applicant's household is means-tested to determine eligibility for support but also that of any children and parents not living in the same household. This rule creates significant inequality and poverty as it does not depend on whether relatives actually provide any care or income support and is unfit for purpose in an increasingly individualistic society where values have changed. There is a strong case for further easing (and eventually phasing out) the family support obligation, as was done in other OECD countries that previously had comparable rules including Austria, Belgium or France; in Germany, a similar rule is still operated but only in cases where relatives actually provide regular payments. Abolishing the family support obligation could potentially double or more than double the BLSP caseload, according to some estimates. A further expansion of the caseload seems justified given the relatively low share of working-age individuals who receive BLSP. Nevertheless, older people would probably benefit the most from a lowering and elimination of the family support obligation.

Any expansion of BLSP coverage should ensure to continue the strong activation of *conditional* claimants. To this effect, social, welfare, health and financial services could be better harmonised to address all labour market barriers. Ideally this should be done under the responsibility of the Employment Centres, to ensure that the necessary services reach beneficiaries with the highest needs. The current co-location of various counselling services and dispatching of local welfare officers, who remain under local government control, is only a second-best solution. It bears the risk for beneficiaries to be handed over from one service body to another, diluting the necessary focus on employment promotion.

Further expansion of BLSP eligibility conditions should bring more low-income jobseekers with work capacity under the measure. Further monitoring and strengthening of job-search requirements of these conditional BLSP recipients – by, for example, harmonising them with the behavioural requirements of EI recipients – would help make the entire process more efficient. It is important in this regard to enforce conditionality and job-search requirements for all BLSP household members of working age, as foreseen in the legislation, not only the main applicant or household head.

Maximising the impact of activation under ESPP

ESPP is a well-designed labour market programme targeting jobseekers not entitled to EI, especially those with low incomes, thus capturing some of those moving in and out of unemployment and low-paid, precarious work. ESPP offers customised job-search support and, if necessary, training. Intervention is structured in three phases lasting a total of 9-12 months and unsuccessful jobseekers can reapply after 3-30 months.

ESPP fills the large gap between EI and BLSP in a rather effective way, with a potential target group of, initially, close to 4 million people (all working-age individuals with an income below 60% of the median) and possibly many more given that more recently some discretionary target groups (youth and certain vulnerable groups including lone parents and disabled people, among others) can participate without a means test. ESPP eligibility has been broadened continuously since its introduction in 2009 and the caseload has increased accordingly. Nevertheless, there is still considerable room for further expansion of, perhaps, 3-5 times the current number of participants.

A significant further expansion of the programme will require a corresponding increase in the number of ESPP counsellors as well as continuous quality improvements. The latter will require: a) additional resources to reduce the current caseload of 100-120 participants per counsellor nearer to the lower number in the first years of the measure; b) better training for counsellors; and c) more ambitious targets on employment outcomes for each Employment Centre, varied according to the local economic situation and the degree of participants' disadvantage or distance from the labour market.

Strengthening private employment service provision under ESPP

The recent expansion of ESPP has encouraged many new private providers of employment services to emerge. While low-income and disadvantaged groups are currently served by public Employment Centres, ESPP services for all other participants (including in particular youth) are subcontracted to private providers.

The measurement of provider performance could be broadened further to ensure only the most effective providers delivering a high-quality service remain in place. Like in Australia's *Star-Rating System*, provider placements and outcomes could be made public with regression adjustments taking client characteristics and the state of the local labour market into account. Meanwhile, the short duration of private providers' contracts should be reconsidered: at just one year in length, Korea's short contracts are likely to hinder longer-term investment in specialised competencies among providers. Australia and the United Kingdom, for example, have shifted towards contracts for private providers lasting several years following such an experience.

Another question is whether the chosen split in participants between public Employment Centres and private service providers is efficient and can be maintained under any future expansion of ESPP. Australia and the United Kingdom, again, have chosen to outsource employment services irrespective of participants' vulnerability or disadvantage as it is not clear public providers would necessarily serve them better nor in a more cost-effective way. Both countries keep the monitoring of behavioural conditions and participation requirements exclusively under the control of public authorities, however. Under an expanding ESPP caseload, such an approach could also be worth considering for Korea.

Developing ESPP into an unemployment assistance measure

One option for ESPP would be to expand eligibility conditions and its payment level in such a way as to reach out in a more comprehensive way to jobseekers ineligible for both EI and BLSP benefits. One concrete proposal made along these lines by the Korea Labor Institute suggests a "Korean-style unemployment assistance scheme" could reach twice ESPP's current number of participants (jobseekers earning less than 60% of the median income) and provide a benefit worth 20% of the average wage for up to 12 months. This would certainly be one valuable way to expand ESPP. The current government has plans to take steps into this direction, with higher benefits in a first step provided to youth participating in ESPP and at a later stage, from 2020 onwards, also to other groups.

How widely ESPP can be expanded in terms of scope and coverage entirely depends on what additional public investments are willing to be made. Evidence suggests that ESPP significantly improves employment outcomes among all types of participants, including the most disadvantaged, and in a cost-effective way. An expanded ESPP measure could eventually reach all jobseekers earning below 60% of median income, irrespective of their employment history, delivering to them income support, customised employment support and opportunities for training.

ESPP has a number of features in common with unemployment assistance measures found in other OECD countries, including its benefit component and means-testing requirements. Nevertheless, unemployment assistance measures only exist in a minority of OECD countries and their characteristics vary considerably: some target new labour market entrants predominantly while others are oriented towards jobseekers that have exhausted their entitlement to contributory unemployment benefits. Similarly, benefits in some countries may be paid indefinitely but only for a limited period (typically up to one year) in others. The main aim of an expanded ESPP measure might be to bring effective employment services to more people in dire need of them, alongside a modest benefit component. The ESPP's current design reflects this goal very well.

ESPP's current income support is relatively low (about 10-15% of the median wage, taking all payments into account) and its structure strongly geared towards promoting employability and lasting employment outcomes. This payment structure should be maintained if participation is further expanded in order to keep work incentives high. Raising the payment level, however, will be necessary both to increase the motivation of people to actively participate in the measure and to ensure participating households gain adequate income support. A fixed-rate benefit worth 20% of median income for all participants could be a good starting point and would be in line with similar payments provided in other OECD countries – although the short duration of participation in ESPP could enable higher payments. Indeed, in no other OECD country is the gap between the minimum unemployment insurance benefit and the unemployment assistance benefit (where such benefit exists) as large as in Korea. This implies a strong case for Korea for lowering the EI benefit floor in exchange for higher ESPP payments.

Increasing support for in-work poverty

Better supporting low-income jobseekers will be important for Korea but not sufficient. More can be done to boost support for Korea's working poor, most of whom are own-account or non-regular workers and many of them in older age. Today, 60% of Korea's working poor (defined as everyone earning less than 60% of the median wage) receive no public assistance at all and 80% are not covered by EI.

EITC was introduced in 2008 to provide some support for such workers in the form of a tax credit, with the credit initially varying by the number of children in a family. In 2014, a separate *Child Tax Credit* (CTC) was introduced and EITC modified to only vary by the number of earners in the family. In 2015, EITC was expanded to include self-employed persons. The take-up of EITC, however, is still low because it is closely targeted to the lowest-income families and phased out completely already at the level of 50% of average household income. Moreover, for those eligible the tax credit itself is also low, amounting to an average claim worth only about 2% of the average wage per year.

Take-up of EITC should be promoted more actively among groups not sufficiently covered by other measures. Korea's tax authorities already collect excellent records on this and may be well placed to more proactively enlist workers entitled to EITC but not claiming it. In addition, EITC take-up of low-income households could also be increased through modified assets tests while smoother taper rates would maximise the work incentives of qualifying households.

EITC is not the only labour market institution geared at helping workers make ends meet. The Korean government has announced to increase the statutory minimum wage from its current KRW 51 760 per day, for 2017, to KRW 80 000 by 2020. The average daily wage for a regular salaried worker in Korea, by comparison, was KRW 92 100 in August 2016, according to the *Economically Active Population Survey*. Such a rapid increase in the minimum wage by 2020 would represent a compound average rise of 15.6% per year – probably fast outpacing the growth of Korea's average wage and increasing the ratio between the two to above its current 50-55%. Such a significant increase will bring a rapid pay rise to Korea's formal low-wage workers, with likely knock-on effects for those in the informal sector, too, as other countries have experienced.

Although its benefits may be debated, a minimum wage increase of such magnitude will have important consequences on social protection measures further down the line. It is, therefore, important for policy makers to investigate and fully understand the direct interactions EI, BLSP and EITC have with the minimum wage.

If the increase in the minimum wage and further promotion and expansion of EITC fail to reduce in-work poverty to the intended extent, BLSP could also provide a stronger top-up for low-income working households. Providing in-work benefits through a central social assistance measure of this kind is, indeed, a common practice in many OECD countries.

Helping sick workers stay in employment

Korea's social protection system is especially weak for workers who encounter temporary work incapacity due to acute or chronic health problems. Korea is among a small minority of OECD countries without a statutory (or a coherent privately-regulated) cash sickness benefit measure to help this group.

Limited support may reach sick workers in Korea, under two sets of circumstances. *First*, jobseekers who encounter sickness when they are already receiving EI benefits – and are thus prevented from looking for a new job – can continue receiving EI until the end of the regular entitlement period. *Second*, workers working in an EI-affiliated job who are forced to quit because of a sickness can postpone their EI claim for up to a maximum period of four years until they are well enough to look for work. They are not entitled to any income support during this period but can delay the start of their claim period until after they have recovered. Entitlement criteria are relaxed somewhat for these workers who can qualify for EI when "it is difficult for them to perform their job due to lack of physical strength, mental and physical disability, illness or injury".

Less than 20 000 people every year profit from these two regulations, however. The large majority of workers gain no support in Korea in case of sickness or temporary work incapacity. None will gain any income support for as long as they are in employment and those who want to retain their jobs have virtually no avenue of support open to them. Consequently, many may not regain their original job and face difficulties in entering a new one and, thus, often face long periods out of work. This is likely to have a negative impact on i) their wellbeing and recovery, further delaying their return to work and entrenching an overall loss of productivity, as well as ii) the labour market and the economy, as these workers and their capacities remain unused or underutilised.

The experience of many other OECD countries has demonstrated such workers find it much easier to return to their original positions (or take on another role with their original employer) than to gain an altogether new employment. Therefore, every effort should be made to improve job retention of workers experiencing health problems. Introducing a period of liability for sickness upon employers would go a considerable way in mitigating the chances of a return to work. Further introducing a statutory cash sickness benefit – either under an expanded mandate for EI or as a stand-alone social protection measure – would increase the chances workers with health problems have of staying in work.

Employers in most OECD countries are liable for part of the risk associated with temporary work incapacity among their workers. In most countries, such obligations cover between a week and a month of absence or, in some cases, much longer (for example, up to 36 weeks in Italy and up to two years in the Netherlands). During this time, employers are obliged to pay all or part of their absent workers' wages. Introducing such a mechanism in Korea could secure a minimum level of protection for all salaried workers. Regulating workers' minimum entitlement to payments in case of sickness would end the large discretion employers currently have over this area, thus acting to reduce labour market duality. Such mechanism would also safeguard the jobs of hitherto disadvantaged workers who would otherwise have lost them under such circumstances.

Cash sickness benefits are provided in almost all OECD countries in addition to a period of employer liability. In most countries, such benefits are contributory (financed from premiums collected from both employers and employees) and form part of a common insurance fund: either a broader health insurance fund; a broader employment insurance fund; or as a stand-alone measure with its own individual fund. Though all three kinds of arrangements exist in OECD countries, most operate cash sickness benefits through their general health insurance plans.

For Korea, this approach could provide a more level playing field for all workers, given the high coverage rates already achieved under the existing health insurance measure. Nevertheless, perhaps the most straightforward option for Korea would be to link cash sickness benefits directly with EI, as Canada and Ireland do, and use the existing EI infrastructure to administer it. This would be a big advantage for salaried workers in Korea by providing them the support they need for their recovery and, thereafter, enabling them to return to their original jobs instead of having to re-enter the labour market afresh. Such a solution, however, would make it even more important to broaden EI coverage to a larger share of the working population.

Under all scenarios it would be important that any new cash sickness benefit measure is coupled with a robust rehabilitation component, which includes tools to help recovering workers to return to work; clear protocols defining the rights of workers and employers as well as doctors and insurance authorities; and regular work capacity reassessments.

Korea's progress on implementing smooth and effective social protection measures over the past 20 years has been exemplary. Starting from a very low base around the time of the Asian Economic Crisis, Korea's social protection institutions now provide income and employment support to millions of households in need. What is more, Korea has successfully navigated many of the pitfalls other OECD countries have faced – not least in light of its highly robust approach to activation. Taking this powerful momentum forward, Korea is now very well placed to go further: addressing its remaining coverage gaps; strengthening the implementation of what is already legislated for; and designing effective new ways to address the many troubles faced by workers who become sick and, upon recovery, help ensure their timely return to work.

Key recommendations

The Korean government should consider taking the following policy actions:

- Expand EI coverage further by: a) seeking effective ways to ensure coverage of self-employed workers, especially dependent self-employed, possibly by making EI contributions mandatory for this group; and b) retaining EI entitlement for workers who leave their jobs voluntarily, including a benefit suspension for a suitable period instead of disqualifying them outright.
- Better enforce EI regulations by: a) expanding the resources and mandate of the relevant authorities to help ensure all workers are formally documented and offending employers sanctioned; b) promoting and rigorously applying the use of EI's arbitration procedure through which initially undocumented workers can claim their EI entitlements retrospectively; and c) sharing information by the tax authority and the Korean Workers' Compensation and Welfare Service to bring EI coverage in line with the higher coverage rates already achieved by IACI.
- In the light of a reconsideration of recent EI developments: a) decide on the future structure of payments – whether to return to earnings-related EI benefits or instead turn to a purposefully flat-rate measure; b) make the Social Insurance Premium Subsidy Program more targeted and temporary; and c) abolish the ineffective Early Re-employment Allowance.
- Improve the situation of workers with health problems by: a) introducing a statutory employer liability of several weeks for workers' sick pay; b) introducing a cash sickness benefit, perhaps integrated into a somewhat broader EI measure and implemented through its existing infrastructure; and c) matching the new benefit with a strong focus on rehabilitation and return to work.
- Maximise the impact of ESPP by: a) continuously increasing the number of people participating by promoting the programme among low-income jobseekers and providing higher income support; b) increasing the number of ESPP counsellors and providing them with better training; and c) improving the performance measurement framework for local Employment Centres.
- Strengthen private ESPP service provision by: a) expanding services in line with increases in the ESPP caseload; b) possibly reconsidering the current split in responsibilities between private providers and public entities; and c) expanding the duration of contracts with these providers while strengthening guidance and performance assessment.
- Ease access to BLSP by: a) phasing out the family support obligation; b) strengthening the activation approach for conditional BLSP recipients; and c) better co-ordinating and integrating social, welfare, health, financial and employment services, under the responsibility of the Employment Centres.
- Help the large group of working poor by: a) actively reaching out to people who should be eligible so as to expand EITC coverage to a wider range of poor people; b) investigating the implications of the planned increase of the minimum wage on labour market outcomes and on EI, EITC and BLSP; and c) if in-work poverty remains high, promoting the use of BLSP as a top-up to low income.

Chapter 1. Korea's economic and labour market situation

This chapter provides a concise overview of labour market trends and challenges in Korea. It describes how Korea's vast economic and social development has shaped its labour market over the past five decades. The analysis highlights Korea's predominance of micro-enterprises with low productivity; widespread culture of subcontracting practices; high incidence of non-regular work; and the impact of these phenomena on labour market dualities and ongoing weaknesses around job quality and labour market inclusiveness. The chapter also discusses the challenges vulnerable groups – particularly women, youth and older workers – face within the labour market.

The statistical data for Israel are supplied by and under the responsibility of the relevant Israeli authorities. The use of such data by the OECD is without prejudice to the status of the Golan Heights, East Jerusalem and Israeli settlements in the West Bank under the terms of international law.

Economic and labour market development in Korea

Economic growth and remaining challenges

Korea has made tremendous progress over the past five decades. Overcoming extreme poverty and destruction during the Korean War of the early-1950s, Korea became the world's 12th largest economy and the 7th largest exporter in 2015. Real economic growth in Korea has somewhat slowed down over this time, though it was the highest of any OECD country for long periods of time during the 1970s, 1980s and early-1990s and still remains higher than the OECD average (Figure 1.1, Panel A). Per capita income rose from 15.3% of the OECD average in 1970 (controlling for purchasing power parities) to 61.5% in 1996 – the year Korea joined the OECD. By 2016, this figure had risen to 91.9%, placing Korea 19th from the top among the 35 OECD countries (Figure 1.1, Panel B).

Figure 1.1. Korea's economic development has been impressive

Percentages (Panel A) and thousands of US dollars (USD) at constant prices and 2010 PPPs (Panel B)

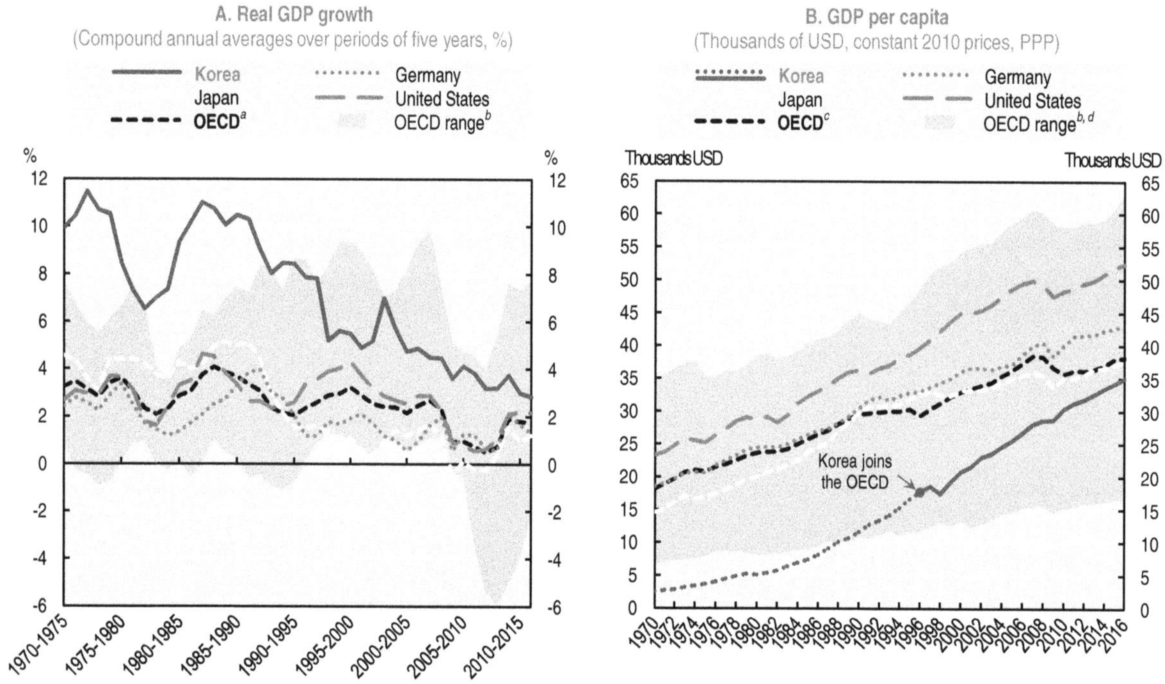

Note: GDP: Gross domestic product. PPP: Purchasing power parity.

a) Weighted average of the 35 OECD countries.

b) Shaded area highlights the minimum and maximum values of OECD countries (excluding Korea).

c) Maximum figure excludes Luxembourg, which attained a GDP per capita of USD 90 600 in 2016.

d) Unweighted average of OECD countries, excluding non-members in any given year.

Source: OECD Annual National Accounts Database, Main Aggregates, "Table 1. Gross domestic product (GDP), Gross domestic product (annual)" [Variable VOB: Constant prices, OECD base year, National currencies, 2010 (expenditure approach)] for Panel A, http://stats.oecd.org/index.aspx?queryid=9185 (accessed on 29 September 2017); and Main Aggregates, "Table 1. Gross domestic product (GDP): GDP per head, US $, constant prices, constant PPPs, reference year 2010" [Variable Gross domestic product (expenditure approach)] for Panel B, http://stats.oecd.org/index.aspx?queryid=60707 (accessed on 29 September 2017).

StatLink http://dx.doi.org/10.1787/888933644547

Korea's economic growth has also entailed significant social progress. Health and education outcomes have improved especially fast. Life expectancy at birth in Korea rose by 23.5 years between 1970 and 2014 – the largest increase in the OECD countries. Korea's population has become more educated with 45% of persons aged 25-64 having completed tertiary education in 2015 – considerably higher than the OECD average of 35%.

Such a rapid process of economic development over the past five decades has shaped Korea's industrial and labour market characteristics. During the 1960s, industrialisation was driven by an export-led growth strategy that attracted the most productive resources into the manufacturing sector. Manufacturing enjoyed a number of advantages including a devalued currency and various fiscal incentives. Following a decade of unprecedented economic growth, the government decided in 1973 to shift from general export promotion towards a more targeted approach focusing on heavier industries and chemicals manufacturing. This enabled Korean exports to maintain strong growth despite increased competition for light manufactures from other emerging economies. This broad strategy led to the development of a highly competitive manufacturing sector in Korea, dominated by large firms, alongside a relatively less productive services sector dominated by small and medium-sized enterprises (SMEs) (OECD, 1994[1]).

Starting in around the early 1990s, Korea began to face still greater competition from emerging economies – and China, in particular – coupled with rising wages at home. In response, large firms began to outsource various production processes to lower-cost SMEs in order to boost price competitiveness and refocus internal processes on technology-intensive, higher value-added tasks. The Asian Economic Crisis of 1997 further accelerated the subcontracting processes and enlarged the wage gap between SMEs and larger enterprises (Kim, 2015[2]).

Today, Korea's export-led economy competes not only with emerging East and South-east Asian rivals but also with more advanced economies in higher-end markets. Domestic demand, on the other hand, is constrained by structural factors. Household debt, for example, has risen steadily in Korea from 40% of GDP in 1990 to around 90% by 2016. Stagnant productivity within the services sector and struggling SMEs have also weakened domestic demand in Korea (Zoli, 2017[3]).

Figure 1.2 shows that Korean companies with fewer than 300 employees accounted for larger shares of non-agricultural employment than anywhere else in the OECD. While SMEs accounted for a relatively common 45% of total value-added in manufacturing, they accounted for a much higher 85% among services sectors – by far the highest of any OECD country – in 2013. The overabundance of SMEs in Korea's services sector has contributed to their low productivity and, ultimately, to low job quality. Addressing this could bring not only economic gains but also strengthen social outcomes in Korea.

Labour market trends and remaining challenges

Korea's labour market has also undergone profound changes during the past five decades. Starting from a relative abundance of low-skill, rural self-employment, Korea's population now engages in much more highly-skilled work dominated by industry and services. The share of Korean workers employed in agriculture, forestry and fishery declined from 63% in 1963 to 5.2% in 2015. Meanwhile, the share of workers in the services sector including construction and SOC increased from 28.3% to 77.5%. The share of those employed in mining and manufacturing reached a peak at 28.5% in 1988, gradually declining ever since to 17.3% by 2015, in line with other OECD countries.

Figure 1.2. SMEs employ the majority of Korea's workforce, especially in the services sector, but their productivity is low

Contribution of SMEs to total employment and total value added, manufacturing and services sectors, 2013 or latest year available (%)

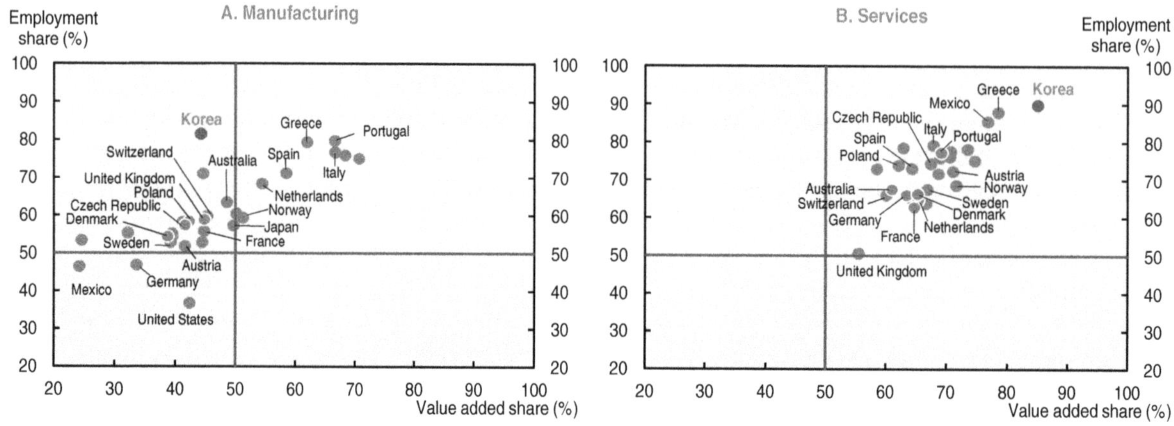

Note: SMEs include firms with 1-249 employees (1-200 for Australia, and 1-300 for Canada, Japan and Korea). Data cover the business economy, excluding financial intermediation. Value-added data refer to *value added at factor costs* in European countries and *value added at basic prices* for non-European OECD countries. Data for Canada, Israel, Japan, Korea, Switzerland and the United States exclude own-account workers. Data for Korea and Mexico refer to establishments. Data for the United Kingdom exclude an estimated 2.6 million small unregistered businesses. Data are for 2013 except Ireland (2011); Japan (2012); and Canada, Israel, Korea and Mexico (2014).

Source: OECD Structural and Demographic Business Statistics (SDBS) *Database*, http://dx.doi.org/10.1787/sdbs-data-en.

StatLink http://dx.doi.org/10.1787/888933644566

The employment rate among those aged 15-64 has risen steadily in Korea over the past two decades from 57% in 1986 to 66.3% in 2016 – just a fraction below the OECD average of 67% (Figure 1.3, Panel A). Better mobilising under-utilised labour resources, especially of women and youth, will be critical not only to increase overall employment, but also to mitigate the difficult economic transition population ageing will be likely to require in the coming decades.

Rapid economic growth reduced the unemployment rate in Korea from 8% in the early 1960s to roughly 2-4% from around the late-1980s to the present day (except for a brief spike that reached 7% at the height of the Asian Economic Crisis). More recently, Korea's labour market has proven to be particularly resilient in the wake of the Global Financial Crisis compared with many other OECD countries (Figure 1.3, Panel B).

A unique characteristic of the Korean labour market is the very low incidence of long-term unemployment. The share of those unemployed for 12 months or longer was only 0.9% in Korea in 2016, compared with an OECD average of 30.5% (Figure 1.3, Panel C). The fact that so many jobseekers move back into work relatively quickly in Korea partly reflects a positive range of opportunities workers find. Nevertheless, at least part of the underlying reason Korea has such low long-term unemployment has to do with a lack of income support for unemployment, which leaves many jobseekers with no alternative other than to settle for a job as quickly as possible, regardless of its quality or the career prospects it might offer. Another underlying reason is that many jobseekers ultimately leave unemployment within the first year by exiting the labour force altogether – and, hence, enter a period of inactivity rather than employment (OECD, 2013[4]).

High rates of inactivity remain a key challenge for Korea's labour market. At 31.3% in 2016, Korea's inactivity rate was some three percentage points above the OECD average – about one percentage point above for men and five points for women (Figure 1.3, Panel D).

Figure 1.3. Key labour market indicators have developed favourably in Korea although inactivity remains high

Employment, unemployment, long-term unemployment and inactivity rates in selected OECD countries, 1980-2015 (percentages)

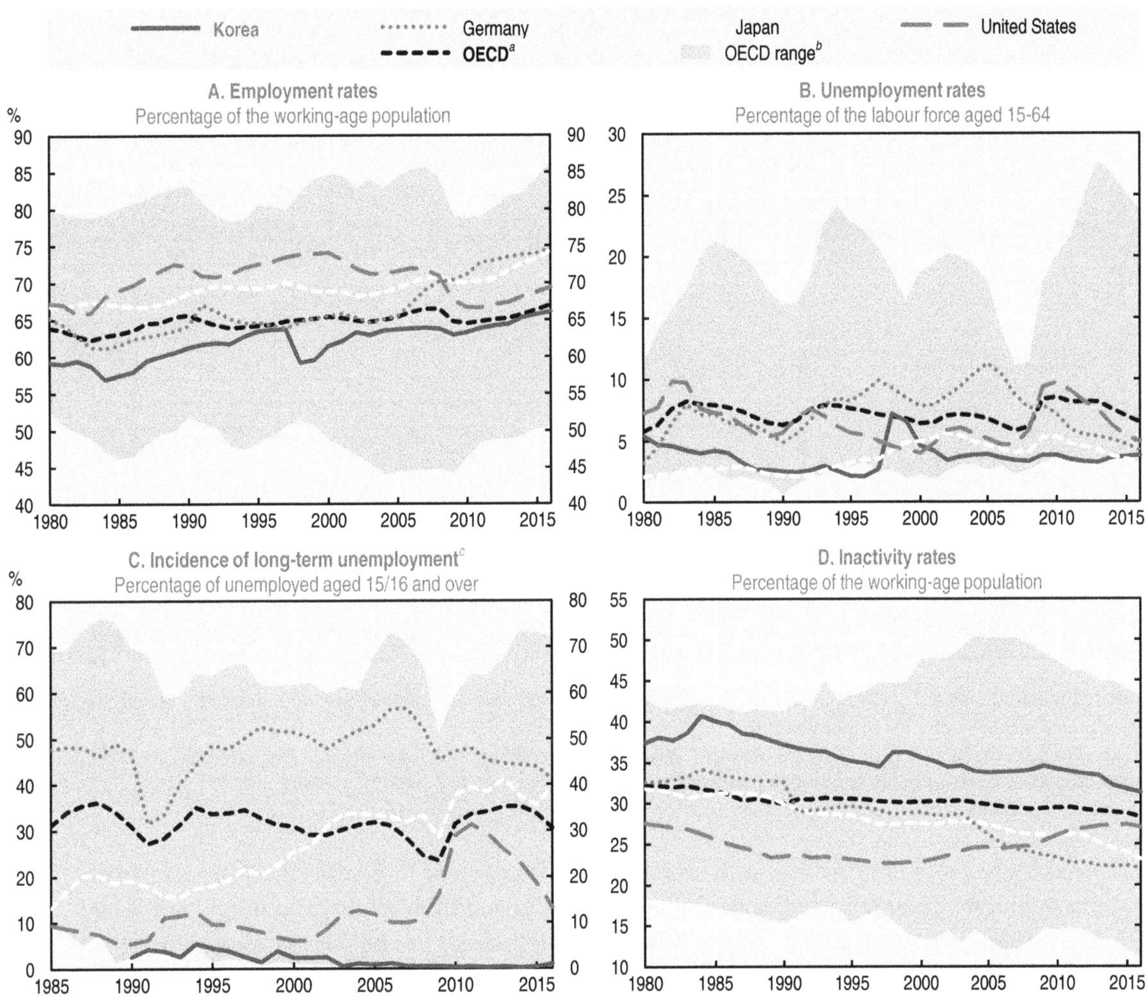

a) Weighted average of OECD countries.

b) Shaded area highlights the minimum and maximum values of OECD countries (excluding Korea).

c) Data refer to people unemployed for 12 months and more.

Source: OECD Employment Database, www.oecd.org/employment/database.

StatLink http://dx.doi.org/10.1787/888933644585

Labour market structure

Perhaps the most distinctive characteristic of Korea's labour market is the combination of a high share of self-employment and the over-representation of non-regular workers in very small firms that are relatively unstable and unproductive. Such features of the labour market exacerbate labour market dualities and earnings inequality among different groups of workers in Korea.

Figure 1.4 shows a comprehensive breakdown of Korea's total employment by status in employment. In 2016, 26.0% of Korea's total employed population were engaged as non-salaried workers: 15.5% of them working on their own account; 6.0% as employers; and 4.5% as unpaid family workers. Of the remaining 74.0% of total employment, around one-third were engaged as non-regular salaried workers: 8.4% of them on non-typical employment contracts; 9.4% working for 35 hours per week or less; and 13.8% engaged on a non-permanent basis.

Figure 1.4. Total employment in Korea has a diverse breakdown

Total employment in Korea by status in employment, 2016 (number of persons and share of total, %)

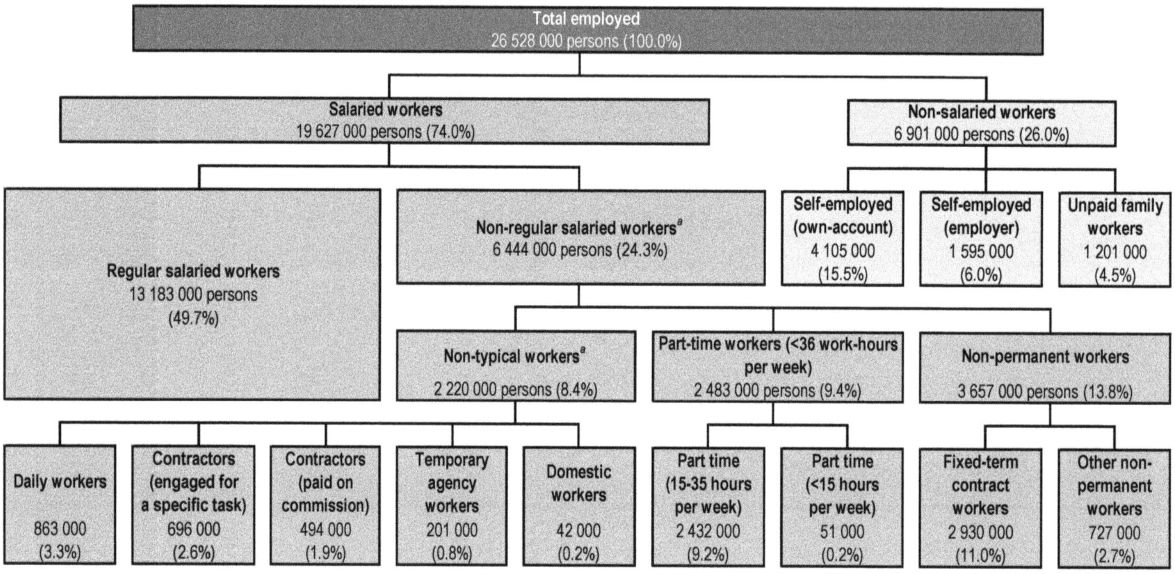

Note: Data include all workers (in both public and private enterprises) aged 15 and above. Numbers in parentheses give the relevant share of the total employed population.

a) Total numbers of "non-regular salaried workers" and "non-typical workers" are smaller than the sum of their consistent parts, due to some overlap in the sub-categories provided.

Source: Statistics Korea (2017), Economically Active Population Survey, August 2016.

Such a diverse labour market in Korea entails a number of important dualities that often result in very divergent outcomes for individuals around job quality, earnings and social protection. The remainder of this sub-section evaluates some of the main characteristics and trends that some of Korea's key dualities entail.

Dualities between salaried and non-salaried workers

The Korean economy has yet to develop sufficiently enough to absorb its large number of non-salaried workers into more regular salaried employment. An abundance of non-salaried workers in Korea – including own-account workers, employers and contributing family workers – has emerged in tandem with the proliferation of micro-enterprises. The share of non-salaried workers in Korea's total employment fell from 61.0% in 1970 to 25.5% by 2016. This remains much higher than the OECD weighted average of 15.3% in 2015 (Figure 1.5, Panel A).

The widespread practice of early retirement from the main job around the age of 45-50 also contributes to the abundance of micro-enterprises in Korea. Many middle-aged and elderly workers in Korea become self-employed upon reaching a mandatory age of retirement with their employer (or taking a form of early-retirement commonly known as "honorary retirement"). According to the *Economically Active Population Survey*, 54.3% of business-owners in Korea were previous salaried workers; 24.0% non-salaried workers; and 21.7% previously non-employed in 2015. The self-employed aged 50 years or more accounted for 62.8% of total self-employment in Korea in 2015 (Figure 1.5, Panel B).

Figure 1.5. Self-employment is declining gradually in Korea but still remains concentred among older workers

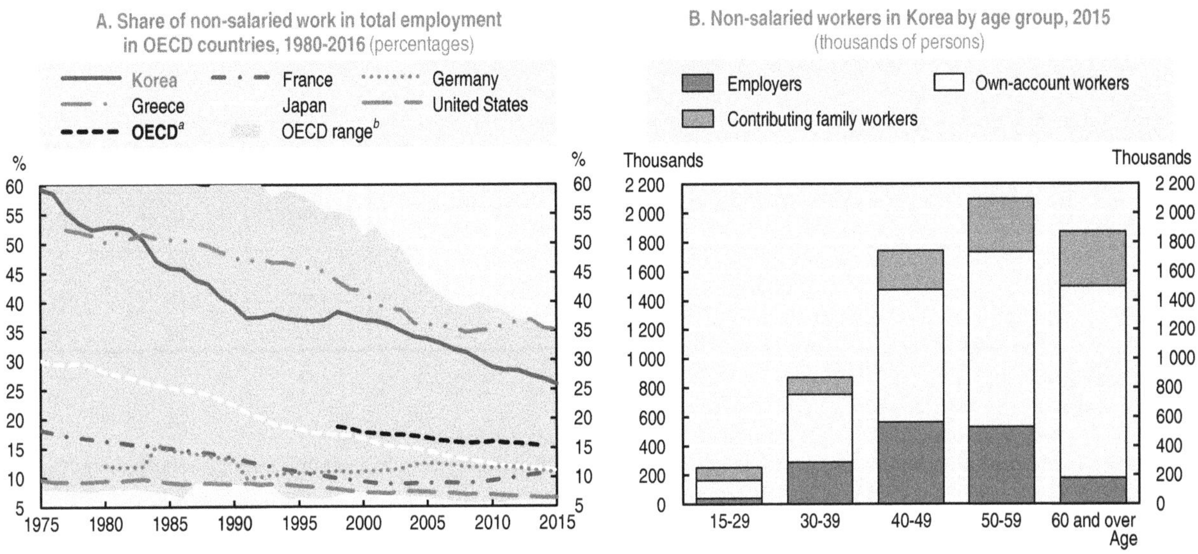

Note: Self-employment includes own-account workers, employers, members of producers' co-operatives, and unpaid family workers. Data for Germany are interpolated for the years 1984-90.

a) Weighted average of OECD countries.

b) Shaded area highlights the minimum and maximum values of OECD countries (excluding Korea).

Source: OECD (2017), "Labour Force Statistics: Summary tables", *OECD Employment and Labour Market Statistics* (database), http://dx.doi.org/10.1787/data-00286-en, Self-employment rate (indicator), http://dx.doi.org/10.1787/fb58715e-en (accessed on 16 May 2017) for Panel A; and Statistics Korea (2015), "Additional Economically Active Population Survey for Non-wage Workers", Korean Statistical Information Services for Panel B.

StatLink http://dx.doi.org/10.1787/888933644623

Dualities between regular and non-regular workers

Korea's labour market displays some clear and very strong dualities. The clearest manifestation of labour market duality in Korea is the high prevalence of non-regular workers who account for a little over one-third of all salaried workers. Non-regular workers' pay and working conditions are considerably less attractive than those of regular salaried workers (Table 1.1). While the share of non-regular employment has remained quite stable since 2003 at around 32-36%, those among them who work part-time increased quite substantially from 19.0% to 38.5% between 2005 and 2016.

Labour market duality is also a major cause of income inequality in Korea. In 2016, non-regular workers were paid 34.6% less per hour than regular salaried workers, even though their skills are broadly the same (OECD, 2015[5]). The wage gap between regular and non-regular salaried workers has gradually increased since the early 2000s and mobility between the two is very low. International comparisons show that temporary workers in Korea appear to be more at risk of becoming trapped in temporary employment or becoming unemployed than their counterparts in other OECD countries (OECD, 2013[6]).

Table 1.1. Non-regular workers account for about one-third of all salaried workers in Korea and they earn much less than regular salaried workers

A. Salaried workers by status in employment[a]

Year	Salaried workers	Non-regular workers		Of which[b]					
				Non-permanent workers, with			Part-time workers	Non-typical workers	
				Fixed-term contract		Open-ended contract[c]		Dispatched	Others[d]
2003	14 149	4 606	*32.6*	2 403	*52.2*	*13.3*	*20.2*	*2.1*	*34.3*
2009	16 479	5 754	*34.9*	2 815	*48.9*	*12.1*	*24.8*	*2.9*	*36.8*
2016	19 627	6 444	*32.8*	2 930	*45.5*	*11.3*	*38.5*	*3.1*	*31.3*

B. Hourly wages of non-regular salaried workers relative to regular workers

Index "Regular worker" = 100

Year	Regular workers	Non-regular workers	Of which[b]				
			Non-permanent workers, with		Part-time workers	Non-typical workers	
			Fixed-term contract	Open-ended contract[c]		Dispatched	Others[d]
2003	*100.0*	*71.6*	*70.7*	*69.1*	*85.1*	*68.0*	n.a.
2009	*100.0*	*61.5*	*65.5*	*58.2*	*56.2*	*69.7*	n.a.
2016	*100.0*	*65.4*	*69.6*	*66.0*	*59.1*	*67.4*	n.a.

n.a.: Not available.

a) Thousands of workers and percentages (shown in blue italics).

b) The sum of the categories of non-regular workers exceeds 100% due to double-counting.

c) Workers whose employment contract term is not fixed but whose employment can continue through repeated renewals of the contract or is not expected to continue due to involuntary reasons.

d) The category *Others* corresponds to three additional types of non-typical employment: independent contractors, daily workers and domestic workers. The hourly wage index for *Others* in Panel B is an employment weighted average for these three employment types.

Source: Statistics Korea, Economically Active Population Survey (EAPS), Supplementary Results of the EAPS by Employment Type (August), for Panel A; and Korea Labor Institute (2016), "2016 KLI Labor Statistics of NRWs" for relative earnings and OECD estimates based on the Ministry of Labor (MOEL) Survey on Labor Conditions by Type of Employment, for Panel B.

StatLink http://dx.doi.org/10.1787/888933645326

Interactions between non-regular work and small firm size

Non-regular work in Korea is largely concentrated in micro-enterprises with relatively low productivity. Indeed, 48.7% of non-regular workers are employed in micro-enterprises with fewer than 10 employees and 72.1% of them in small firms with fewer than 30 employees. Since the incidence of non-regular work is much higher in micro-enterprises and those within the services sector (Table 1.2), there is considerable overlap between the two forms of labour market duality (OECD, 2013[6]).

Larger firms in Korea often prefer subcontracting out work to SMEs than hiring non-regular workers directly. This enables them to maintain low labour costs while enhancing business flexibility. Micro-enterprises, on the other hand, are more likely to hire non-regular workers to reduce their labour costs since subcontracting is usually not a viable option. The fact that nearly half of all non-regular workers in Korea are concentrated in micro-enterprises makes it more difficult for workers to build their way up into more secure, better-paid jobs in larger firms.

Table 1.2. There are very clear differences between regular and non-regular workers within Korea's labour market

Regular and non-regular workers in Korea by individual and firm characteristics, 2016 (%)

	Regular workers	Non-regular workers	Total (all salaried workers)
Age			
15-29 years	18.7	20.5	19.3
30-59 years	76.1	56.7	69.7
60+ years	5.2	22.8	11.0
Gender			
Men	61.5	45.1	56.1
Women	38.5	54.9	43.9
Educational attainment			
Completed middle school or less	7.3	23.9	12.8
Completed high school	35.3	44.3	38.3
Completed tertiary or higher	57.3	31.8	48.9
Occupation[a]			
Assembly and elementary workers	30.5	47.9	36.2
Administrators and managers	27.0	17.1	23.7
Clerks	26.8	10.6	21.5
Others	15.7	24.5	18.6
Economic activity			
Manufacturing	25.5	8.5	19.9
Wholesale and retail	12.2	9.7	11.4
Construction	5.3	11.8	7.4
Other sectors	57.0	70.0	61.3
By size of establishment			
1-9 employees	29.6	48.7	35.9
10-29 employees	22.1	23.4	22.5
30-299 employees	32.3	22.7	29.2
300+ employees	16.0	5.2	12.4
Tenure			
Average tenure	7 years and 5 months	2 years and 5 months	5 years and 9 months
Coverage by social insurance			
Employees' Pension Scheme	82.9	36.3	67.6
Employees' Health Insurance	86.2	44.8	72.6
Employment Insurance	84.1	42.8	69.6

a) Top three occupations for regular workers. The category *administrators and managers* includes engineers.
Source: Statistics Korea (2016), Supplementary Results of the Economically Active Population Survey by Employment Type in August 2016.

StatLink http://dx.doi.org/10.1787/888933645345

The concentration of non-regular workers in small enterprises is a major source of earnings inequality in Korea (Figure 1.6). Average wage levels are much higher among larger enterprises for both regular and non-regular workers, with the impact of firm size being somewhat stronger for non-regular workers (OECD, 2013[6]).

Figure 1.6. Pay is significantly higher for regular workers and workers in large firms

Average earnings in Korea by employment type and firm size, 2016 (thousands KRW)

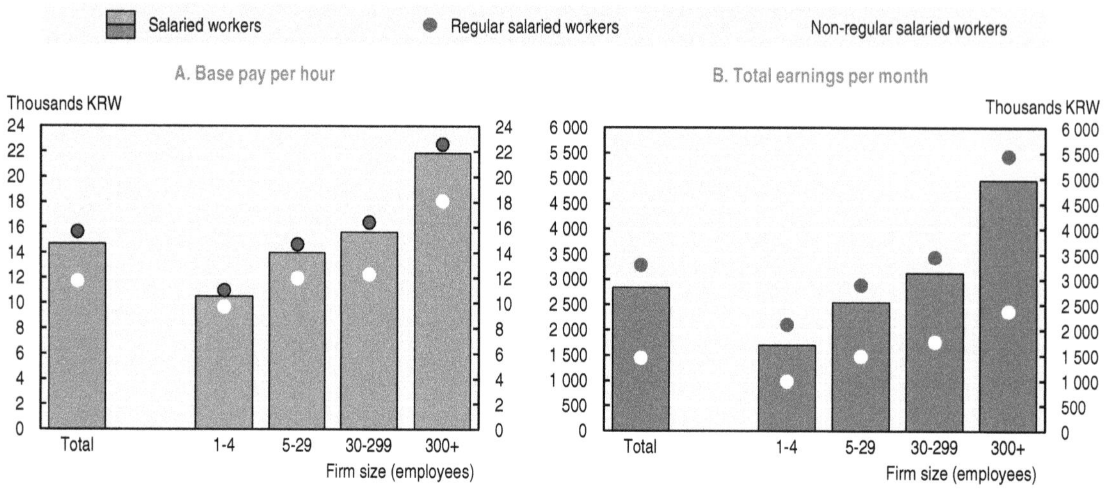

Source: OECD estimates using MOEL (2017), Survey Report on Labor Conditions by Employment Type, http://laborstat.molab.go.kr/newOut/renewal/menu05/menu05_search_popup.jsp, Table "Age, Days, Hours, Payments, Workers by Size, Education, Age".

StatLink http://dx.doi.org/10.1787/888933644642

Indeed, the gap between the wages paid by SMEs and those paid by larger firms is considerable in Korea and has increased continuously over time. Average waged in firms of different sizes were relatively similar during the 1980s, with workers in medium-sized enterprises of 10-39 workers earning within 90%, on average, of what those in the largest enterprises of 300 or more workers were paid. Average wage levels diverged rapidly after that, creating considerable discrepancies among firms of different sizes (Figure 1.7).

Figure 1.7. Wages in Korea's smaller companies have fallen far behind the rest

Average hourly base pay in Korea by establishment size, 1993-2016 (KRW in constant 2015 prices)

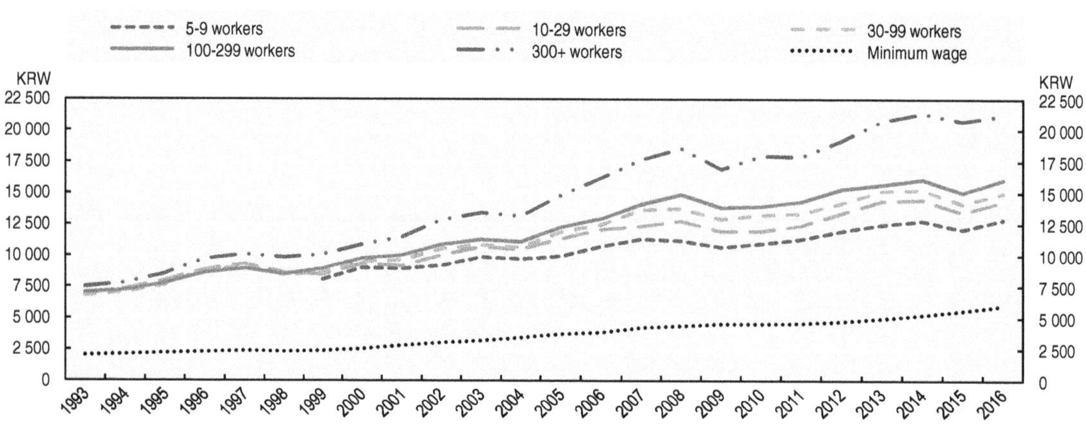

Note: Data refer to real average base pay per regular hour worked in 2015 prices. Data have been deflated using the KOSIS consumer price index (2015 = 100).

Source: Ministry of Employment and Labor, Survey Report on Labour Conditions by Employment Type, http://laborstat.molab.go.kr/newOut/renewal/menu05/menu05_search_popup.jsp, Table "Age, Days, Hours, Payments, Workers by Size, Education, Age".

StatLink http://dx.doi.org/10.1787/888933644661

The combination of firm size and status in employment also results in an elevated incidence of low-paid work in Korea – making it the third highest OECD country after the United States and Ireland. Korea also has one of the highest overall ratios between the top and bottom earnings deciles, third only to the United States and Israel (Figure 1.8).

Figure 1.8. Low-paid work is more frequent in Korea than in most OECD countries and earnings inequality is higher

The incidence of low-paid work[a] and earnings dispersion[b] in OECD countries, 2015 or latest year available[c]

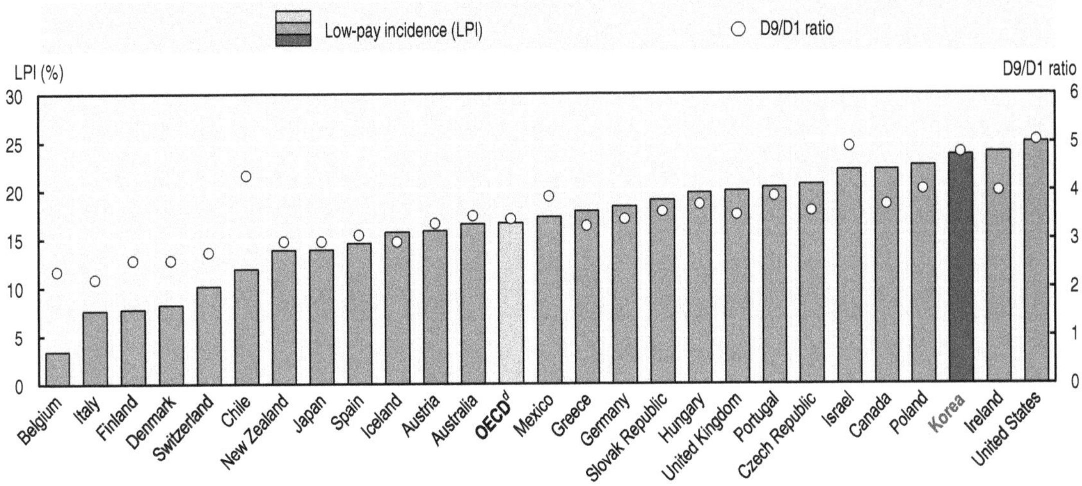

a) The incidence of low pay refers to the share of workers earning less than two-thirds of median earnings.
b) Earnings dispersion is measured by the ratio of 9th to 1st deciles limits of earnings.
c) Data refer to 2015 except: Israel (2011); Spain (2012); and Australia, Belgium, Germany, Greece, Iceland, Italy, Japan, Korea, New Zealand, Poland, Portugal and Switzerland (2014).
d) Unweighted average of the countries shown.

Source: OECD Earnings Distribution Database, www.oecd.org/employment/emp/employmentdatabase-earningsandwages.htm.

StatLink http://dx.doi.org/10.1787/888933644680

Further dualities between smaller and larger firms

Only 13.6% of workers in Korea were employed in large firms with 300 or more employees in 2014. On the other hand, 41.3% of employees work in micro-enterprises (i.e. those with fewer than 10 employees). Work in such enterprises can often be characterised by low wages; a precarious employment status; large gaps in social insurance coverage; and a near-total absence of trade unions (Figure 1.9).

Large firms in Korea used to employ a much larger share of workers before the 1990s – especially in manufacturing. Faced with increasing competition for exports and domestic market liberalization, however, large firms began to boost competitiveness through increasingly low-cost outsourcing. To meet this new demand, medium-sized enterprises also began passing on production processes to yet smaller-scale companies paying still lower wages (Kim, 2015[2]). Such a downward spiral spread widely through the manufacturing sectors and eventually into services sectors.

In 1993, establishments with 300 or more employees accounted for 22.6% of total employment in Korea (34.4% in the manufacturing sector). The share declined rapidly to 12.0% in 2000 before increasing slightly to 13.6% by 2014 (Figure 1.10, Panel A). Conversely, the share of employment among companies with 1-9 and 10-19 employees gradually increased from 37.3% and 8.4% in 1993, respectively, to 41.3% and 10.7% by 2014. Meanwhile, the overall share of employment among medium-sized companies has remained almost entirely flat. These sorts of firm dynamics in Korea stimulated an increase in the number of small companies offering very low pay. Figure 1.10, Panel B, shows the change in the number of companies over the past two decades for each category of firm size. Increases were observed primarily among small companies.

Figure 1.9. Large firms in Korea account for a lower share of salaried workers than in other OECD countries

Persons employed by firm size, 2013 or latest year available (percentages)

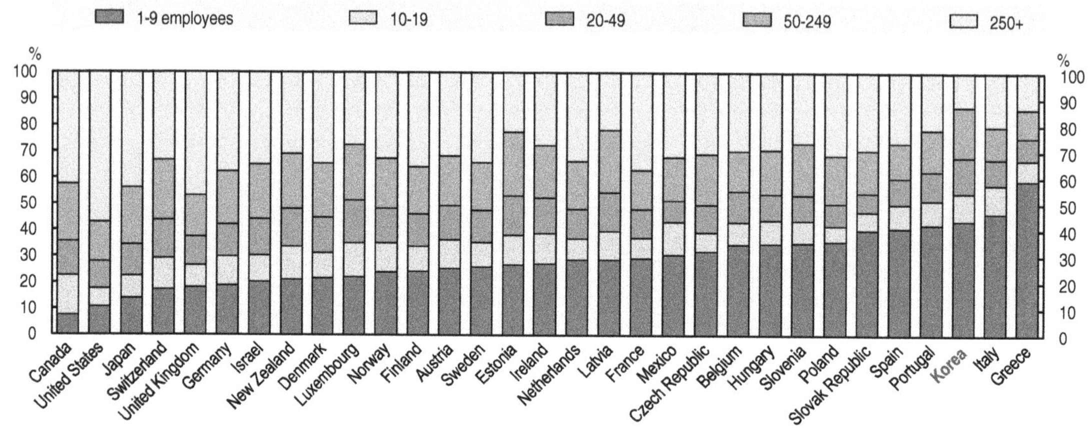

Note: Data cover the business economy, excluding financial intermediation. Firm size breakdowns differ slightly in the following exceptional cases: Canada has four categories referring to 1-4, 5-19, 50-299, and 300+; Japan and Korea have a slightly higher cut-off reference between the two largest categories (50-299 and 300+). Data do not include non-employers for Canada, Israel, Japan, Korea, Switzerland and the United States. Data refer to establishments for Korea and Mexico, which counts branches of a business as establishments and tends to show a relatively higher employment share of SMEs. Data for the United Kingdom exclude an estimate of 2.6 million small unregistered businesses.
Data refer to 2013 except: Ireland (2011); Japan (2012) and Canada, Israel, Korea and Mexico (2014).
Source: OECD Structural and Demographic Business Statistics (SDBS) *Database*, http://dx.doi.org/10.1787/sdbs-data-en.
StatLink http://dx.doi.org/10.1787/888933644699

Figure 1.10. Employment by large firms rapidly declined in Korea during the 1990s

Employees by firm size (percentages) and number of establishments by firm size (in thousands), 1993-2014

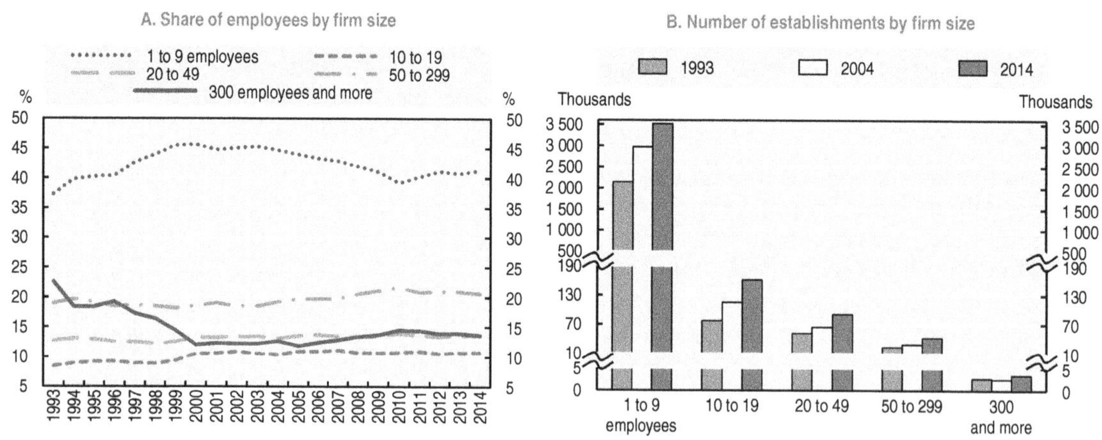

Source: Statistics Korea, Census on Establishments, 2015.

StatLink http://dx.doi.org/10.1787/888933644718

Most start-up enterprises in Korea emerge with extremely small funds: in 2015, 30.4% started out with less than KRW 5 million and a further 19.9% with KRW 5-20 million. Widespread self-employment coupled with limited business experience and small start-up funds largely explain the sharp drop of the survival rate after one or two years in manufacturing in Korea (Figure 1.11). Such instability also leads to the precarious employment conditions they offer workers.

Figure 1.11. Survival rate in Korea drops sharply one or two years after start-up

Enterprise survival rates in manufacturing, 2006 cohort (percentages)

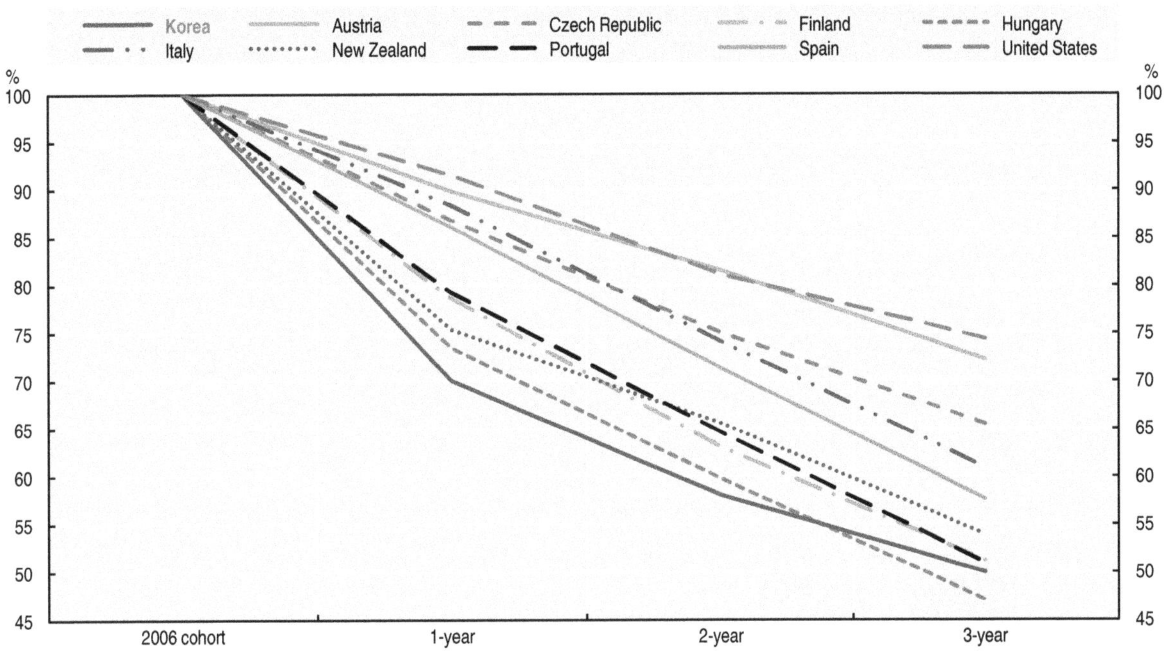

Note: The employer enterprise survival rate measures the number of enterprises of a specific birth cohort that have survived over different years. The *n-year* survival rate for a reference year *t* gives the number of *n-year* survival enterprises as a share of all enterprises registered for the first time in year *t-n.*

Source: OECD Structural and Demographic Business Statistics Database, SDBS Business Demography Indicators (ISIC Rev. 3): Employer enterprise survival rates, http://stats.oecd.org/Index.aspx?DataSetCode=SSIS_BSC_ISIC4# for Finland, New Zealand, Spain and the United States; and OECD (2013), *Entrepreneurship at a Glance*, OECD Publishing, http://dx.doi.org/10.1787/entrepreneur_aag-2013-en, Figure 3.21, p. 52, for Austria, the Czech Republic, Hungary, Italy, Korea and Portugal.

StatLink http://dx.doi.org/10.1787/888933644737

The average job tenure of workers in Korea is lower than six years: the lowest of any OECD country and considerably lower than the OECD average of 9.3 years in 2015. In 2015, 30.9% of employees in Korea were in their jobs for shorter than one year – compared with an OECD average of 17.6%.

Employment in Korea is less stable, on average, among smaller firms. 50.7% workers in enterprises (those with fewer than five employees) have job tenure of shorter than one year in 2015, compared with 12% among enterprises with 300 or more employees (Figure 1.12). Such high employment turnover is closely related to the fact that the share of non-permanent employees in total salaried employment is twice as high in Korea as the OECD average, with most such workers concentrated in micro-enterprises. This presents one of the main obstacles towards enlarging social insurance coverage in Korea.

Figure 1.12. Average job tenure in Korea is very short, especially in smaller firms

Average job tenure (in years) and incidence if job tenure of less than one year (percentages)

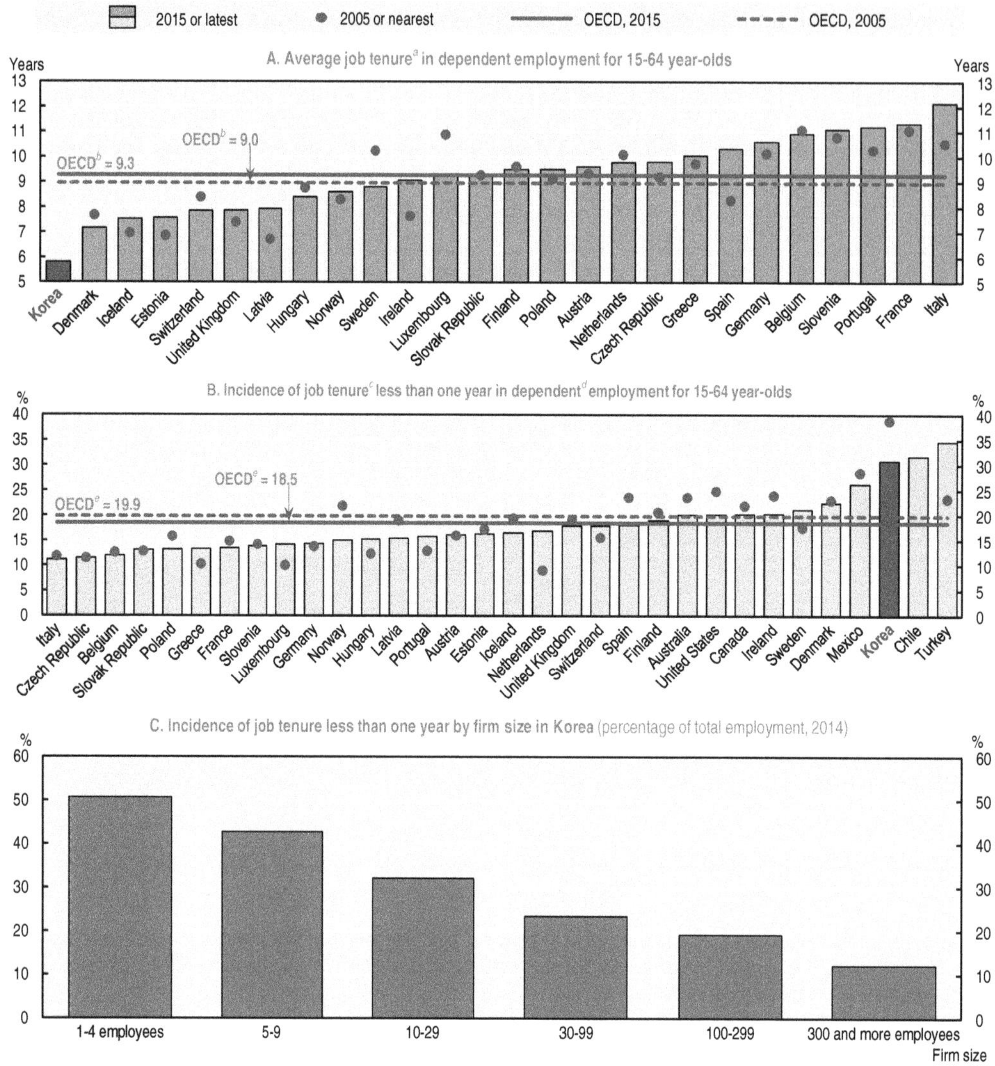

a) Data refer to 2015.
b) Unweighted average of 26 OECD countries (excluding Australia, Canada, Chile, Israel, Japan, Mexico, New Zealand, Turkey and United States).
c) Data refer to 2012 for Japan and 2014 for Austria and the United States.
d) For Japan, data refer to total employment.
e) Weighted average of 32 OECD countries (excluding Israel, Japan and New Zealand).

Source: Statistics Korea, Economically Active Population Survey, 2015 for Panel A. *OECD Job Tenure Dataset*, a subset of the *OECD Employment Database*, www.oecd.org/employment/database for Panels B and C.

StatLink http://dx.doi.org/10.1787/888933644756

Trade unions can bring considerable benefits to workers in terms of their wage levels and status in employment. Trade union members in all OECD countries predominantly have a permanent status in employment – with only 11% of them working on a non-permanent basis (OECD, 2017[7]).

Collective bargaining in Korea takes place predominantly at the level of firms. Trade union density varies considerably across firms of different size, ranging from 0.1% in small enterprises with less than 30 employees to 63% in large enterprises with more than 300 employees (Figure 1.13).

Figure 1.13. Differences in trade union density by firm size are very large in Korea and overall union density is relatively low

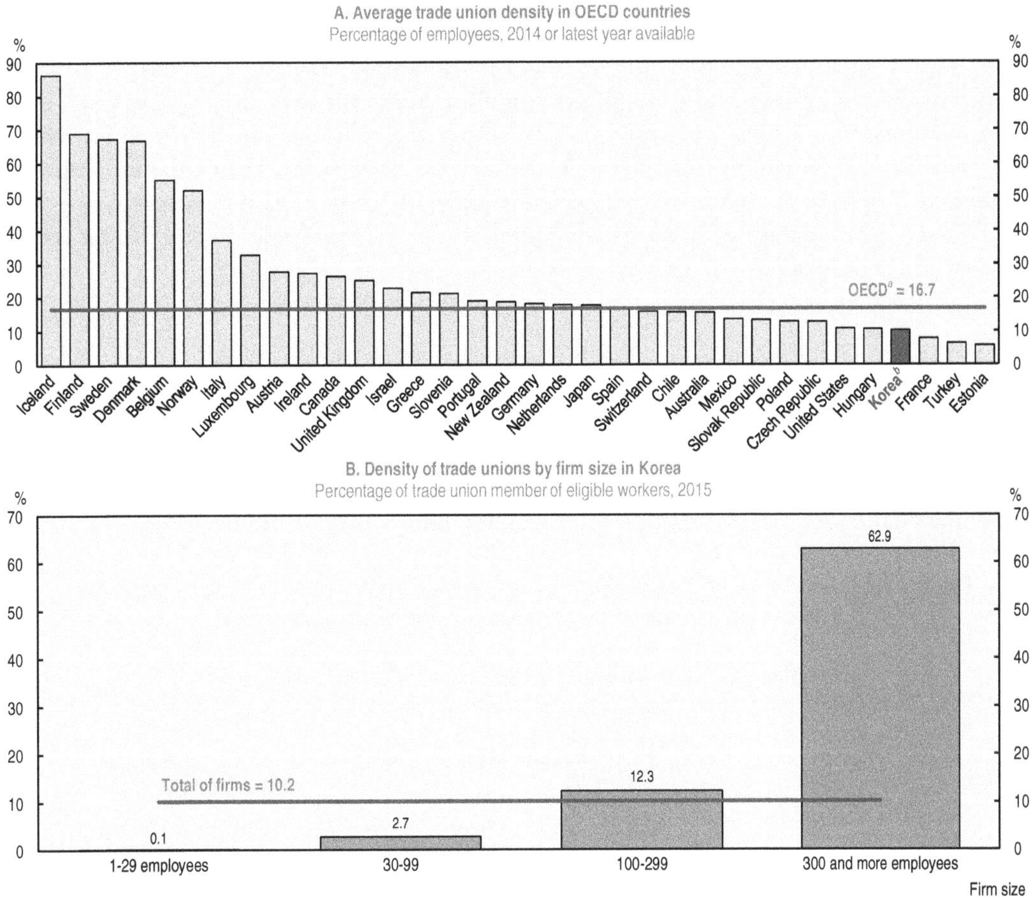

Note: Trade union density corresponds to the ratio of salaried workers that are trade union members, divided by the total number of salaried workers [from the *Employment by activities and status Dataset*, http://stats.oecd.org/Index.aspx?DataSetCode=ALFS_EMP, a subset of the *Annual Labour Force Statistics* (ALFS) *Database*]. Density is calculated using survey data, wherever possible, otherwise through administrative data adjusted for non-active and self-employed members.

a) Weighted average of OECD countries in 2014.

b) For Korea, data refer to 2012.

Source: OECD and J. Visser, *ICTWSS Database* (Institutional Characteristics of Trade Unions, Wage Setting, State Intervention and Social Pacts, 1960-2010), Version 3.0, www.uva-aias.net for Panel A; and MOEL (2016), "Analysis on trade unions based on data at the local labour offices in 2015" for Panel B.

StatLink http://dx.doi.org/10.1787/888933644775

Furthermore, the Labour Standards Act which is one of the most important laws on the working conditions of employees in Korea applies partially to micro-firms with less than five employees. Most of regulations on dismissal and working hour don't apply to the micro-firms. Employers are allowed to dismiss the employees without justifiable reasons. There are no daily or weekly limits on working hours at the micro-firms and the employers don't have to additionally pay 50% of the ordinary wages for extended work.

The near-non-existence of trade unions and the somewhat limited application of the Labour Standards Act also contribute to persistently low wages and precariousness of employment in small firms in Korea.

Labour market situation of specific groups

In Korea, three separate groups of workers are particularly affected by low-quality, low-productivity jobs: women, youth and the elderly. Korea has scope to raise employment rates of women – especially during child-rearing ages. Lowering childcare costs and narrowing the gender wage gap could facilitate women's employment and help more of them move into full-time work. Addressing mismatches between the skills acquired during education and those demanded by firms is a big challenge towards improving employment rates among young people in Korea. Despite a relatively high employment rate among older people in Korea, the problem of low-wage and precarious work arises continually.

Women workers

Despite some improvement in recent years, the employment rate of women aged 15-64 in Korea was only 56.2% in 2016 – almost 20 percentage points below that of men, constituting the fourth-largest gap of any OECD country. Many Korean women currently miss out on a professional career following marriage or childbirth around the age of 30, given the challenges of balancing professional and family duties (Figure 1.14).

Figure 1.14. Unlike many other OECD countries, Korea's female employment rate according to age shows a pronounced M-shaped curve

Employment/population ratios by gender in OECD countries, 2016
(percentage of female, respectively male population in each age group)

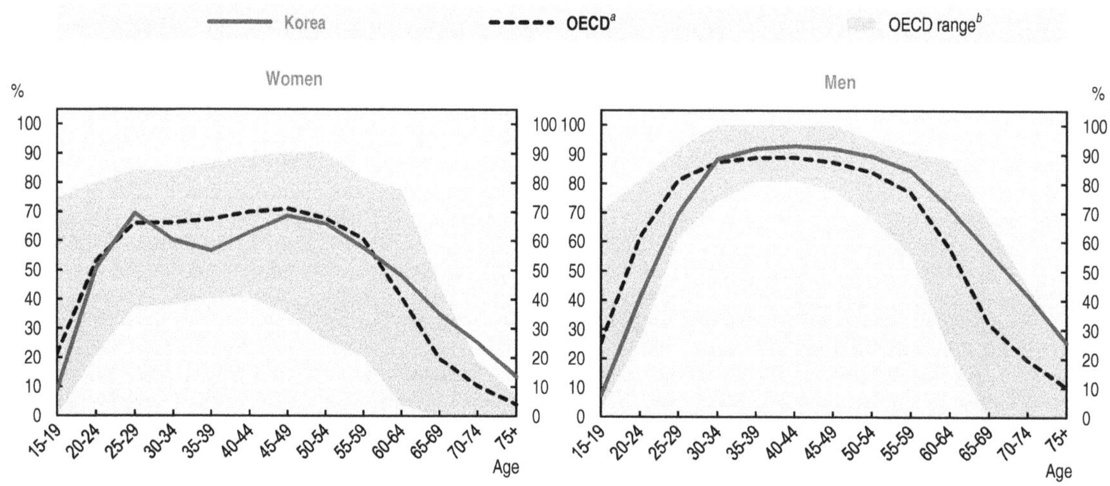

a) Weighted average of OECD countries.
b) Shaded area highlights the minimum and maximum values of OECD countries (excluding Korea).
Source: OECD Employment Database, www.oecd.org/employment/database.

StatLink http://dx.doi.org/10.1787/888933644794

Korean women are more likely than men to work as non-regular employees or be employed in SMEs. While the total share of non-regular employment in Korea is 32.8%, the share among female employees is 41%. Moreover, 23.3% of women in Korea work at very small firms with fewer than five employees, compared with 13.8% of men. These differences contribute to the Korea's gender wage gap, which is the highest of any OECD country at 37% in 2014 (compared with an OECD average of 15%). The second-longest working hours in the

OECD countries and the shortage of high-quality child care options also discourage Korean women from entering or re-entering the labour market following motherhood.

Contrary to any other OECD country, the gender employment gap in Korea is actually higher among the more highly-educated employed population. At 30%, the gender gap in employment is especially large among people with tertiary education – larger than in any other OECD country (Figure 1.15). This is highly inefficient given the high cost of tertiary education and the incredible skilled labour potential lost in this way (OECD, 2015[5]).

Figure 1.15. Contrary to other OECD countries, Korea's gender employment gap increases with the level of education

Gender employment gap by educational attainment in OECD countries, 2015[a] (percentages)

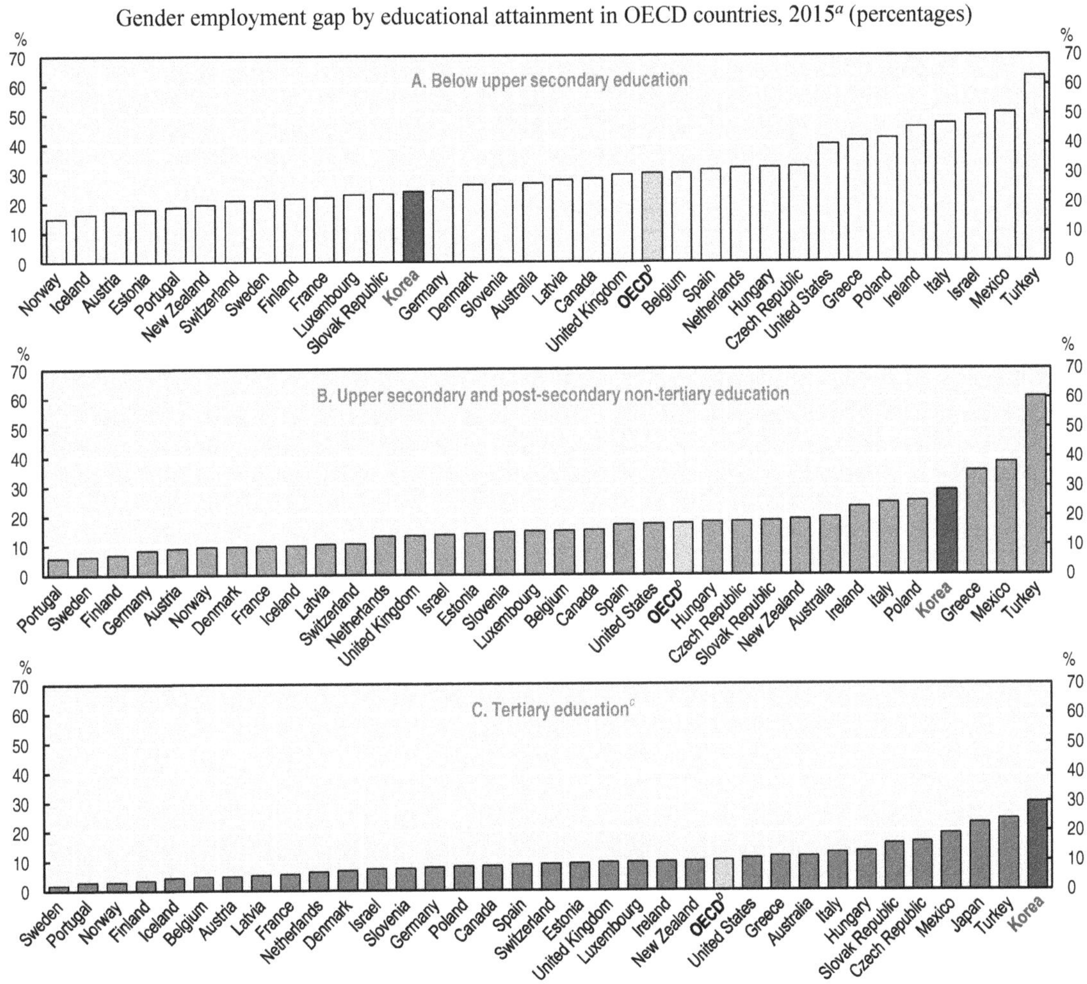

Note: The gender employment gap is calculated as the difference between male and female employment rate as a share of the male employment rate. Data refer to the population aged 25-64.

a) Data refer to 2014 for France.

b) Unweighted average of the 34 OECD countries shown in each panel (excluding Chile).

c) For Japan, data for short-cycle tertiary education and total tertiary education include upper secondary and post-secondary non-tertiary programmes (less than 5% of the adults are under this group).

Source: Educational attainment and labour force status: Employment rates and unemployment rates, by aggregated levels of educational attainment, trends Dataset from the *OECD Education at a Glance Database*, http://stats.oecd.org/index.aspx?queryid=69473.

StatLink http://dx.doi.org/10.1787/888933644813

Young workers

Korean students achieve excellent educational outcomes: in the 2015 PISA study, 15-year-olds ranked second across OECD countries in mathematics and fifth in both reading and science (OECD, 2016[8]). Virtually all young people, 98%, complete their upper-secondary education, and the share of the population with tertiary education is by far the highest in the OECD.

In spite of these impressive education outcomes, young people in Korea find the transition into work quite challenging: reflected in a low youth employment rate and a high share of young people who are not in employment, education or training (NEETs). The employment rate of youth aged 15-29 was 42.3% in 2016, well below the OECD average of 52.6% (Figure 1.16, Panel A). Korea's NEETs rate stood at 18% in 2015 and, thus, above the OECD average of 15%. Moreover, the large majority of NEETs in Korea are inactive – 80% of them, compared with 60% elsewhere (Figure 1.16, Panel B).

Figure 1.16. Korea's youth employment is well below the OECD average and a large share of youth is inactive

Youth employment rate in 2016 and NEET rate in 2015 (percentages)

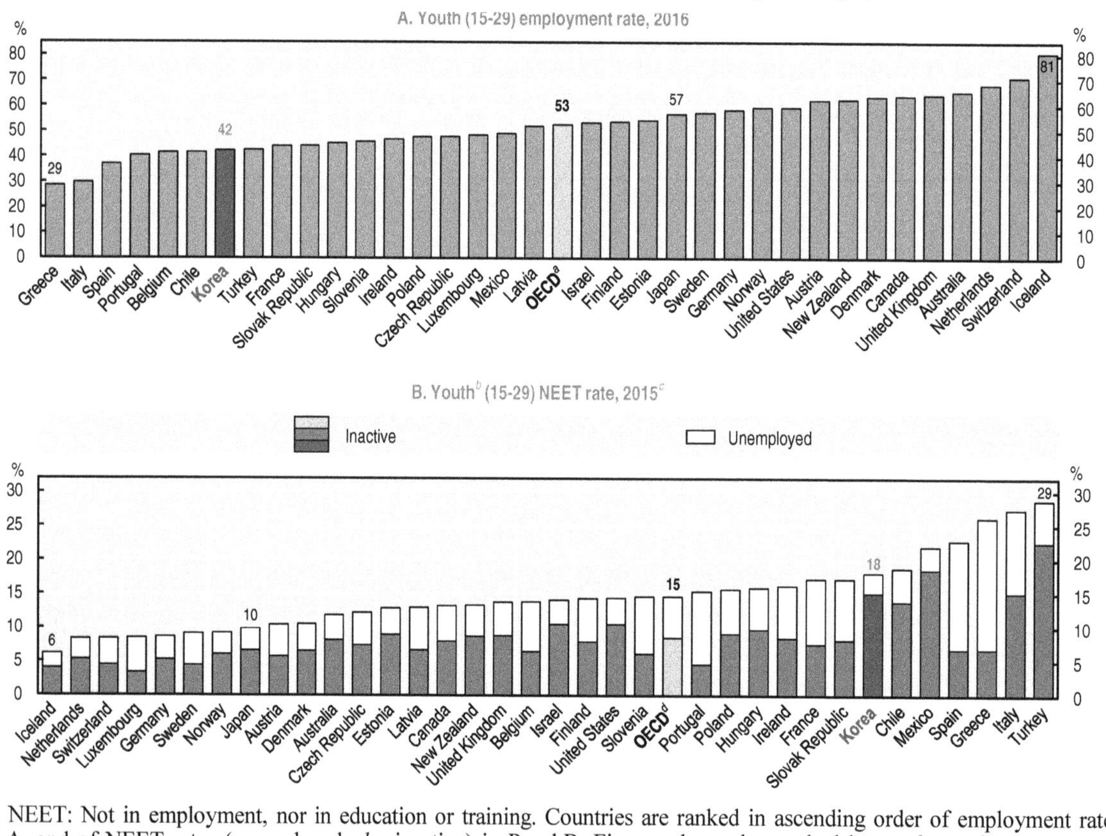

Note: NEET: Not in employment, nor in education or training. Countries are ranked in ascending order of employment rates in Panel A, and of NEET rates (unemployed *plus* inactive) in Panel B. Figures above the stacked bars refer to the NEET rates in Panel B. Due to the fact that youth in informal educational institution is categorized as NEETs in Korea, there is a tendency for the statistical share of NEETs to become larger values.

a) Weighted average of the 35 OECD countries.

b) Instead of 15-29 year-olds, data refer to 15-24 year-olds for Japan, and to 16-29 year-olds for Spain.

c) Data refer to 2013 for Chile and Korea, and to 2014 for Japan.

d) Unweighted average of the 35 OECD countries.

Source: OECD Employment Database, www.oecd.org/employment/database for employment rates; and *OECD, Transition from School to Work Dataset*, a dataset from the *OECD Education and Training Database*, www.oecd.org/education/education-at-a-glance-19991487.htm for NEET rates.

StatLink http://dx.doi.org/10.1787/888933644832

High inactivity rates reflect young people's response to a strongly segmented labour market. In order to increase their chances of being hired by an attractive, large company or a public-sector employer, many young people in Korea try to acquire additional qualifications and certificates after having completed their studies (OECD, 2016[9]). They are counted as inactive NEETs in the labour market statistics, because such learning activities typically take place outside of the formal education system. Unlike in many other OECD countries, the NEET challenge in Korea may thus not reflect young people's lack of skills, but rather an inefficient over-education in the face of labour market segmentation. NEET rates in Korea are nearly identical for young people with and without tertiary education, and the relationship between numeracy or literacy and the risk of being NEET is weaker than in most other OECD countries.

Elderly workers

While the employment rate of Korean aged 55-64 was 66% in 2015, well above the OECD average of 58.5%, many of them work in poor quality jobs, which are insecure and lower-paid. Older workers in Korea are strongly over-represented among non-regular workers. About 34% of Korean workers aged 55-64 hold a temporary job, compared with only 8% on average in OECD countries (Figure 1.17). This reflects the common pattern under which regular workers retire at relatively young ages from their career jobs and then commence "second careers" in non-regular jobs or as own-account workers in the highly competitive, low-productivity service sector.

Figure 1.17. Work of older workers in Korea is often temporary

Incidence of temporary work among older workers in OECD countries in 2015[a] (percentages)

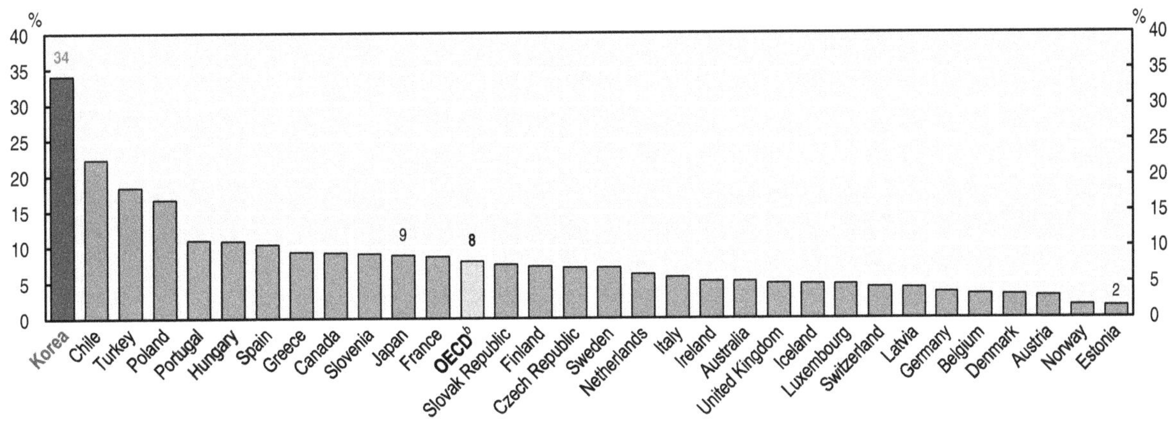

Note: Data refer to dependent employment.

a) Data refer to 2013 for Australia.

b) Weighted average of the 30 OECD countries shown whose data refer to 2015 (i.e. excluding Australia).

Source: OECD Employment Database, www.oecd.org/employment/database.

StatLink http://dx.doi.org/10.1787/888933644851

According to the Supplementary Results of the Economically Active Population Survey for the Elderly in August 2016, the average age of separation from the main job (i.e. the job with the longest duration) for the labour force aged 55-64 was as low as 52 years old for men and 47 years old for women. The strong seniority-based wage system associated with a huge skill gap between younger and older people make businesses reluctant to hire or retain older people as permanent workers (Figure 1.18).

Figure 1.18. Korea's seniority-based wage is strong, especially for male employees

Age-earnings profiles in Korea compared with selected OECD countries (latest available year), Index, 25-29 year-olds = 100

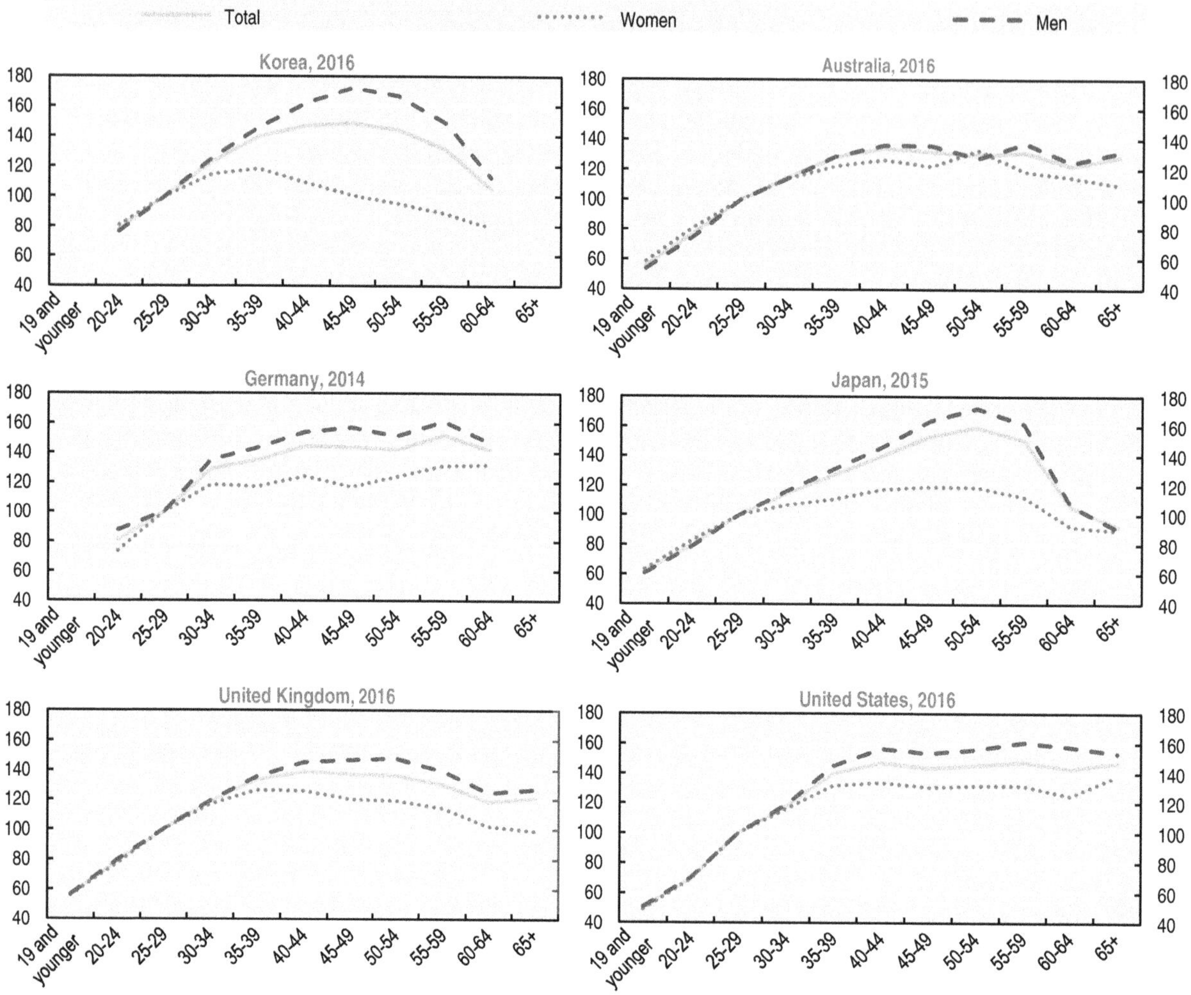

Note: Data refer full-time workers.
Source: OECD Earnings Database for age-earnings profiles.

StatLink http://dx.doi.org/10.1787/888933644870

Conclusion

Korea has gone through remarkable economic development during the past five decades, coupled with considerable social transformation. While overall employment has grown and unemployment and long-term unemployment are remarkably low, labour market developments have not kept pace with Korea's overall economic development. Job quality and job security, in particular, remain poor for many Korean workers, highlighting pronounced labour market dualities. This, in turn, enables many of the lowest-paid, lowest-skilled workers to go undocumented, reducing their access to social protection.

The labour market faces a number of big challenges including, above all, a high prevalence of: a) non-regular employment; b) self-employment; and c) very small micro-businesses. These factors are associated with poor job quality and low pay. Strong labour market duality and inequality affects women more than men and older workers more than other groups. Moreover, many young people with tertiary education struggle to find adequate employment.

The peculiarities of the Korean labour market have shown to be persistent and a common practice of outsourcing of poor-quality jobs to SMEs – in particular those in the services sectors characterised by low productivity – has reinforced existing labour market dualities. To fulfil Korea's growth potential, labour market problems will have to be addressed.

References

Kim, J. (2015), "Promoting Good-Quality Job Creation in the Sector of SMEs", *KDI Focus*, Vol. 29, http://econpapers.repec.org/article/kdikdifoc/v_3a29_3ay_3a2015_3ap_3a1-13.htm (accessed on 05 July 2017), pp. 1-13. [2]

OECD (1994), *OECD Economic Surveys : By Country, 1993-1994 Korea.*, OECD. [1]

OECD (2013), *Korea: Improving the Re-employment Prospects of Displaced Workers*, OECD Publishing, http://dx.doi.org/10.1787/9789264189225-en. [4]

OECD (2013), *Strengthening Social Cohesion in Korea*, OECD Publishing, http://dx.doi.org/10.1787/9789264188945-en. [6]

OECD (2015), *OECD Skills Strategy Diagnostic Report: Korea*, OECD Publishing, http://www.oecd.org/skills/nationalskillsstrategies/OECD-Skills-Strategy-Diagnostic-Report-Peru-2016.pdf (accessed on 07 July 2017). [5]

OECD (2016), "PISA 2015 Results in Focus", https://www.oecd.org/pisa/pisa-2015-results-in-focus.pdf (accessed on 07 July 2017). [8]

OECD (2016), *OECD Economic Surveys: Korea 2016*, OECD Publishing, http://dx.doi.org/10.1787/eco_surveys-kor-2016-en. [9]

OECD (2017), *OECD Employment Outlook 2017*, OECD Publishing, http://dx.doi.org/10.1787/empl_outlook-2017-en. [7]

Zoli, E. (2017), "Korea's Challenges Ahead—Lessons from Japan's Experience", IMF, https://www.imf.org/en/Publications/WP/Issues/2017/01/18/Koreas-Challenges-Ahead-Lessons-from-Japans-Experience-44549 (accessed on 07 July 2017). [3]

Chapter 2. Strengths, gaps and weaknesses in Korea's income and employment support measures

This chapter looks at the development, take-up and effectiveness of the main systems in place in Korea to support jobseekers and the working poor in finding employment and earning a decent income. The discussion focuses on four schemes: the Employment Insurance (unemployment benefit), the Basic Livelihood Security Programme (social assistance), the Employment Success Package Programme (employability support) and the Earned Income Tax Credit (in-work support). The chapter also discusses how the programmes are administered and delivered. It concludes that better enforcement of the systems already in place could go a long way in closing the social protection gaps as Korea strives to create a more robust and mature welfare state.

The statistical data for Israel are supplied by and under the responsibility of the relevant Israeli authorities. The use of such data by the OECD is without prejudice to the status of the Golan Heights, East Jerusalem and Israeli settlements in the West Bank under the terms of international law.

The development of the Korean welfare state

Over the past few decades, Korea has not only seen fast economic growth and transformation but also rapid social development and eventually, since the mid-1980s, the construction and gradual expansion of a social protection system that better aligns with the country's state of development. There is still a long way to go for Korea to achieve a mature and effective benefit system and employment service. In the years to come it will be important to take the right decisions on which parts of the system to expand, which new elements to introduce, if any, and how to better enforce the system and regulations currently in place. This chapter discusses this process and in particular the extent to which the main components of Korea's social protection system succeed in providing adequate income and employment support to low-income jobseekers and the working poor.

Towards effective social security and activation

Public social spending as a percentage of GDP is still low in Korea, compared with other OECD countries, but has increased continuously since the Asian financial crisis in the late 1990s. In 2016, *gross* public social spending stood at 10.4% of GDP – the second lowest in the OECD (after Mexico), well below the OECD average of 21.0% and only one-third of the level in many European countries, including France and Italy (Figure 2.1, Panel A1). The gap with the OECD average is slightly smaller when also including *private* social spending, mandatory or voluntary, and looking at *net* spending which takes into account the extent to which social benefits are taxed away. Because of the low tax burden in Korea, total public and private net social spending is about two percentage points higher, each year, measured as a share of GDP (Figure 2.1, Panel A2).

Korea is among the few OECD countries still expanding their social protection system. This is reflected in the continuous growth in public social spending which more than doubled since 2000. The increase in real terms outpaced the growth rate in most OECD countries. The introduction of a public pension system (in 1988), universal health insurance (in 1989), mandatory employment insurance (in 1995) and a national social assistance programme (in 2000) all contributed to this increase. Also the increase since 2000 in the absolute share of GDP allocated to public social spending – almost six percentage points in the case of Korea – was larger than in most countries.

Rapid population ageing is the biggest factor in recent years in social spending increases in other OECD countries, more influential than system reform. This factor will be a key driver of further change in the coming years in Korea's rapidly ageing society: social expenditure in Korea is projected to increase rapidly to at least 26% of GDP by 2050, even without further social benefit reform, because of the shift in the age structure and the gradual maturing of the current social protection system (Won and Kim, 2013[1]).

Figure 2.1. Social expenditure in Korea increases continuously but is still rather low

Public and private social expenditure in percentage of GDP, Korea and selected OECD countries, 1990-2016

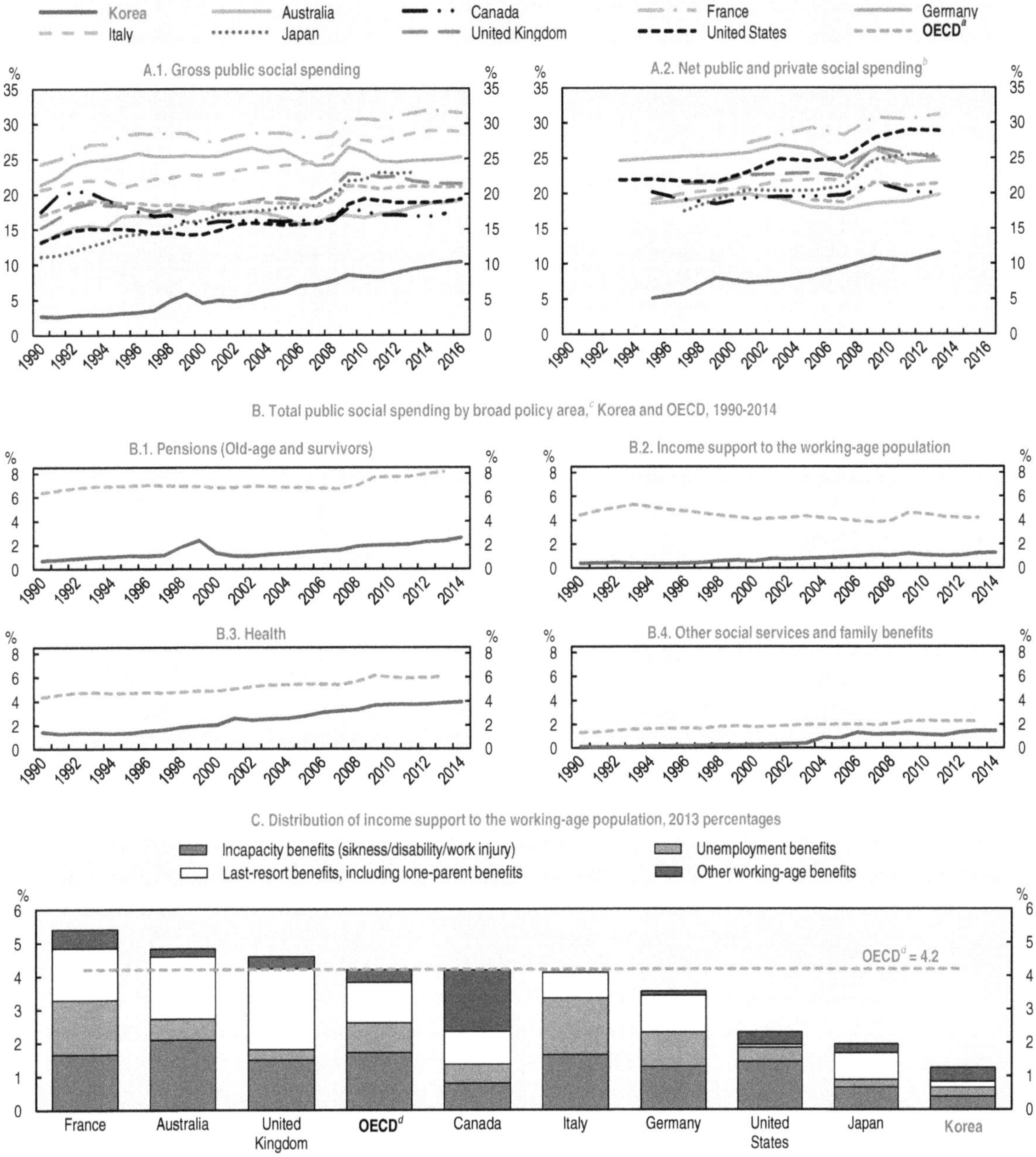

Note: GDP: Gross domestic product.

a) For gross and total public social spending: unweighted average of the 35 OECD countries; 1990-99 data are trended from 23 countries (Panel A1 and Panel B). For net public and private social spending: unweighted average of 27 OECD countries for which data are available from 2005 onwards (Panel A2).

b) Net public and private social spending are reported only for odd years. For even years, data have been interpolated from data related to odd years, for all countries and the OECD.

c) Data do not include spending on Active Labour Market Programmes which cannot be split into cash and service spending.

d) Unweighted average of the 35 OECD countries.

Source: OECD Social Expenditure Database, www.oecd.org/social/expenditure.htm.

StatLink http://dx.doi.org/10.1787/888933644889

The importance of population ageing for the cost of social protection is also reflected in the structure of public social spending. The largest and fastest increasing components of Korea's social expenditure are pensions (which target older people only) and health care (which targets older people predominantly). This is similar in most OECD countries (Figure 2.1, Panel B) but the situation in Korea is exceptional in several ways, as emphasised in earlier OECD work (OECD, 2013[2]):

- Pension spending, although increasing continuously since 1990, is still relatively low – around 2.6% of GDP in 2014 – because the system has yet to mature fully but also because entitlements are lower than in many other OECD countries.
- Health spending which more than doubled in the same period, to around 4% of GDP in 2014, is predominantly in the form of services because contrary to other OECD countries Korea does not have statutory sickness benefit insurance.
- Korea's outlays on income support to the working-age population (unemployment benefits, incapacity benefits and last-resort benefits),[1] at 1.3% of GDP in 2014, are among the lowest in the OECD area, less than one-third of the OECD average of 4.2%. This is only partly explained by the low unemployment rate in Korea.
- Within the latter group, Korea spends much less than other OECD countries on all risks that the working-age population is possibly facing: unemployment, poor health and low income (Figure 2.1, Panel C).

Comparative OECD statistics also reveal some of the strengths of the Korean social protection system: a system which was built much later than in other countries and thereby avoided some of the mistakes of "early" welfare states. Most importantly, Korea avoided creating a social protection system with strong disincentives to work and high benefit dependence through a combination of three factors: a) a focus on activating jobseekers and the provision of active labour market programmes (ALMP), including training; b) relatively modest benefit levels and relatively strict entitlement conditions; and c) low tax rates which contribute to making work pay.

Since 2009, ALMP spending in Korea has been higher than the country's spending on unemployment benefits (as was also the case until 2002). This is different from most other OECD countries. On average across the OECD, ALMP spending equals only around 60% of a country's unemployment benefit spending, with some countries showing shares much lower than this (e.g. 20% in Italy and the United States or 40% in Australia and Canada). In most countries the ratio of active to passive spending dropped after the global financial crisis in 2008-09, because of the sharp rise in unemployment and corresponding spending on unemployment benefits. Korea and, to a lesser extent, also Japan, are exceptions to this trend: ALMP spending was increased after the crisis, initially through a stronger focus on job creation and more recently in the case of Korea through business start-up incentives and more investment in training. A similar picture emerged in Korea in the aftermath of the Asian crisis in the late 1990s, while in the period 2003-08 total ALMP spending was below the country's total unemployment benefit spending (Figure 2.2). The relatively high level of active spending, relative to passive spending, is a good starting point for achieving strong reemployment outcomes for jobseekers in Korea.

Figure 2.2. Overall ALMP spending in Korea is high relative to the country's unemployment benefit spending

ALMP spending in percentage of unemployment benefit spending, Korea and selected OECD countries, 2000-14

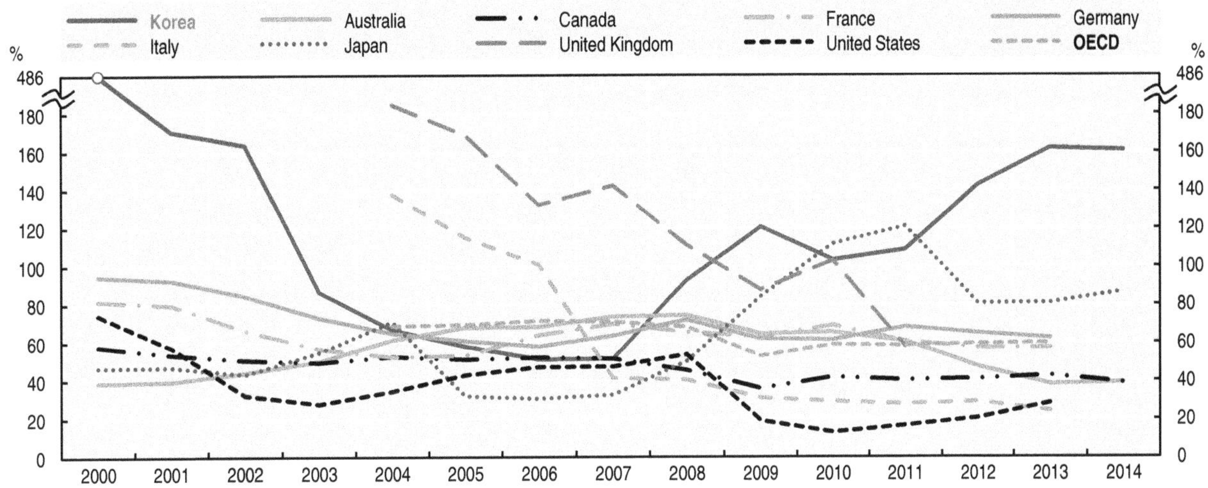

Note: ALMP: Active labour market programmes. Unweighted average of OECD countries for which ALMP spending for active measures (Categories 1 to 7) are available from 2004 onwards. For unemployment benefit spending, unweighted average of the 35 OECD countries; 1980-99 data are trended from 23 countries, as information for Chile, the Czech Republic, Estonia, Hungary, Iceland, Israel, Korea, Mexico, Poland, the Slovak Republic and Slovenia is not available from 1980.

Source: OECD/Eurostat Labour Market Programme Database, http://dx.doi.org/10.1787/data-00312-en for ALMP and *OECD Social Expenditure Database*, www.oecd.org/social/expenditure.htm for unemployment benefit spending.

StatLink http://dx.doi.org/10.1787/888933644908

However, the composition of Korea's ALMP spending is lagging behind the developments in many of the OECD countries which are in the forefront of labour market policy. Total spending on ALMP, at 0.42% of GDP, is at the OECD average. However, spending in Korea is still largely concentrated on direct job creation in the public sector (Figure 2.3, Panel A). Most OECD countries have downsized considerably such community employment programmes which were popular especially in the 1990s as these programmes failed to bring people back into the regular labour market. Spending on training, employment incentives and other programmes to help jobseekers of all ages improve their employability and find stable employment in the private sector is lower in Korea than in the average OECD country.

There is another factor which reduces the actual impact of ALMP spending in Korea on employment. According to administrative data, almost 80% of direct job creation is targeted at workers *above* the retirement age of 65 years. This type of social spending, which can be seen as a welfare programme for older workers to tackle the high poverty rates of this group, comprises roughly 40% of Korea's total ALMP spending. Effective ALMP spending for the working-age population is therefore much lower. Would Figure 2.2 be adjusted accordingly, by removing ALMP spending for workers above age 65, Korea's ratio of active spending to passive spending for 2014 would drop from 160% to just 100% – which is still above but much closer to the OECD average.

Figure 2.3. Compared with other OECD countries, Korea spends little on the administration of its Public Employment Service

Expenditure on PES administration and on active labour market programmes by main category as a percentage of GDP, selected OECD countries, 2014[a]

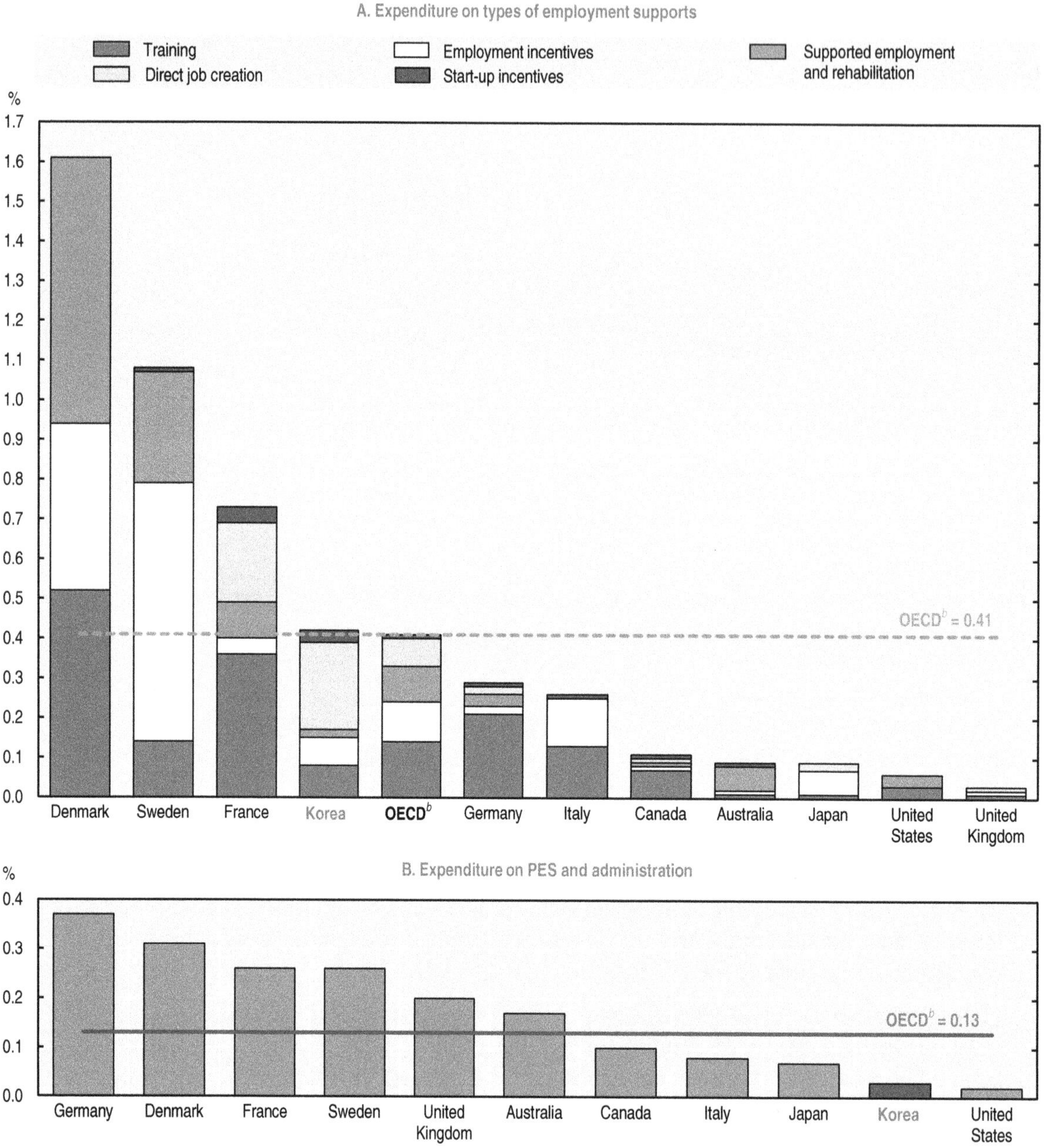

Note: GDP: Gross domestic product; PES: Public Employment Service. Countries are ranked in decreasing order of expenditure in each respective panel.

a) FY 2011/12 for the United Kingdom.

b) Weighted average of the 35 OECD countries.

Source: OECD/Eurostat Labour Market Programme Database, http://dx.doi.org/10.1787/data-00312-en.

StatLink http://dx.doi.org/10.1787/888933644927

Moreover, Korea spends comparatively little – merely 0.03% of its GDP which is less than 10% of the entire ALMP budget – on the administration of its Public Employment Service (PES) and on counselling and case-managing of jobseekers. Partly this is due to the relatively low level and short average duration of unemployment. However, low spending on administering employment services limits the effectiveness of the PES as research from around the world has shown: intense counselling of jobseekers (Crépon, Dejemeppe and Gurgand, 2005[3]; Pedersen, Rosholm and Svarer, 2012[4]), regular monitoring of their job-search requirements (Klepinger et al., 2002[5]; Borland and Tseng, 2007[6]; McVicar, 2008[7]) and low clients-per-counsellor caseloads (Hainmueller et al., 2011[8]; Hofmann et al., 2012[9]) are very effective means to achieve sustained reemployment. Most OECD countries use much larger parts of their ALMP budget to manage the PES and its clients, sometimes as much as 50% of the total funds or even more than this, like in Australia, the United Kingdom or the United States, and typically around 25% (Figure 2.3, Panel B).

Korea will have to make critical choices when further expanding its welfare state, especially the part directed to the working-age population. A main challenge will be to expand the system while keeping work incentives and the activation orientation high. Finding the right balance between entitlements and obligations and between benefits and work incentives has shown to be a challenge in many countries, especially for low-income groups. Any easing of eligibility criteria; any increase in payment levels; and any introduction of new system components to close current gaps in the system must, therefore, go hand-in-hand with expanded and strengthened activation efforts to avoid undesirable benefit dependence and assure high and sustained rates of employment and reemployment of low-income jobseekers and the working poor.

Key outcomes delivered by the social protection system

Expanding social protection will be necessary for Korea to make sure jobseekers receive the employment and income support they need to make ends meet and to find adequate and sustained employment. There are gaps in the Korean system – in the Korean literature commonly referred to as "blind spots" (Yoo, 2013[10]) – which must be fully understood and addressed in an effective and efficient way. Not all groups of people are well included in the labour market, some groups of jobseekers are poorly supported when out of work and in-work poverty is also a prevalent phenomenon to be tackled.

Job quality and labour market inclusiveness

In a nutshell, the Korean labour market is characterised by low unemployment but only average levels of employment due to relatively poor labour market integration of disadvantaged groups as well as women (Figure 2.4). Moreover, many workers work in poor-quality jobs with high levels of job strain and rather low earnings. Income security in case of job loss appears to be high but this is only true for people who are entitled to unemployment benefits and many in the Korean workforce are not.

In other words, there is significant room for improvement in labour market outcomes in various areas. Governments have a number of tools at hand to influence labour market developments, many of which are not the main focus of this report. Solid social protection that allows jobseekers to find a good-quality job that matches their skills is one such tool which could be effective if complemented by well-targeted support to improve jobseekers employability and enable them to find a new job. The low social and labour market spending of the Korean government directed towards the working-age population hinders these labour market institutions from unfolding their full potential. Consequently, for many Koreans good-quality employment remains unachievable.

Figure 2.4. Korea's labour market has a number of strengths but also weaknesses

OECD Scoreboard of labour market performance: job quality, job quantity and labour market inclusiveness

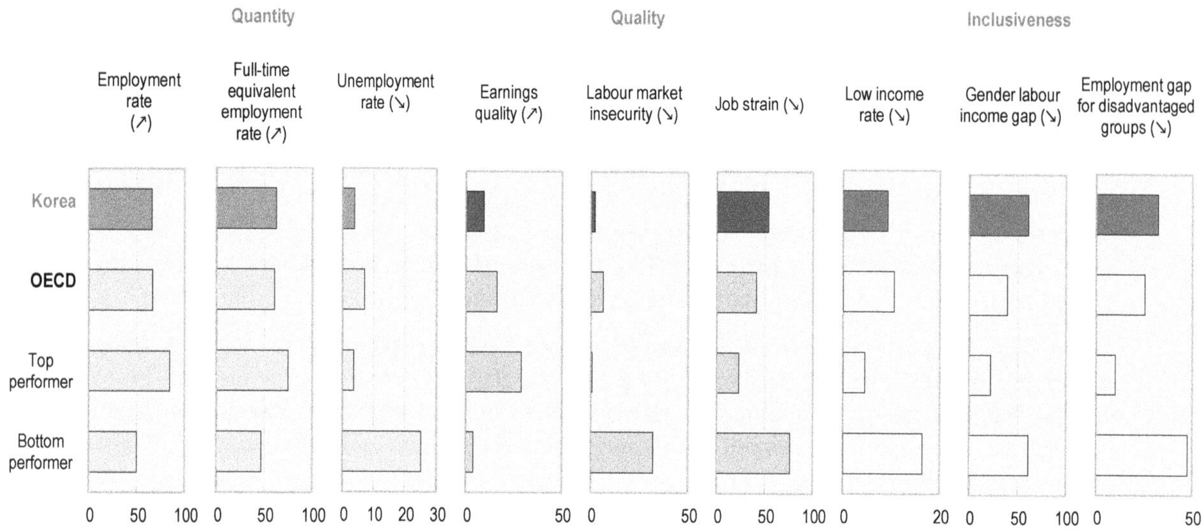

Note: An upward ↗ (downward ↘) pointing arrow for an indicator means that higher (lower) values reflect better performance.

Definitions: Earnings quality: Gross hourly earnings in USD adjusted for inequality. *Labour market insecurity:* Expected monetary loss associated with becoming unemployed as a share of previous earnings. *Job strain:* Percentage of workers in jobs characterised by a combination of high job demands and few job resources to meet those demands. *Low income rate:* Share of working-age persons living with less than 50% of median equivalised household disposable income. *Gender labour income gap*: Difference between average per capita annual earnings of men and women divided by average per capita earnings of men. *Employment gap for disadvantaged groups:* Average difference in the employment rate for prime-age men and the rates for five disadvantaged groups (mothers with children, youth who are not in full-time education or training, workers aged 55-64, non-natives, and persons with disabilities) as a percentage of the employment rate for prime-age men.

Source: OECD calculations using data for 2015 or latest year available from multiple sources. See *OECD Employment Outlook 2017*, http://dx.doi.org/10.1787/empl_outlook-2017-en, Table 1.2, http://dx.doi.org/10.1787/888933478165 for further details.

StatLink http://dx.doi.org/10.1787/888933644946

Take-up of working-age benefits

The availability of effective income and employment support is important, for at least two reasons: First, people outside the social benefit system rarely receive, or seek, targeted employment support, in Korea as much as in other OECD countries. Second, to make ends meet jobseekers not entitled to any support will have to accept jobs of any quality or will be pushed into low-quality self-employment. This is certainly happening in Korea.

In all OECD countries, including Korea, there is a big discrepancy between being unemployed and actually receiving income support and, possibly, employment support. There are many reasons why unemployment benefit take-up tends to be low: i) eligibility criteria that, legally or effectively, exclude self-employed people and certain groups of workers depending on firm size or type of contract; ii) non-eligibility in many countries for all those who quit their job voluntarily; iii) strict entitlement conditions which exclude some of those who would otherwise be eligible for support but have not been in their job long enough; iv) a mismatch between regulations and actual enforcement of legislation; and v) people's own behaviour when temporarily unemployed, such as not claiming a benefit because people found a new job quickly or thought they will find one easily.

All these reasons play a role in Korea in explaining why only very few people who lose or leave their job actually receive any benefits, and some of them play a bigger role than in other countries. For instance, the size of the groups effectively excluded is large; the exclusion of voluntary job leavers is strict; and the enforcement of legislation is weak.

Estimating the share of job changers and job losers who access unemployment benefits is not straightforward and only possible with the use of panel survey data. Analysis based on the Korea Labour and Income Panel Survey (KLIPS) suggests that about one in ten Koreans who lost or changed a job in a given year or had an intermittent period of non-employment during that year actually received unemployment benefit.[2] This is lower than corresponding benefit take-up rates in other OECD countries for which comparable data are available. For instance, in Canada and the United States where voluntary job leavers are also excluded from unemployment benefits the corresponding take-up rates are just over 30% and just below 20%, respectively. Also the figure for Australia, at close to 18%, is above the take-up figure for Korea although the Australian unemployment benefit is entirely means-tested; however, in Australia people leaving their job voluntarily can claim unemployment benefit after a period of around ten weeks of unemployment.

KLIPS analysis further suggests that also the take-up of social assistance benefits is low for the same group of people losing or changing their job in a given year. At 1.25%, the share receiving social assistance is lower than in most other OECD countries because in Korea people with work capacity hardly ever access such payments.

Poverty outcomes for the working-age population

While trying to keep a balance between the provision of income and work incentives, one critical role of a country's benefit system is to prevent people from falling into poverty when losing their job. Comparing various Korean data sources (Survey of Household Finance and Living Conditions, Household Income and Expenditure Survey, KLIPS) with data for OECD countries, Korea finds itself in a rather unique position in regard to poverty outcomes, in several ways.

- *First*, overall poverty rates of the Korean working-age population are very similar to the OECD average rate of 16%.
- *Second*, the labour force status distribution of poverty deviates strongly from that of other countries. Korea has a relatively high rate of poverty among employees – explaining the in-work poverty discussion in the country – but a low poverty rate for unemployed and inactive people. Like in most OECD countries, unemployed people in Korea face higher poverty rates than inactive people.
- *Third*, the small difference in poverty rates between employed and unemployed people in Korea is *not* a result of the transfer system: Contrary to most other OECD countries, in Korea the benefit system has relatively little impact on ultimate poverty outcomes.

The rather limited impact of the benefit system in Korea on people's household income situation, which was already discussed in earlier OECD publications (OECD, 2013[2]), partly reflects the low take-up of social benefits among working-age individuals and Korea's low overall level of public social spending. In the typical OECD country, the tax and transfer system through redistribution eliminates around half of the poverty level that the market income distribution alone would create. This is not the case in Korea where, on the other hand, the market income distribution of households seems to be flatter than in other OECD countries.

This is surprising at first sight because of the large difference in Korea in job quality and earnings between regular and non-regular employees and the large gender wage gap. Data from the Survey of Household Finance and Living Conditions for example suggest that market income poverty rates for those in employment range from only 5% for regular workers to almost 30% for daily workers. However, market income differences seem to be compensated to a considerable extent by the composition of households. After all, it is women who are highly over-represented among those working under precarious employment conditions. Many of them are second earners who live in a household with a first earner who is in regular employment. In turn, the ongoing trend in Korea towards smaller households and less stable family relations is likely to have a considerable impact in the medium term on income distribution and poverty outcomes.

The special situation of people with health problems

One group of people in Korea seems to suffer a much greater poverty risk: people with health problems. KLIPS data suggest that their poverty risk is almost twice as high as for people in good health. This is also the case in some other OECD countries, such as Australia, Belgium, France, Slovenia and the United States, but different from the situation in most OECD countries in which poverty risks for people in bad health are typically only slightly higher than for their healthy peers.

The poverty outcome for people with bad health might be related to the accessibility of a country's benefit system. Across OECD countries, people in bad health tend to depend on social benefits to a larger extent, with their more frequent benefit take-up partly compensating their lower employment rate although this also depends on the value of the benefits available to this group. In Korea, social benefit take-up hardly varies by health status; people in bad health have a less comprehensive, less mature safety net available in case of unemployment or incapacity. This issue deserves special attention.

The main elements of Korea's support system for the working-age population

Four pillars to support the unemployed and the working poor

Korea can do more to support unemployed people but also those who have a job but do not earn enough to sustain a living above the poverty threshold. Korea has four main support systems in place to assist the unemployed and the working poor:

- Unemployment benefit provided by the *Employment Insurance* (EI);
- Social assistance provided by the *Basic Livelihood Security Programme* (BLSP);
- Employability support with a benefit component provided under the *Employment Success Package Programme* (ESPP); and
- In-work support provided through the *Earned Income Tax Credit* (EITC).

In total (if only considering recipients of working age) these four systems catered for 3.88 million people in 2015, which corresponds to around 10% of the working-age population. This is one million more than just four years ago, in 2011, largely because of the expansion and maturing of EITC and ESPP. Total annual spending on these four support programmes was over 10 trillion KRW in 2015, up from around 8 trillion in 2011 (Table 2.1).[3]

Table 2.1. Korea's spending on the Employment Success Package and Earned Income Tax Credit is low compared with Employment Insurance and Basic Livelihood Security

Recipients, total spending and annual spending per recipient of Korea's four main social protection programmes for the working-age population, 2011 and 2015, numbers and percentages

	Year	Employment Insurance	Basic Livelihood Security	Employment Success Package	Earned Income Tax Credit	Total
Participants (thousands and percentages)	2011	1 202	831	64	752	2 849
		42.2	*29.2*	*2.2*	*26.4*	*100.0*
	2015	1 271	931	295	1 379	3 876
		32.8	*24.0*	*7.6*	*35.6*	*100.0*
Spending (billion KRW and percentages)	2011	3 561	3 900	0.11	614	8 075
		44.1	*48.3*	*0.0*	*7.6*	*100.0*
	2015	4 544	4 744	166	1 028	10 482
		43.3	*45.3*	*1.6*	*9.8*	*100.0*
Spending per person (million KRW)	2011	3.0	4.7	0.0	0.8	
	2015	3.6	5.1	0.6	0.7	

Note: Data only include Basic Livelihood Security Programme spending and recipiency for the working-age population (15-64). Percentages are shown in blue and italics in the table.
Source: OECD compilation based on administrative data provided by the Ministry of Employment and Labor.

StatLink http://dx.doi.org/10.1787/888933645364

In short (with more details below), EI provides support and income replacement benefits for workers who lose their job involuntarily, provided they are insured and eligible for payments. BLSP provides a means-tested safety net for people living below the poverty line, provided they fulfil all entitlement conditions. Given the strictness of both EI and BLSP criteria, many Koreans will not be eligible for payments from either of the two support programmes. ESPP covers some of this gap for a small number of jobless people needing particular help to access the labour market. EITC covers some of the income gap for workers who earn too little to support their families. The size of the non-protected group, however, remains large.

Table 2.1 also shows that the size and weight of the four schemes in the overall policy package has changed considerably. EITC, after a large expansion in the past few years, now has the largest number of participants but, because spending per participant is low, EITC spending is only about 10% of the total spending on these four programmes. BLSP has the highest per-recipient cost and is therefore the largest programme in terms of total costs (again, only including BLSP recipients of working age). EI has more participants than BLSP but per-recipient spending is lower and so is total EI spending. ESPP, finally, despite its recent expansions still plays a minor role in terms of both recipients and spending. In the coming years, ESPP and EITC recipient numbers will probably increase further but the overall spending composition will change little without further reform.

Protecting the unemployed: Employment Insurance

Korea introduced its EI programme in mid-1995; much later than most other OECD countries and also considerably later than its own *Industrial Accidents Compensation Insurance* (IACI), which was introduced 30 years earlier. EI is a comprehensive labour market and social security measure including i) the employment security and vocational skills development programmes aimed at preventing joblessness, promoting employment and improving workers' vocational skills; and ii) the unemployment insurance component providing income support to displaced workers (see Box 2.1 for more details on some of the key characteristics of Korea's EI).

Box 2.1. Key characteristics of Korea's Employment Insurance (EI) system

Benefit coverage

Eligibility: EI in principle covers all employees on a mandatory basis, except for most persons working less than 60 hours a month or 15 hours a week, and family labour. Most self-employed can opt in on a voluntary basis. *Entitlement*: a beneficiary must have at least 180 days of coverage during the last 18 months, be registered at an employment security office, capable of work and available for work. Unemployment must not be due to voluntary leaving, misconduct, a labour dispute, or the refusal of a suitable job offer.

Benefit level and duration

EI beneficiaries receive 50% of their previous average gross wage. EI benefits are paid in instalments of 14 days, every two weeks. The *minimum* daily benefit is set at 90% of the minimum wage, whereas the monthly *maximum* was originally fixed at a constant level of KRW 40 000 but increased to KRW 43 000 in 2015 and KRW 50 000 as of April 2017. When EI was first introduced, the minimum benefit was around a fifth of the maximum but as the minimum grew rapidly, in line with increases in the minimum wage, and the maximum remained largely untouched, this is no longer the case.

The EI *payment duration* has not changed since the introduction of the system. Payment duration increases with age at the time of job loss and the length of the insurance record, ranging from 90 days for people insured for less than a year, irrespective of age, to 180 days for people under age 30 who are insured for 10 or more years (or 210 days if aged 30-49 and 240 days if aged 50 or older or if having a recognised disability).

Special benefits

Extended EI benefits exist in several forms. *Individual extended benefits* are offered to jobseekers who, after having been referred to job vacancies three or more times by a Job Centre, fail to gain employment and are considered needy. They can receive 70% of their previous EI benefit for an additional period of 60 days. *Benefits for extended training* are offered to jobseekers with difficulties in finding work because of a lack of skills. Such individuals are ordered to take training and can receive 100% of their previous EI benefit for a period of up to two years, as long as they receive training. *Special extended benefits* are offered to jobseekers whose unemployment benefit period has expired and who have difficulties in finding new employment due to a sudden rise in unemployment, during a period designated by the Minister of Employment and Labour. These beneficiaries can receive 70% of their previous EI benefit for an extended period of up to 60 days. Such benefits were provided three times during the crisis of 1998, but have not been offered since. Finally, a *beneficiary who falls ill* can receive 100% of the EI entitlement until being well enough to resume job search, up to a maximum of four years.

Funding mechanism

The EI system is co-funded from employee and employer contributions. Unemployment benefits are funded by 1.3% of the worker's gross wage, with the cost shared equally by employer and employee. Depending on firm size, employers have to pay an additional contribution ranging from 0.25% of the wage sum (less than 150 employees) to 0.85% of the wage sum (over 1 000 employees) to cover the cost of the employment security and vocational skills development programme. (For comparison, industrial accident insurance is fully covered by employers who pay a risk-rated premium ranging from 0.70% to 32.3% of the wage sum – the average being 1.70%). The EI contribution for voluntarily insured self-employed is equal to 2.25% of a self-chosen monthly remuneration level.

EI covers most salaried workers on a mandatory basis and they are entitled to payments if they have been dismissed involuntarily and paid contributions for at least 180 days out of the past 18 months. EI is co-funded by employer and employee premiums. At around 2% of the wage, total EI contributions in Korea are lower than in other OECD countries with an (un)employment insurance, with premium rates typically in the order of 4-8%.

In the current blind-spots discussion in Korea, the benefit side of EI dominates the debate, for obvious reasons. EI benefits have long suffered from the low coverage of the programme and more recently face the additional challenge of having turned over time into a relatively low and de-facto flat-rate payment. Both EI coverage and EI payment levels will have to be addressed vehemently in the coming years.

Despite a series reforms, EI coverage issues remain urgent

Despite continuous expansion of the programme since its introduction, the biggest problem of Korea's EI scheme remains the low number of workers insured and the low number of jobseekers entitled to a benefit. Korean governments at all times tried to tackle this weakness. In the late 1990s, legal coverage was gradually extended from companies with 30 and more ordinarily employed workers to all companies, irrespective of the number of workers employed. In the 2000s, coverage was extended to include not only regular but also most groups of non-regular employees, including part-time workers and daily workers. And most recently, since 2012, own-account workers and employers with less than 50 employees can also choose to be insured on a voluntary basis.[4]

EI take-up, however, remains low, for a number of reasons. *First*, there are still certain groups of salaried workers legally excluded from EI. This includes: a) employees who work less than 60 hours per month or 15 hours per week; b) businesses with less than five employees in the agricultural, forestry, fishery and hunting industries; c) most foreign workers; and d) workers aged 65 and over.[5] *Second*, while self-employed workers can in principle choose to opt-in they almost never do so in practice – despite the high flexibility of the regulation and affordable premium rates.[6] This is very important in a country where self-employment accounts for roughly one quarter of the total workforce and where many jobless people have no other choice than own-account work to make a living. *Third*, while EI is legally mandatory for all groups of employees not explicitly excluded, many of these employees are not insured, especially when they work in very small businesses with less than five employees (see below); again, this is a very strong limiting factor in a country dominated by such micro-businesses.

Figure 2.5 shows the blind spots of EI enrolment in Korea in more detail. Overall, in 2016 only just over half, or 53.2%, of the employed population in Korea had access to an unemployment safety net, either through EI (47.6%) or through other schemes for special groups of (public) workers (5.6%). Of the remainder, 14.9% were wage workers not enrolled in EI although they should be enrolled; 5.8% were excluded wage workers (mostly workers over age 65 or non-standard contracted workers); and the remaining 26% were non-enrolled self-employed (mostly own-account workers but also employers and unpaid family workers). In other words, many Koreans are still excluded despite a drop in the excluded share from 58.5% in 2006 to 53% in 2010 and 47% in 2016. In the period 2006-10, most of the improvement resulted from structural labour market changes (i.e. a decline in self-employment and unpaid family work over this period). In the period 2010-16, over half of the improvement was due to a decline in non-enrolment, and the rest was due to structural change.

Figure 2.5. Blind spots in Korea's Employment Insurance are manifold and still large

Distribution of the employed population in Korea by employment status and EI coverage (percentages)

A. Share of workers *with* and *without* employment safety net by gender and age as a percentage of employed people, 2016

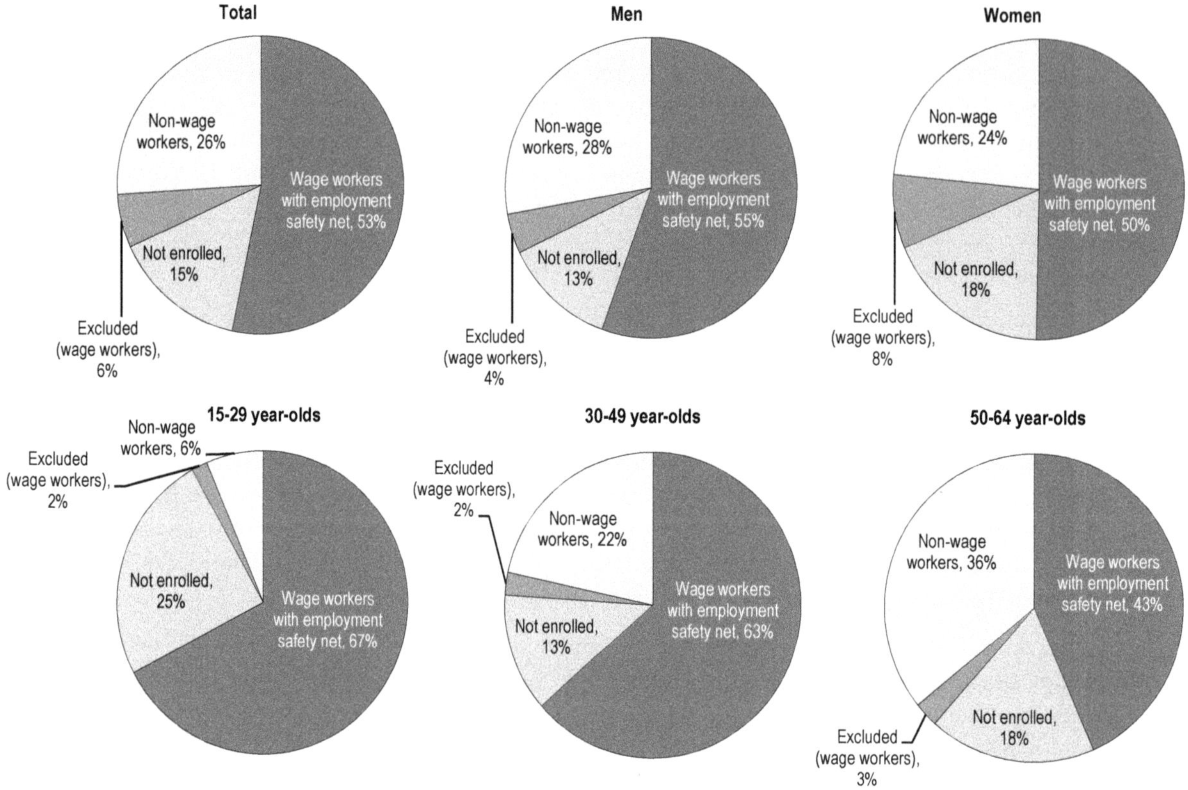

B. Distribution of workers *with* and *without* employment safety net by gender and age as a percentage of employed people, 2006, 2010 and 2016

		Wage workers *with* employment safety net	Workers *without* employment safety net					
			Not enrolled	Excluded (wage workers)	Non-wage workers			
					Employers		Self-employed	Unpaid family workers
					Firms with 5 or more employees	Firms with less than 5 employees		
Total	2006	41.4	20.1	4.8	2.4	4.8	19.8	6.8
	2010	46.9	18.6	5.5	1.8	4.3	17.3	5.5
	2016	53.2	14.9	5.8	1.7	4.4	15.5	4.5
Men	2006	49.3	13.6	3.0	3.7	6.1	22.8	1.3
	2010	51.1	15.3	3.5	2.7	5.4	20.6	1.4
	2016	55.4	12.4	4.3	2.4	5.4	19.0	1.0
Women	2006	30.3	29.1	7.4	0.5	2.8	15.5	14.5
	2010	41.1	23.3	8.2	0.6	2.8	12.7	11.3
	2016	50.3	18.3	7.9	0.6	2.9	10.7	9.2
15-29 year-olds	2010	61.6	29.3	1.8	0.2	0.6	4.0	2.4
	2016	67.3	24.6	1.8	0.1	0.8	3.4	2.0
30-49 year-olds	2010	54.0	17.6	3.6	2.2	5.4	13.1	4.2
	2016	63.5	12.5	2.4	1.8	5.0	11.6	3.2
50-64 year-olds	2010	34.5	19.0	3.8	2.5	5.3	26.7	8.1
	2016	43.5	18.0	2.6	2.4	5.6	21.8	6.1

Note: This figure adapts and updates a similar figure published in KDI Focus by Yoo (2013[10]).

Source: Supplementary results of the Economically Active Population Survey by employment type in August 2006, August 2010 and August 2016.

StatLink http://dx.doi.org/10.1787/888933644965

There are significant age and gender differences in non-enrolment. *First*, women are more likely than men to be excluded from EI although this gender gap is closing rapidly both because of a larger drop for women in EI non-enrolment – from 29% in 2006 to 18% in 2016 – and the drop in the number of unpaid family workers who are women in most cases. *Second*, workers over the age of 50 are less likely than their younger peers to be covered by EI – 43% of the 50-64 year-olds have a safety net compared with 67% of the 15-29 year-olds. The age gap in non-coverage is also closing but only very slowly: EI non-enrolment has fallen much faster for workers under age 50 while the decline in self-employment has affected workers over age 50 more than other age groups.

Lowest coverage for non-regular workers in micro-businesses

Two characteristics of the Korean labour market explain much of the low EI coverage: non-regular work and work in micro-businesses with less than five workers. Both forms of work are widespread in Korea, with one in three salaried workers having a non-regular work contract and four in ten working in a micro-business (see Chapter 1).

EI coverage for regular workers reached over 90% more than ten years ago and is now at around 95%. But among non-regular workers, even in 2015 only about two-thirds are covered by EI despite a continuous increase in this share which stood at only 50% of all non-regular workers ten years ago (Figure 2.6).

Figure 2.6. Non-regular salaried workers in small Koreans firms face the lowest employment insurance coverage

Share of workers covered by employment insurance by firm size and type of employment, 2006-15

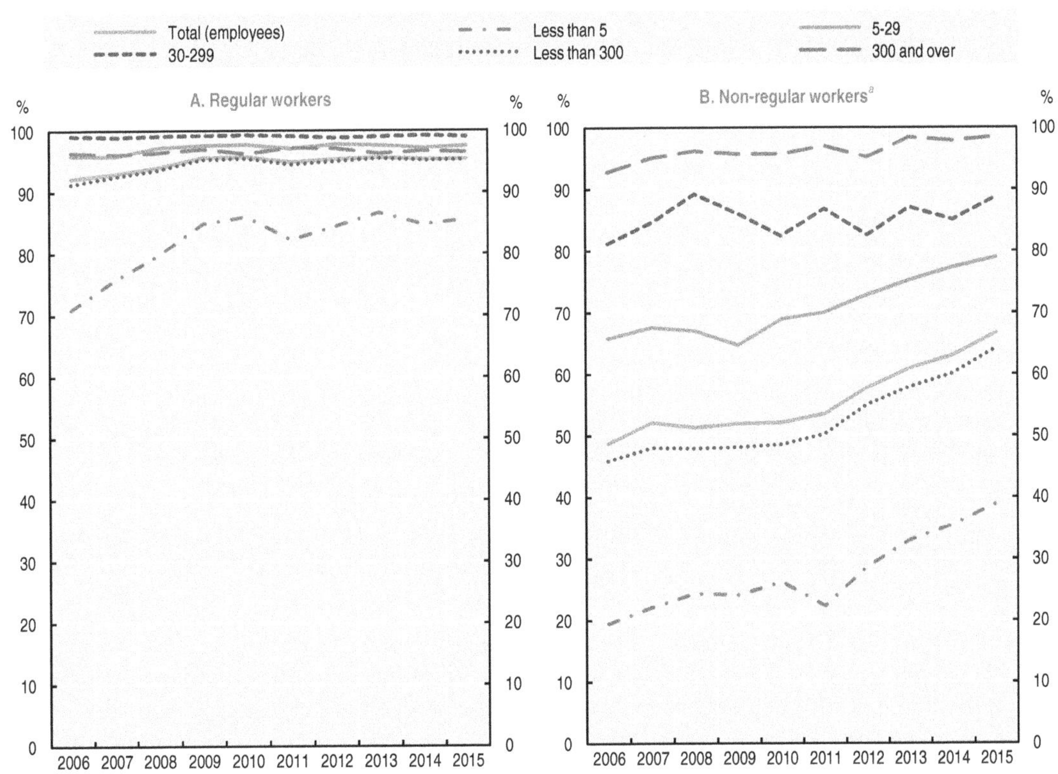

a) Excluding independent contract workers.

Source: Ministry of Employment and Labor, Survey on Labor Conditions by employment type, 2006-15.

StatLink http://dx.doi.org/10.1787/888933644984

Comparable inequality in EI coverage is found by firm size. Workers employed in large companies with more than 300 employees have EI coverage rates near to 100%, irrespective of whether they have a regular or non-regular work status. Similarly, the type of employment has a limited impact in firms with 30-299 employees in which also among non-regular workers around 90% are covered by EI. The situation is much worse for workers employed in micro-businesses. Non-regular workers in these firms have EI coverage rates below 40%, despite a 15 percentage-points increase in the past four years. In such micro-businesses, even one in seven regular workers miss out on EI coverage, with no further improvement for this group in the past six years.

Non-regular work in a micro-business has the lowest odds of providing EI coverage. This is worrisome for at least two reasons: *First*, non-regular work is often involuntary and taken up because people need immediate income. Only about one-quarter of all regular workers (i.e. half of those who are in such a job voluntarily) claim to be satisfied with their working conditions (Table 2.2). *Second*, the chances to transition from non-regular to regular work are poor in Korea: previous OECD analysis using self-assessment data has demonstrated that one year after, 70% of those workers are still in non-regular employment and only 12% have become regular workers, and that the probability to make a successful transition falls further over time; in other words, non-regular work in Korea is quite persistent (OECD, 2013[2]).

Table 2.2. Non-regular employment in Korea is often not a question of choice

Reasons given by non-regular workers for accepting non-regular employment, 2016 (percentages)

	Total	Temporary workers	Part-time workers	Atypical workers
Voluntary non-regular workers	**53.1**	**57.3**	**57.8**	**37.7**
Satisfied with working conditions	50.3	56.5	43.1	48.8
To obtain job security	16.6	22.7	4.2	14.0
To build up career for next job [a]	21.8	14.9	40.5	12.9
To have more flexibility in working hours [b]	11.3	5.9	12.2	24.3
Involuntary non-regular workers	**46.9**	**42.7**	**42.2**	**62.3**
To obtain immediate income	77.8	77.8	68.7	85.1
Cannot find a desirable job	13.1	14.5	15.9	9.5
To build up career for next job	7.3	6.8	13.7	2.9
To have more flexibility in working hours	1.7	0.8	1.7	2.4

a) Includes balancing work with family responsibilities or training, and to accumulate job experience.
b) Includes obtaining performance-based pay.
Source: Supplementary results of the Economically Active Population Survey by employment type, August 2016.

StatLink http://dx.doi.org/10.1787/888933645383

Recent efforts to expand EI coverage had some effect but at a high cost

In 2012, the Korean government introduced a premium subsidy scheme, generally known as the Duru-Nuri Social Insurance Premium Subsidy Programme, to overcome some of the shortcomings of the EI system. The main purpose of the scheme is to raise the number of undocumented low-wage workers legally guaranteed EI but not actually enrolled – the *effective* blind spot. Duru-Nuri provides financial assistance to low-wage salaried workers at workplaces of up to ten employees and their employers. Initially, a pilot programme was launched in selected counties of 16 provinces. Since July 2012, the programme has been in effect nationwide. Eligibility criteria and the size of the subsidy were changed several times. Until 2016, the wage level up to which workers can qualify was gradually raised to KRW 1.4 million per month – corresponding to roughly 125% of the minimum wage. The share of the premium subsidised through the programme was increased to 60% for all newly enrolled contributors, for as long as one year, and lowered to 40% of the premium for all other currently enrolled workers (previously the rate was 50% for both groups). Employers receive the same subsidy for their part of the contribution. In 2016, the number of workers who received an EI premium subsidy was just over 700 000 and the number of employers benefitting from a subsidy was just below 340 000.[7]

Recent analysis by the Korea Development Institute, using about 900 000 observations on the number of registered workers in small establishments over three years – 1.5 years before and 1.5 years after the introduction of Duru-Nuri –, suggests that the subsidy programme increased the number of EI registered workers by 1.36%. Approximately 98.5% of the programme cost was a deadweight loss: the large majority of subsidised people would have been insured also without the subsidy (Kim, 2016[11]). Put differently, for every 1 000 subsidised employees Duru-Nuri created 15 new covered employees, implying a cost per new EI enrolment of around KRW 50 million – roughly three times the person's annual wage. Premium subsidies alone do not seem to solve the problem of low EI coverage in Korea in very small businesses, which emerge and disappear with high frequency, in an effective manner. Many employees apparently do not consider the incentive provided by the subsidy strong enough.[8]

Two factors explain the ineffectiveness of the programme: The permanence of the subsidy and the fact that, for reasons of fairness, it is also paid to low-wage workers already insured. Other OECD countries do not have insurance premium subsidies of a nature comparable to Duru-Nuri. More common are reductions in insurance contributions for employers as an incentive to hire workers who are disadvantaged (e.g. young people, older workers, people with a disability) or in economically difficult times. But also such more targeted schemes struggle with high deadweight losses, even though contribution reductions tend to be given on a temporary basis.

The premium subsidy scheme could also be seen as a complement to another regulation in Korea, already in place since the inception of EI in 1995 that enables undocumented workers to claim EI benefits they should have been due. Such workers for whom EI contributions have not been made but who otherwise fulfil the eligibility and entitlement criteria and have been dismissed involuntarily can request a "confirmation of insured status" from their local Employment Centre and become eligible for EI payments in retrospect. The worker has to demonstrate the existence of the employment relationship and pay, ex post, the EI and national pension contributions that would have to be paid during the undocumented period of employment, for up to a maximum of three years. The employers who neglected to document such workers are mandated to pay their part of the contributions plus a one-off fine of KRW 300 000 per worker. The arbitration procedure nicely complements the Duru-Nuri scheme: employers have an obligation to document their workers and can receive a subsidy as an incentive to register low-paid workers but if they fail to do so, they may have to pay all EI premiums plus a fine.

In practice retrospect payment of EI premiums in order to secure EI entitlement is rare. In 2016, only 1 802 workers applied for an arbitration procedure of which 950 cases were approved (the remaining cases were rejected because entitlement criteria had not been fulfilled). The number of cases has remained relatively stable over the years. There is no research available on the reasons for the low number of cases but it is likely that these workers, typically non-regular workers in small firms, and presumably also their employers, are largely unaware of the possibility to request insured status in retrospect. It is also probably difficult for such workers to prove their employment relationship.

Enforcement of EI legislation and premium collection

With every reform step, EI coverage has improved but often only by a small margin. The slow expansion of coverage despite a series of comprehensive changes indicates that the structure of the Korean labour market has not responded sufficiently or perhaps remained unaffected. In particular, informal work – however defined – is still widespread in Korea and the life span of small businesses is still very short. This raises the question how much additional legal change would be able to achieve and, conversely, how the quite inclusive legislative framework could be better enforced.

In a recent paper, Lee (2012[12]) finds that on the basis of 2011 data around 40% of all wage workers in Korea engage in some form of informal work, defined as work that is not fully covered by minimum wage regulation, labour standards and social insurance. Notably he concludes that only 20% of this informality is due to a lack of regulation applicable in those workplaces while in all other cases non-coverage of this work is the result of non-compliance with existing legislation. Echoing the findings described above, non-compliance is more widespread in non-regular than in regular employment and far more frequent in small and micro-businesses than in larger companies.

Korea can do more to improve the enforcement of its EI and other labour legislation. Enforcement is difficult in a situation in which 1 300 labour inspectors have to inspect 1.86 million workplaces. Data from the late 2000s, when the number of labour inspectors fluctuated around 1 200, suggest that in any given year only about 1-2% of all workplaces were inspected but also that in 75% of these cases a violation was detected (Lee, 2012[12]). The planned gradual increase in the number of labour inspectors by 1 000 people until 2018 is welcome; however, even the larger number of inspectors will not be enough to inspect workplaces regularly and forcefully.

Employers have an obligation to report their workers acquisition of EI insurance status to the authorities[9]: Failure to do so can result in a penalty of KRW 30 000 per employee not reported (up to a KRW 1 million maximum) or KRW 50 000-100 000 (and a maximum of KRW 3 million) in case of false reporting of, for example, the wage level or date of employment. If a breach of obligation is discovered, the authority can enrol the employee into EI or correct false facts with no further action from the employer. However, not only are per-person fines low but data from the Ministry of Employment also suggest that fines are seldom used: In 2016, penalties were given for a total of just over 250 000 employees not reported and just over 60 000 employees falsely reported. The low fine and the low likelihood of its application are unlikely to pose a real threat to employers.

Another way to improve EI coverage is by better identifying workplaces that should be formalised and covered. Social insurance premium collection is an important aspect in this regard. While in the past the four social insurances (pensions, health, employment, industrial accidents) operated independently, since 2011 the government has allowed the insurances to integrate the collection of their premiums at the National Health Insurance Corporation. This has led to a minimal integration of the premium collection system: today, a company receives only one envelope rather than four, but the four insurances continue to perform their main tasks (such as application, enrolment and benefit payment) independently. Better integration of tasks would be a step in the right direction because insurance cover varies by type of insurance. Health and pension insurance coverage is even lower than EI coverage for most types of non-regular work but IACI coverage is high for all workers and in most cases has been high for many years (Table 2.3). The high IACI coverage rate has yet to be achieved for the other branches of social insurance.

Table 2.3. Insurance coverage is still low for many non-regular workers in Korea

Share of salaried workers covered by social insurance by type of insurance and type of employment, 2007-15

	All salaried workers	Regular salaried workers	Non-regular workers (excluding independent contract workers)						
			All non-regular salaried workers	Family workers	Agency/ Sub-contract workers	On-call workers	Part-time workers	Fixed-term workers	Contingent workers
A. Employment Insurance coverage									
2007	85.2	93.0	52.1	19.5	88.5	31.7	28.3	80.6	24.6
2009	85.9	95.6	51.9	15.2	90.4	36.8	27.1	81.5	25.1
2011	85.1	94.9	53.5	16.2	87.1	44.6	28.9	83.1	25.5
2013	88.6	95.6	60.9	54.5	90.0	44.6	50.5	85.3	34.7
2015	89.3	95.4	66.7	67.2	93.5	46.0	65.0	87.0	38.0
B. Industrial Accident Compensation Insurance coverage									
2007	95.0	95.8	90.9	69.1	94.8	90.9	79.1	94.7	86.0
2009	96.2	97.0	92.3	73.5	95.0	92.3	82.9	96.3	84.2
2011	96.3	96.8	94.2	74.4	96.8	95.9	86.2	96.9	88.1
2013	97.5	97.8	96.4	97.8	94.9	97.8	94.4	98.3	93.1
2015	97.6	98.0	96.4	93.2	97.9	97.4	94.2	98.3	87.6
C. Health Insurance coverage									
2007	86.6	94.7	49.6	19.4	88.3	14.1	26.9	82.5	19.0
2009	87.4	96.6	49.7	18.3	90.3	14.8	25.4	84.3	17.5
2011	87.2	96.4	50.6	18.6	89.1	14.0	26.8	89.5	17.5
2013	87.6	97.4	50.6	58.9	90.7	10.7	44.7	90.3	24.4
2015	88.4	97.9	55.5	68.6	92.2	8.5	59.6	92.6	26.6
D. National Pension Insurance coverage									
2007	86.2	94.2	47.3	18.6	87.3	13.4	26.2	80.3	18.3
2009	87.1	96.4	46.8	21.0	88.8	12.5	24.7	81.2	17.7
2011	87.0	96.1	48.1	19.0	87.7	13.6	27.8	84.5	15.8
2013	87.6	97.2	47.0	56.3	88.3	9.5	42.1	85.5	22.5
2015	88.7	97.8	52.7	70.6	90.1	9.0	56.4	88.5	25.9

Note: Information on this table is limited to salaried workers, either regular or non-regular, but does not include non-salaried workers (employers, own-account workers and contributing family workers).

Source: Ministry of Employment and Labor, Survey Report on Labour Conditions by Employment Type, http://laborstat.molab.go.kr/newOut/renewal/menu05/menu05_search_popup.jsp, 2007-15.

StatLink http://dx.doi.org/10.1787/888933645402

A recent change through which, as of 2017, the Korea Workers' Compensation and Welfare Service (KOMWEL) became responsible for EI applications of both workers and employers (in addition to IACI applications), could be an important step. This could contribute to a further increase in EI coverage among salaried employees and improve the link with the tax authority. The latter is important because in Korea work not covered by social insurance (be it non-regular work or own-account work) is generally registered for tax purposes; it only remains informal or undocumented for insurance purposes.

Over time, EI has turned into a flat-rate payment

A second problem of the EI scheme is the gradual erosion of the level of payments. Unemployment benefits in Korea have never been particularly generous in an international comparison but for many workers their value has fallen over time. For an average wage worker, EI initially replaces around 50% of the worker's wage – compared to an OECD average of around 65% (Figure 2.7, Panel A). The situation deteriorates if looking at the situation of workers unemployed for a longer period, even though long-term unemployment is low in Korea:[10] averaged over one year of unemployment, the income replacement rate is only 32% (because EI is only paid for a relatively short period), unless the person becomes eligible for BLSP. These benefit levels are among the lowest in the OECD; the OECD average for one year of unemployment is over 50%.

Figure 2.7. For most Korean workers the value of unemployment benefits has fallen over time

Net replacement rates (NRR) of EI entitlements across countries (Panel A) and over time (Panel B) and development of minimum and maximum thresholds of daily EI entitlements since 1995 (Panel C)

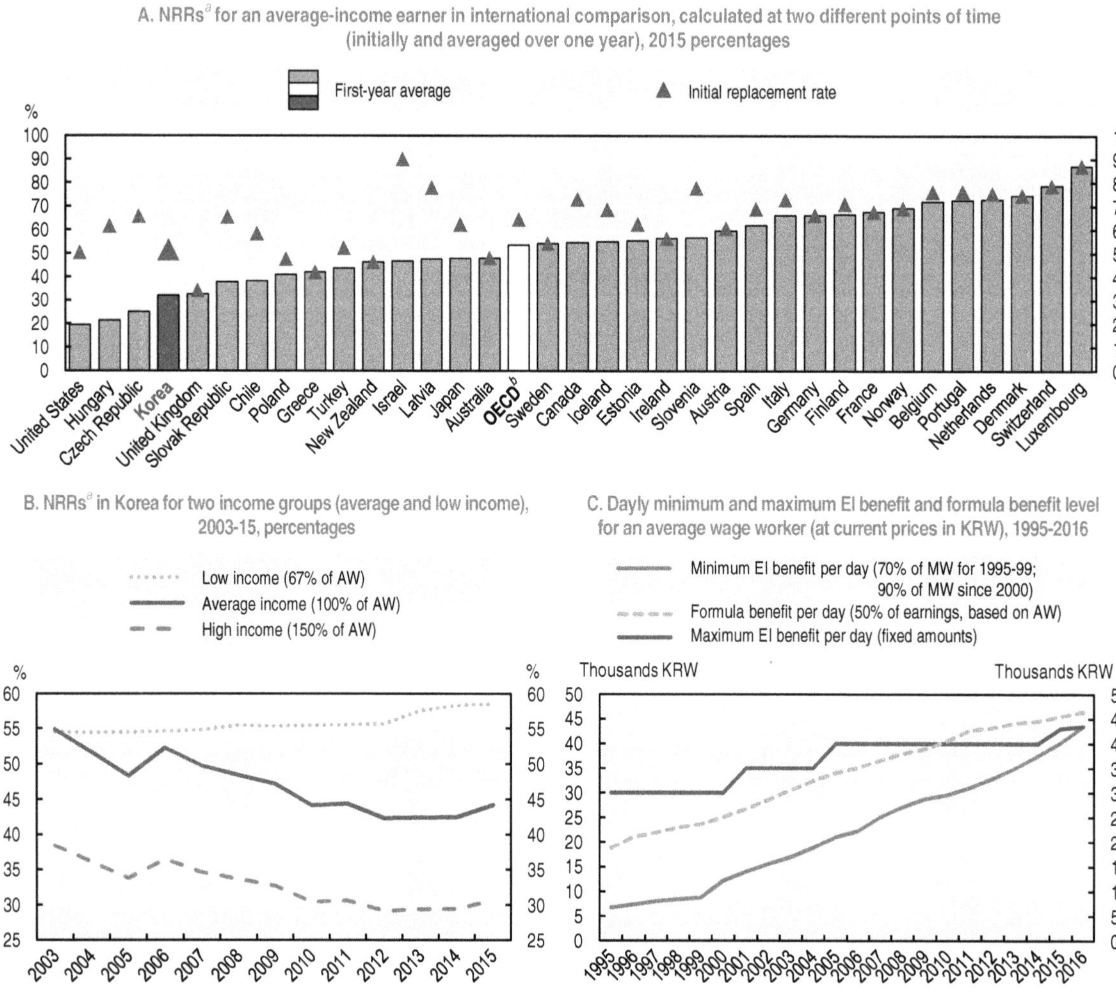

Note: AW: Average worker. EI: Employment insurance. KRW: Korean won.

a) Net replacement rate (NRR) is the ratio of net income out of work to net income while in work. Calculations consider cash income as well as income taxes and mandatory social security contributions paid by employees. Social assistance and housing-related benefits potentially available as income top-ups for low-income families are not included. Family benefits are included, while entitlements to severance payments are excluded. NRRs are calculated for a 40-year-old worker with an uninterrupted employment record since age 22. They are averages over four different stylised family types (single parents and one-earner couples, with and without children) and two earnings levels on the lost job (67% and 100% of average full-time wages). The one-year average is a somewhat artificial number insofar as the unemployment benefit payment duration is shorter than one year in around half of the OECD countries. Due to benefit ceilings, NRRs are in most countries lower for individuals with above-average earnings (see also Chapter 3).

b) Unweighted averages of the 34 OECD countries shown in Panel A above (excluding Mexico).

Source: OECD Tax and Benefit Models, www.oecd.org/els/social/workincentives for Panels A and B; and author's own compilation for Panel C.

StatLink http://dx.doi.org/10.1787/888933645003

Figure 2.7 (Panel B) also shows that, today, EI initially replaces close to 60% of the net wage for a low-income earner, around 45% for an average earner and around 30% for a high-income earner – suggesting considerable progressive redistribution within the EI scheme. Replacement rates have fallen sharply in the past decade for most workers except those earning a low income. For workers earning the average wage or more, the initial net replacement rate has fallen by around 10 percentage points in only ten years.

How is this fall in replacement rates explained? Korea has seen an unusual development in the past two decades by way of which the EI system has gradually moved away from its original structure. The maximum EI payment has remained largely unchanged ever since the introduction of the system whereas the minimum EI payment, fixed at 90% of the minimum wage, has gradually increased in line with the minimum-wage increase. As a consequence, today the minimum EI payment is almost equal to the maximum. This is very different from the situation in 1995, the year when EI was introduced: back then the minimum EI payment corresponded to one-fifth of the maximum (Figure 2.7, Panel C).

Panel C also shows the "intended" daily benefit for an average earner. In 1995, this intended payment was right between the minimum and the maximum. In the mid-2000s, however, an average earner hit the EI maximum and ever since then the actual payment was lower than the intended one. If the rapid increase in the minimum wage planned by the new government materialises – a 15% increase for three consecutive years – both the minimum and the maximum EI entitlement and the actual payment for all EI recipients would increase accordingly. In this case, the current somewhat unusual situation of a minimum that equals the maximum would continue.

Some EI features and developments could be reconsidered

It is surprising that this shift in payment structure could happen with so little resistance. It appears that EI premium increases which would be needed to re-establish the original payment features of the system and to raise benefit payments back to their level initially agreed more than 20 years ago are highly unpopular – more unpopular than the ongoing erosion of the system. Partly this development can be explained by the fact that the Korean EI scheme was introduced at a time of very low unemployment. The crisis in the late 1990s resulted in some increase in EI premiums to cover the fast increasing number of unemployed at the time but the appetite for a sufficiently large premium increase to fund a true insurance for all workers was lacking.

Whether the current situation is sustainable in the long run remains to be seen. For many jobseekers and their families EI entitlements are no longer providing a sufficient income to maintain the level of living. This has been accepted so far because of the low average duration of unemployment in Korea and maybe it has also contributed to that low duration because workers have strong incentives to find a new job quickly.

The reluctance to increase EI premium rates is understandable insofar as higher non-wage labour costs potentially reduce international competitiveness; this is especially relevant for the export-oriented industrial production which is still at the heart of Korea's economy. But the current situation arose from political decisions, not out of necessity. Over 20 years, benefit entitlements have fallen so drastically that resurrecting the initial situation would indeed require an increase in premium rates. It will require a political discussion on what the future EI benefit level should be to keep the system economically viable and socially sustainable. In the past, EI surpluses have been used to introduce new tasks, such as maternity leave and parental leave benefit which were introduced without a corresponding increase in premiums or additional dedicated tax funding.

The EI scheme in Korea also includes elements the existence of which might have to be reconsidered. Employment promotion allowances were introduced as an incentive for EI benefit recipients to find new employment quicker. There are three forms of such allowances but only the *Early Re-employment Allowance* (ERA) is relevant in practice. ERA is offered to benefit recipients who find stable work before the end of their EI entitlement period. After a series of reforms, the allowance now equals 50% of the remaining benefit entitlement (or two-thirds if the EI recipient is over the age of 55 or has a disability). To be entitled, a recipient must: a) find a new job in the first half of his entitlement period; and b) have been employed (or engaged in his/her own business) for a period of at least 12 consecutive months. Until the late 2000s, ERA entitlement criteria have been much laxer and total ERA spending corresponded to about 15% of total spending for job-seeking benefits. After the recent reforms, the ERA spending level dropped to less than 5% of this. The various changes and corresponding cuts in both ERA recipients and ERA spending were justified because of analysis which showed that ERA came with considerable deadweight effects (Hwang, 2013[13]). It remains to be seen whether this is not the case any longer with the revised ERA criteria.

Preventing poverty and exclusion: Basic Livelihood Support Payment

The second most important social benefit programme in Korea is BLSP, a means-tested social assistance programme providing cash and in-kind benefits to eligible persons living in absolute poverty. BLSP was put in place in 2000 in response to the rapid increase in the number of poor and unemployed people in the aftermath of the Asian financial crisis of the late 1990s.[11] BLSP was long criticised for its strict eligibility criteria that exclude many deserving families and for a payment structure which creates dependence on rather low financial support. Both issues have been addressed recently but certain problems continue. In addition, there are issues around the group of *conditional* BLSP recipients – a small group that could grow bigger and would benefit from more attention.

An increasing number of recipients but eligibility remains strict

Local governments are in charge of determining BLSP entitlement and providing corresponding benefits and services.[12] In order to receive BLSP, an applicant has to meet both income and family requirements. Household income (income and assets converted into income) must be below a given threshold level, which is determined in relation to standardised median income – objectively derived from a household survey – and varies by household size and type of benefit (Table 2.4). Before mid-2015, thresholds had been defined by the government every year in relation to the minimum cost of living. The current thresholds imply that a family or household of four people would only be entitled to living benefit (the main component of BLSP) if having a total income similar to Korea's minimum wage although such household could possibly still be entitled to other BLSP components. The steep increase in thresholds with household size implies that BLSP is designed as a payment to support larger families.

Table 2.4. Income thresholds for BLSP entitlement vary by type of payment

Monthly BLSP income thresholds (in KRW) by type of cash benefit and size of household, 2017

	Size of household (persons)					
	Single	Two	Three	Four	Five	Six
Living benefit (30% of SMI)	495 879	844 335	1 092 274	1 340 214	1 588 154	1 836 093
Medical benefit (40% of SMI)	661 172	1 125 780	1 456 366	1 786 952	2 117 538	2 448 124
Housing benefit (43% of SMI)	710 760	1 210 213	1 565 593	1 920 973	2 276 353	2 631 733
Education benefit (50% of SMI)	826 465	1 407 225	1 820 457	2 233 690	2 646 923	3 060 155

Note: BLSP: Basic Livelihood Security Programme provides seven different benefits, mostly paid-out in cash, of which four are main benefits. SMI: Standardised median income is derived from and similar to the minimum cost of living. For comparison: the monthly minimum wage in 2017 was KRW 1.45 million.
Source: Ministry of Health and Welfare.

StatLink http://dx.doi.org/10.1787/888933645421

The family requirement implies that applicants cannot receive benefits if they have a close family member (a parent, child or spouse) capable of supporting them – the so-called *family support obligation rule*. Eligibility does not depend on whether such family support is actually provided. The capacity of family support is measured by the family members' income and assets. The crux is that relatives with a relatively low income are supposed to support their income-poor family member even though, in 2015, the government raised the threshold income to be accepted as an incapable legal supporter from 130% of the minimum cost of living to 100% of median income.

Income requirements and the family support obligation both keep the BLSP caseload under control. Today, about 1.7 million Koreans receive one or several BLSP benefits, corresponding to around 3.2% of the population. This level is similar to the OECD average but low in comparison with OECD countries with an otherwise stringent and immature social protection system – despite a significant increase recently (up from 1.33 million in 2014) because of changes in the income thresholds for applicants as well as potential supporting relatives.

Unpublished estimates suggest that without the family support obligation rule the number of BLSP recipients in Korea could be roughly twice as high as it is today.[13] This is relevant for two reasons:

- *First*, family relations and household composition have changed drastically in Korea in the past few decades. The average household size, for example, declined from 4.7 people per household in 1980 to 2.7 in 2016 and the share of one-person households increased from only 5% to almost 25% in the same period (Figure 2.8); both trends will continue into the future. Accordingly, family ties are also changing. Not the least because of such changes in household and family structures, rules similar to Korea's family support obligations have been abolished or reduced in other OECD countries which had or still have comparable rules on paper, such as Austria, Belgium, France, Germany, Japan or Switzerland.[14]
- *Second*, relative to the total number of poor working-age individuals, social assistance take-up is relatively low in Korea: BLSP covers around 13% of that population compared with an (unweighted) OECD average of around 30% (Figure 2.9). Abolishing the family obligation rule would bring Korea closer to this OECD average on this measure.

Figure 2.8. Korean households are becoming smaller and living alone is becoming common, similar to other OECD countries

Average household size (Panel A), distribution of households by number of persons (Panel B) and distribution of one-person households by age (Panel C), 1980-2016

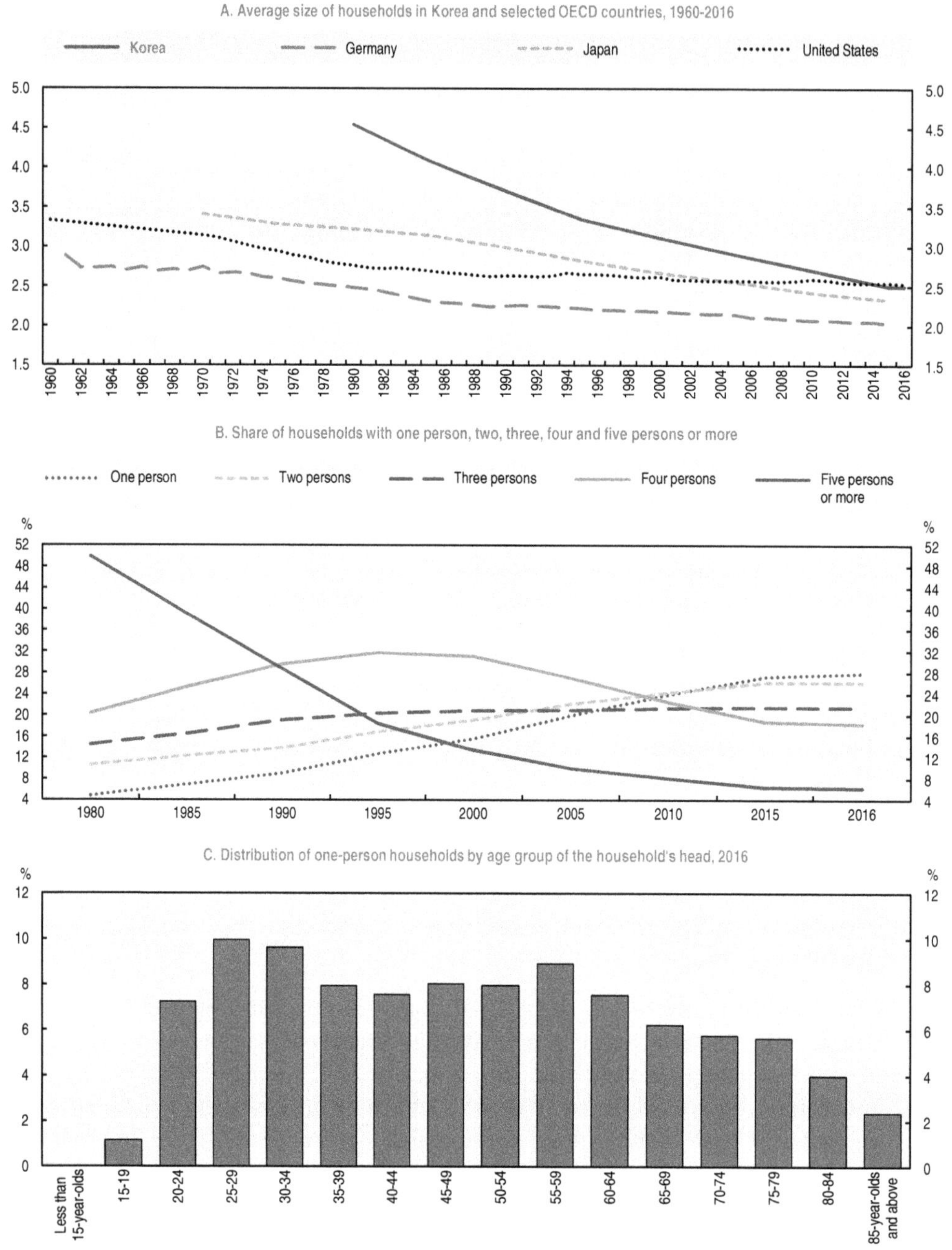

Source: Korean Statistical Information Service (KOSIS), http://kosis.kr/statHtml/statHtml.do?orgId=101&tblId=DT_1JC1611&conn_path=I3 (accessed on 6 October 2017). For Germany, see Table 6 for Western Germany from www.bib-demografie.de/SiteGlobals/Forms/Suche/EN/Servicesuche_Formular.html?nn=3214948&resourceId=3075566&input_=3214948&pageLocale=en&templateQueryString=household+size&sortOrder=score+desc&searchArchive=false&searchIssued=false&submit.x=0&submit.y=0 (accessed on 24 October 2017); and for the United States, US Census Bureau; Bureau of Labor Statistics, "America's Families and Living Arrangements: 2016", www.statista.com/statistics/183648/average-size-of-households-in-the-us/ (accessed on 24 October 2017).

StatLink http://dx.doi.org/10.1787/888933645022

Figure 2.9. In Korea, a relatively low share of poor people receives social assistance

Recipients of social assistance or lone parent benefits as a share of poor working-age individuals, selected OECD countries, 2013

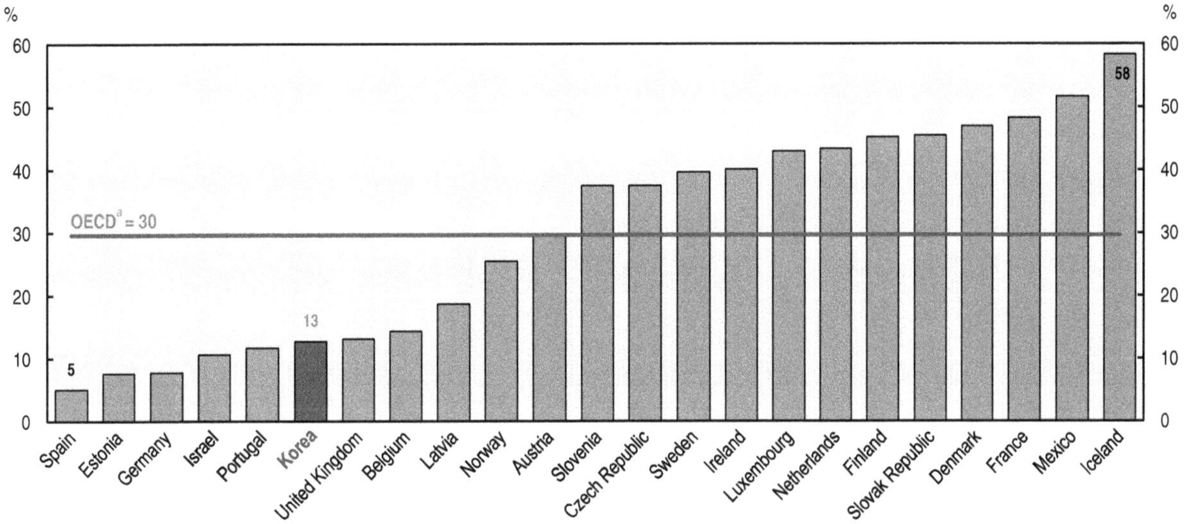

Source: Calculation based on *OECD Social Benefit Recipients Database*, www.oecd.org/fr/social/recipients.htm.

StatLink http://dx.doi.org/10.1787/888933645041

A more customised benefit with flexible entitlements

A second main issue for Korea's BLSP concerns its benefit level and structure. BLSP provides seven different benefits[15] and, until recently, one of the biggest problems was that the income thresholds for all types of benefit were identical. This meant that recipients received all or nothing, and that those receiving benefit had a strong motivation to remain on benefits. This is confirmed by evidence showing that about one quarter of all recipients have been on BLSP for more than ten years and roughly half of them for more than five. The 2015 reform of BLSP eligibility criteria addressed the benefit accumulation issue by de-linking the various benefits and transforming BLSP from a single payment to a more *customised* payment. The four main types of benefits are now phased out gradually: living benefit is phased out first and education benefit last (see Table 2.4).

It is too early to assess the full impact of the 2015 BLSP reform. In the first instance, the more customised payments improve the income situation of a number of recipients and their families. This is reflected in the overall increase in BLSP recipiency after the reform and a particularly fast increase in the number of education benefit recipients, as well as somewhat higher average payments. Improved entitlements for certain groups of BLSP recipients were well justified. Comparing pre-reform net income levels of families relying on social assistance suggested Korea found itself in the lower third of OECD countries for most family types (OECD, 2013[2]). Updated post-reform estimates of net income levels of these groups suggest that lone parent and two-couple families with two children who rely on BLSP still find their income considerably below a relative poverty threshold, with the maximum disposable income provided to these families being at or somewhat below 40% of equivalised medium income, taking cash housing benefit entitlements into account. However, the 2015 estimates put Korea closer to the middle of OECD countries for most types of families (Figure 2.10).

Figure 2.10. BLSP entitlements in Korea keep families below a low income threshold but are comparable with other countries' cash minimum income benefits

Net income value of cash minimum income benefits as a percentage of median household income for two family types, selected OECD countries, 2015

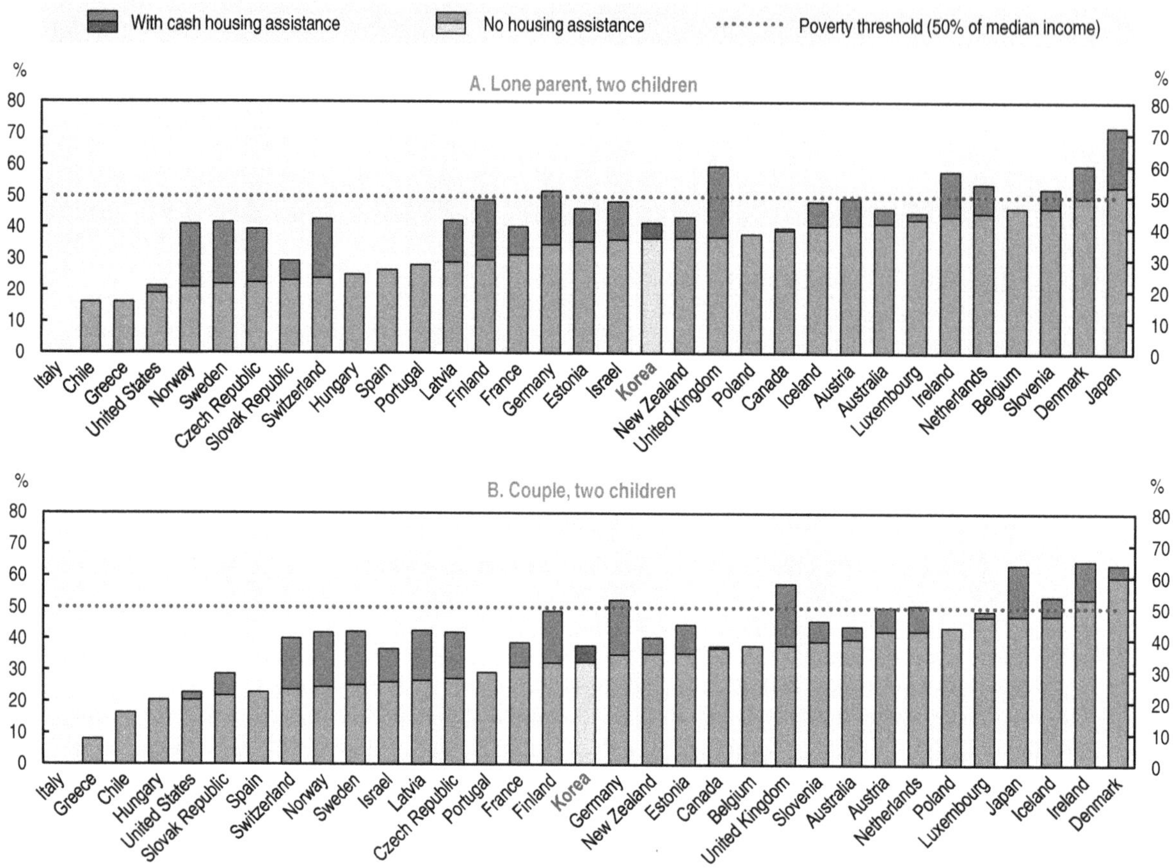

Note: Details of assumptions made in the calculations are available in the table "Income Adequacy" which is available under the statistics heading on the Benefits and Wages website referenced below. Countries are ranked in ascending order of the category "No housing assistance".

Source: OECD Tax and Benefit Models, www.oecd.org/els/social/workincentives.

StatLink http://dx.doi.org/10.1787/888933645060

The longer-term impact of the reform on, for example, the duration of benefit payments or benefit dependence and the number of people moving off benefit remains to be seen (Wan, 2016[14]). Earlier analysis by the OECD has suggested that BLSP, mainly because of the low tax burden imposed on Korean workers, generally creates less of a poverty trap than minimum-income systems in many other OECD countries – although effective tax rates when taking up work can potentially be high for some income and family situations (OECD, 2013[2]). This situation should have improved further with the more customised phase-out of the various payment components of BLSP.

Very few BLSP recipients with work capacity

A discussion about improved work incentives and reduced benefit dependency may, however, be relatively fruitless in relation to BLSP. A closer look at BLSP beneficiaries reveals that among all recipients of the living benefit only some 75 000 (or 6% of the total) are so-called *conditional* recipients. Various medical evaluations can be performed by the pension insurance authority, on request of the local welfare office, to assess whether or not living benefit recipients have the ability to work. If so, they receive a conditional benefit and must get in touch with the local Job Centre where they are entitled to services to help them find and access employment. Virtually all other OECD countries employ similar activation measures as part of their social assistance measures, although the extent of enforcement varies considerably across countries and localities.

The low share of conditional recipients suggests that BLSP in Korea is largely a payment for people unable to work.[16] This partly explains the large gaps in Korea's social safety net: for those who are no longer (or never were) entitled to EI, there is effectively no other support available for a person able to work in principle but not able to find a job or to access the labour market. This can be a particular problem for people with health issues. The situation is very different in most other OECD countries in which one or more of the following situations may arise (see Chapter 3): a) social assistance schemes may cater for a larger number of people who are able to work but have exhausted their unemployment benefit entitlements; b) special unemployment assistance schemes may provide benefits for jobseekers in long-term unemployment or those not entitled to unemployment benefits in the first place; and c) additional other systems might be available to help people temporarily unable to work because of sickness, disability or care obligations. Neither of these options is available in Korea.[17] Instead, a large share of BLSP recipients of working age are classified as unable to work and, thus, as non-conditional recipients because of disability or lone parenthood.

What is happening with the small group of conditional BLSP recipients in Korea? Conditionality implies they have to participate in the Self-Reliance Programme (SRP)[18] organised by the Ministry of Health and Welfare or the Employment Success Package Programme (ESPP) provided by the Ministry of Employment and Labor. Of the roughly 49 000 individuals annually who have participated in SRP, one-third became self-reliant – meaning that they either found employment or started a business or stopped receiving BLSP payments. A more rigorous evaluation of the cost-effectiveness of SRP, however, is not available. Of the roughly 26 000 BLSP recipients who participate in ESPP (see more on this group further below), one in eight succeeded in finding work or starting a business immediately. In the future, efforts could be made to improve these success rates, especially in the event of a further easing of BLSP eligibility criteria whereby the number of conditional recipients with work capacity would increase and the issue of work activation and labour market reintegration would become more pressing.

Supporting jobseekers actively: Employment Success Package Programme

Well aware of the gaps in the social protection system, the Korean government introduced the ESPP scheme in 2009 as a way of helping jobseekers neither entitled to EI nor receiving BLSP but facing considerable disadvantages, especially in the form of low income. ESPP combines targeted employment support with some income support. Over the years, ESPP was expanded rapidly in many different ways and the programme still has considerable potential for further expansion. The challenge for the government is to expand programme capacity as well as quality at a fast enough pace and, at the same time, to raise participation and make it attractive for those eligible to participate.

Assessing the effectiveness of ESPP

ESPP provides targeted, case-managed job-search support as well as training to improve employability, but also various flat-rate allowances as an incentive to participate in the programme and in training and as a reward for having found a job (see Box 2.2).

Box 2.2. The three stages of Korea's Employment Success Package Programme (ESPP)

ESPP is a comprehensive employment service operated by the Job Centre or contracted out to private employment agencies. The programme can last for up to 12 months (it ends as soon as the participant finds a job), with the possibility of re-referral after a suspension period of varying length. ESPP was first introduced for low-income jobseekers only but later on expanded to also include other risk groups, some of them (notably eligible youth) irrespective of their income situation. The programme consists of three stages:

First stage

The main purpose of the first stage, which is obligatory and lasts at least three weeks, is to clarify people's ability and enhance their motivation to work. It includes individual counselling, group counselling, vocational psychological testing, an evaluation of the employability, and the preparation of an Individual Action Plan (IAP).

The counsellor profiles the participants into one of four levels of employability (very low, low, normal, and high), depending on individual barriers and labour market experience. Services are provided in line with the level of employability. Participants must prepare an IAP at the end of the first stage, after a minimum of three face-to-face sessions with their counsellor, which should include relevant personal and career information and a plan for vocational training. Those who complete an IAP are paid a *basic participation allowance* of KRW 150 000 (about EUR 115). If a participant attends special programmes, an *additional allowance* of up to KRW 100 000 is paid (varying by type of participant).

Second stage

The purpose of the second stage is to provide the vocational training and job experience needed to strengthen the participant's employment competence. This stage can last for 6-8 months but is not obligatory if no training needs have been identified in the first stage.

Participants choose services based on their IAP, in consultation with their counsellor. The tuition fee of KRW 3 million is provided as a training subsidy (some participants have to cover a co-payment of 5-50%). During the training, participants receive a *training participation allowance* of KRW 284 000 per month and a monthly *support allowance* of KRW 116 000 to cover expenses occurring during the period of vocational training. There is also special training for those who want to run their own business.

Third stage

The purpose of the third stage, which is obligatory and can last for up to three months, is to help participants find employment through intensive job-placement services provided by either the Job Centre or a private employment agency.

Services include searching for the best job match for each participant based on vocational preferences, aptitudes and participation history in the second stage of the programme. Participants can also receive coaching on job-interview skills and be accompanied during their job interviews. In 2016, the average number of direct referrals at the third stage was 1.63 referrals per participant. During this stage, participants receive KRW 20 000 per month to cover their costs. Type I participants (low-income jobseekers) who obtain a job of more than 30 hours a week which also has EI coverage can receive an *employment success allowance* worth up to KRW 1.5 million in total and paid in three instalments, as follows: KRW 300 000 after three months in the job, another KRW 400 000 after six months, and another KRW 800 000 after 12 months. As of 2018, youth participants will also be entitled to payments worth KRW 900 000 (three times 300 000).

The programme was introduced at a time when a lot was known from other OECD countries on how to set-up and structure an effective activation programme and Korea did not shy away from taking other countries' experiences into account. The programme has many features that were shown to be essential, such as frequent face-to-face counselling, well-customised intervention, strong user involvement, and a strong degree of flexibility in the type and timing of interventions. ESPP also has a good balance of incentives and requirements in place for those who (could) participate.

ESPP reaches out to a number of target groups, classified into type I and type II. Type I participants include jobseekers with less than 60% of median income (the biggest group), various groups of disadvantaged jobseekers e.g. disabled people, lone mothers or youth at risk (with no income threshold), and conditional BLSP recipients. Type II participants include jobseekers aged 35-64 (with up to 100% of median income) and young jobseekers under age 35 (without any income threshold). The classification matters mostly for how services are provided (see below).

The result of the strong programme features is that the majority of participants complete the programme and that ESPP has promising employment outcomes. Of all participants in 2015, over 80% started a job in the course of the programme including just a little less than 80% of the low-income group. However, the quality of the jobs that these jobseekers find is debatable. First, less than half of all ESPP participants find a job that pays more than KRW 1.5 million or 60% of median income. This is not surprising given that ESPP is predominantly targeted to low-income jobseekers who struggle in finding employment. Secondly, and more importantly, only four in five ESPP participants keep their job for more than three months and six in ten of them for more than six months, even though four in five jobs come with EI coverage (Table 2.5). It is not known if and how fast these people find another, maybe better job. Fast job turnover is not uncommon in the Korean economy that is dominated by short-term and other forms of atypical employment. In view of the labour market disadvantage of most ESPP participants, however, more can be done to connect people with more sustainable jobs.

Table 2.5. Participants in Korea's Employment Success Package Programme generally find employment but wages and employment stability are low

Selected ESPP statistics in 2015: participants, programme completion, post-programme employment and employment retention, Employment Insurance coverage and low-wage prevalence

	Participants (units)	Programme completion	Post-participation employment rate	Share of employed insured by EI	3-month employment retention	6-month employment retention	Share of employed earning KRW 1.5 million or more
		Percentages					
Low-income people	137 332	98.4	78.3	79.3	78.9	64.3	43.7
Young people	133 472	99.0	86.8	89.9	79.2	64.3	53.0
Mature people	24 599	99.1	82.1	85.8	79.1	64.5	43.3
Total	**295 403**	**98.7**	**82.5**	**84.9**	**79.1**	**64.3**	**48.3**

Source: Administrative data provided by the Ministry of Employment and Labor.

StatLink http://dx.doi.org/10.1787/888933645440

More in-depth performance evaluation by Lee (2016[15]) suggests ESPP is quite effective in bringing programme participants into employment. Comparing the experience of ESPP participants with that of non-participants, i.e. comparable groups of people who had applied for ESPP but were not selected into the programme, shows that ESPP has a positive employment effect for all people and especially so for some of the most disadvantaged groups; only initially employment effects are masked by a lock-in effect. For low-income clients of ESPP, for example, employment rates are 16 percentage points higher one year on compared with those people not admitted to the programme, and 22 percentage points higher three years on (Figure 2.11). The effect is just a fraction smaller for vulnerable groups (lone parents or disabled people), young people and middle-aged and elderly people. For conditional BLSP recipients who are referred to ESPP the effects are smaller in the first year but also reach 15 percentage points after three years. Over time, the effects were relatively stable for all groups but with a clear tendency towards improved ESPP effectiveness between 2009-2011 and 2014. This suggests that the competence of caseworkers and the quality of services is improving, although it could also reflect the improved economic and business conditions.

Figure 2.11. ESPP participation has clear employment effects for all client groups

Employment rates six months, one year, two years and three years after application for participation in ESPP, participants versus non-participants, by type of participant, 2014 (percentages)

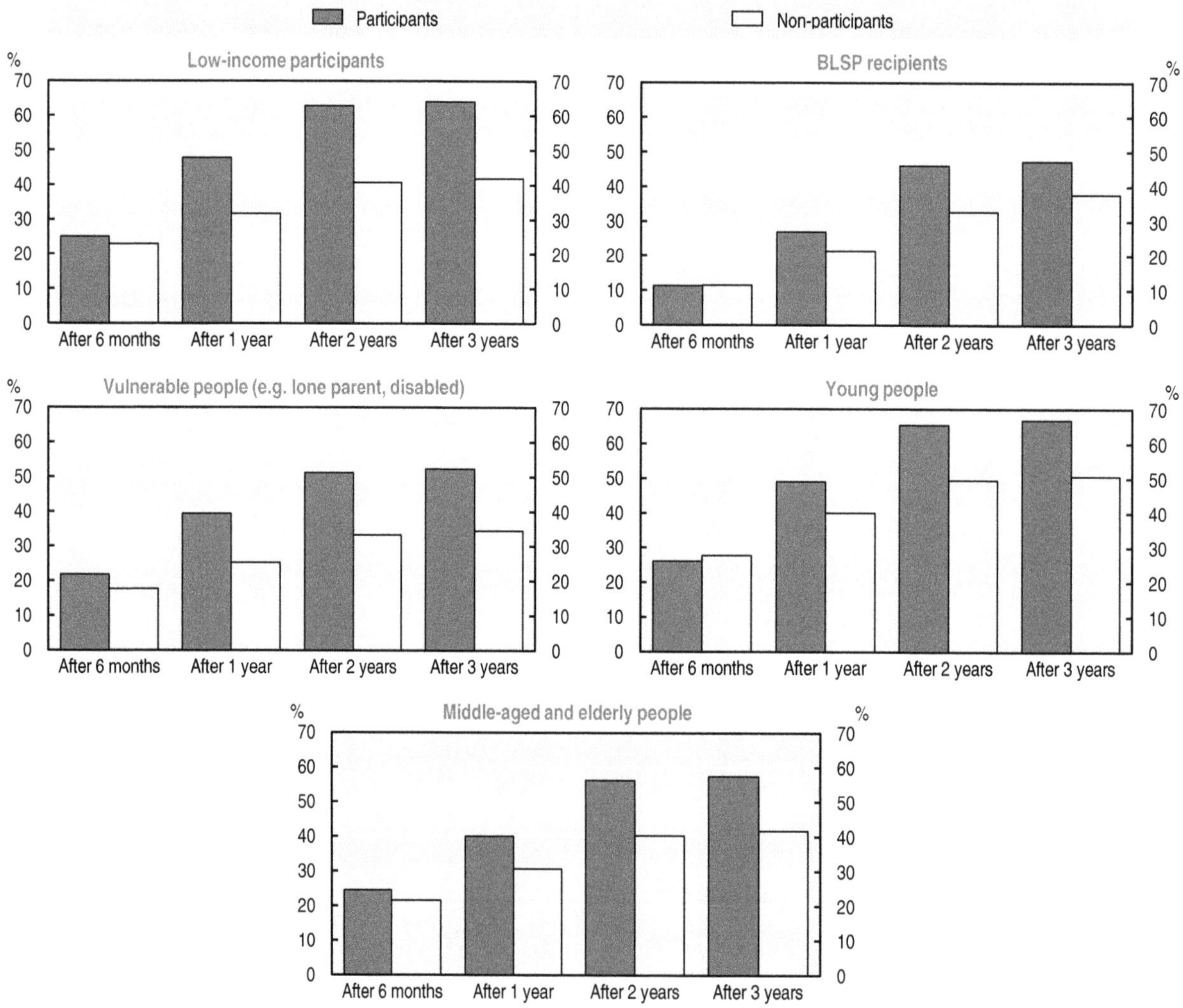

Note: BLSP: Basic Livelihood Security Programme; ESPP: Employment Success Package Programme. Non-participants are people who have applied for ESPP but were not selected into the programme.

Source: Lee (2016[15]), *An evaluation of the employment impact of the Employemnt Success Package Program*, KLI, Seoul..

StatLink http://dx.doi.org/10.1787/888933645079

Expanding the capacity of a promising programme

Creating an effective programme of such size and type more or less from scratch is a very ambitious task in terms of building the sheer capacity of the service. The number of ESPP participants increased from 10 000 in 2009 to 300 000 by 2015. Initially, the programme was developed for low-income jobseekers only – people living below 60% of the median income level (previously measured as 150% of the minimum cost of living) – but, over the years, in recognition of the power of the programme, ESPP was expanded to other target groups.[19] In 2015, 47% of all participants belonged to the low-income group.

Korea has done well in developing and expanding ESPP services. The ESPP budget has increased 32-fold between 2009 and 2015 to reach KRW 217 billion in 2015. Funding comes from general taxation, with a drawback being that it is a "budget programme", with the budget set every year. ESPP was gradually rolled out in all 94 Job Centres under the responsibility of the Ministry of Employment and Labor and the number of staff assigned to ESPP has been increased accordingly. However, the staff increase could not fully keep pace with the increase in the number of participants: since 2009, the caseload has increased from 80 clients per ESSP counsellor to 100 clients and must be expected to rise even higher in the coming years (the caseload of the Job Centres increased particularly fast in 2012 and 2013).

The fast increase in service capacity could not have been stemmed by the PES alone. In parallel, a private employment service market was created and a share of the task entrusted to private service providers. As of 2017, this market includes 333 private employment agencies (plus 399 branch offices) which in total employ slightly more ESPP counsellors than the Job Centres. Building this market was not straightforward and the role of private providers has changed over time. Initially they had responsibility for a certain share of the target group – at that time, jobseekers with very low income. The latest change in 2015 meant that Job Centres gained full responsibility for all low-income clients, while all other clients are now serviced by private providers.

Whether this is the right way of splitting the task is unclear and there is no evidence available which would prove that more vulnerable clients had not been served well before the latest change.[20] For the future, therefore, other ways of sharing of tasks between public and private providers could still be envisaged. Private employment service providers in Korea not only provide services but are also responsible for all client contact. This is unusual among OECD countries which usually tend to keep much of the job-search monitoring and activation process of clients under public supervision and outsource employment service delivery only. This is the case, for example, in Australia and the United Kingdom – the two OECD countries that have gone the furthest in terms of privatising employment services (see Box 2.3).

Assuring high-quality employment services

A main challenge in the course of such rapid service capacity expansion is to ensure high quality services. This is particularly challenging because in Korea contracts with private providers only last for one or two years. Quality assurance happens in three ways in Korea. *First*, the law specifies minimum requirements for private providers such as the minimum room capacity available at the agency, the number and qualification of counsellors and the maximum allowed number of clients per counsellor (which is now 120 clients). In addition, Job Centres have some role in monitoring the legal correctness of the operation of private services, including an occasional inspection of services.[21]

Box 2.3. Subcontracting of employment services to private providers: The cases of Australia and the United Kingdom

Australia and the United Kingdom are the two OECD countries which have gone furthest in subcontracting and privatising its employment services. The idea in both countries is that providers are paid on the basis of the employment outcomes they achieve for their clients – a novel approach which under balanced conditions should maximise employment outcomes in a cost-effective way.

In both cases, outcomes were somewhat disappointing initially and provisions adapted several times over the years to improve outcomes. In particular, both countries gradually strengthened payments for longer-term outcomes and reduced payments for the initial intake of clients. This is a thorough approach which should incentivise private providers to make the investments necessary to not just place jobseekers into any job but to achieve sustainable employment outcomes. Important steps in this regard are to create regional competition to assure private providers improve their services, to measure outcomes and services accurately and rigorously, and to ensure only successful providers stay in the market. An important step in both countries was the extension of the duration of service contracts to assure longer-term investments, in the case of Australia for example from three years in the first contract period to six years in the third period.

Both countries have chosen to outsource employment services but to leave the monitoring of jobseekers largely in public hands. But there are also very notable differences in the approach. Australia steers the process and outcomes through a rigorous quality assurance framework, the star-rating system, and gradually strengthened prescription of service standards. The latter include, for example, engagement in training and work-experience measures for long-term unemployed people. The United Kingdom, on the contrary, has gone much further in setting financial incentives for providers to deliver predefined (longer-term) outcomes but leaves it entirely in the hands of the providers to decide how best to achieve them; the types of services provided in the United Kingdom is a business secret and thus a black box, making evaluation somewhat more difficult.

Outcomes measurement is still not perfect in both countries. Results in Australia suggest that initially outcomes remained largely unchanged but were delivered at a lower cost than before the start of subcontracting. Over time, outcomes have improved. Results in the United Kingdom were satisfying for the average client but failed grossly for hard-to-place clients, especially people with reduced work capacity who are since the shift to the Work Programme serviced by the same providers as all other jobseekers. This is different in Australia which maintained a network of disability employment specialists in parallel to the service provider market. The difficulties in achieving good outcomes for more difficult clients suggests that differentiating providers' outcome payments more seriously by the degree of complexity of the clients' labour market barriers will be essential. Fee variation by client group is also important to lower deadweight costs. Allocating clients to specific providers to avoid cherry picking can also be part of a solution. Finally, care must be taken to minimise red tape so that spending goes to clients mostly rather than being eaten up by cumbersome administrative procedures.

Source: OECD (2013[16]) and OECD (2015[17])

Second, the Korea Employment Information Service evaluates the performance of all private agencies every year. Until 2016, the evaluation included five criteria: a) the post-service employment rate (40% of the evaluation); b) the employment retention rate (20%); c) the better job[22] employment rate (20%); d) the customer satisfaction rate (15%); and e) the level of co-operation with the Job Centre[23] (5%). As of 2017, the five criteria were changed as follows: a) the post-service employment rate (45% of the evaluation); b) the implementation of key employment policies (25%); c) the implementation of HR investment plans (10%); d) the level of customer satisfaction (17%); and e) guidance and inspection results (3%). In addition, minimum performance indicators include an achieved overall employment rate of 53% and a share of disadvantaged participants among all participants of at least 30%.

Each private agency is given one of five levels (A to E) which approximately follow a normal distribution. Level A refers to the 10% of private providers with the highest scores in their performance evaluation and level E to the 10% with the lowest performance scores (level B 25%, level C 30%, and level D 25%). Private agencies with levels A to D can keep their contracts, while the contracts of agencies with level E should be cancelled if they have at least one indicator below the minimum performance criterion in 2017 or if they were graded into group E for two consecutive years. In the past, provider contracts were rarely terminated probably because of the fast growth in the number of ESPP participants: in 2015, the contract of just one out of 309 private agencies was terminated because of poor results and in 2016 this happened for just three out of 288 contracts. For 2017, the 11 lowest-graded institutions from the 2016 evaluation will be excluded from the tender. Overall, there seems to be considerable room for a stricter quality assessment and contract termination for poorly-performing service providers.

The *third* element in Korea's quality assurance framework is financial incentives for providers to deliver employment outcomes. Like in the United Kingdom and Australia, providers are paid for their performance with payments depending on the speed and duration and, since recently, the quality of the employment outcomes they achieve. Until 2016, a provider could earn up to KRW 1 million for one client (in addition to the basic subsidy of KRW 400 000) if a lasting job was found within six months from the start of initial counselling. As of 2017, the employment incentive component was changed to reflect the quality of employment (measured by the person's annual wage) rather than its sustainability and the maximum possible payment was increased to KRW 1.9 million (Table 2.6). In other words, almost 80% of the total possible maximum payment is now paid for employment outcomes (previously 70%), thereby providing a strong incentive for providers to deliver good-quality services. It would be vital, however, to evaluate the payment mechanism rigorously to see if and how it contributes to better results for the users of services; also because the public Job Centres, which deliver similar services to the most vulnerable, low-income jobseekers, lack comparable quality incentives. The frequent changes in payment rules might also have an impact on employment outcomes as providers have to adapt very quickly to new situations.

Increasing take-up and providing income support

Expanding service capacity and assuring quality service provision is one side of the coin. The other is to assure a corresponding growth in ESPP participation, especially since the programme is voluntary in most cases. The biggest factor in explaining the fast expansion in the ESPP caseload is the widening of eligibility criteria and corresponding inclusion of groups hitherto ineligible, i.e. type II clients more generally and among them especially youth. But there are various other measures and regulations that contribute to the growth in the ESPP caseload.

Table 2.6. Private employment service providers in Korea have strong incentives to deliver satisfactory services and achieve good outcomes

Thousands KRW

A. Basic and employment incentive subsidies paid to private employment service providers until 2016

	Total maximum payment	Basic subsidy	Employment incentive subsidies		
			Better job incentive	3-month tenure incentive	6-month tenure incentive
Employment within 6 months[a]	1 400	400	300	300	400
Employment within 12 months	1 200	400	300	200	300
Employment within 15 months	1 000	400	300	100	200

B. Basic and employment incentive subsidies paid to private employment service providers as of 2017

	Total maximum payment	Basic subsidy	Employment incentive subsidies			
			Wage below 1.4 million	Wage below 1.8 million	Wage below 2.3 million	Wage above 2.3 million
Employment within 6 months[a]	1 900	400	600	800	1 000	1 500
Employment within 12 months	1 700	400	400	600	800	1 300
Employment within 15 months	1 400	400	200	400	600	1 000

a) Number of months from the date of initial counselling.
Source: Administrative data from the Ministry of Employment and Labor.

StatLink http://dx.doi.org/10.1787/888933645459

Most important in this regard are the participation incentives paid to programme participants, echoing the incentives for private providers. In the first stage, participants are paid a one-off participation allowance of KRW 150 000-250 000; in the second stage they can receive a monthly training participation allowance worth KRW 400 000; and in the last stage type I participants can receive an employment success allowance paid in steps and in total worth up to KRW 1 million (as of 2017, up to 1.5 million; see Box 2.2). These payments are not very high; neither in international comparison nor relative to any EI or BLSP entitlement. However, it must be emphasised that ESPP recipients are not entitled to any other social benefits. One would need a rigorous evaluation to assess whether or not these participation incentives work, although the caseload growth suggests that they play a certain role for prospective service users.

Conditional BLSP recipients are the only group of people for which ESPP participation is *not* voluntary. Once classified as conditional recipients, they have to go to the Job Centre which will stream them into one of three categories. If they have a high probability to get a job immediately, they are assigned to the first stage of ESPP for at least one week. If they have the possibility of employment but need to remove short-term barriers to employment, they are provided case-managed services for six weeks during the first stage of ESPP. If they have only a low possibility of employment due to more limiting employment barriers, they will be referred to the SRP. As discussed above, about one in three conditional BLSP recipients are referred to ESPP directly. Any future and likely increase in the number of conditional BLSP recipients, therefore, would automatically have a large impact on the operations of ESPP.

A third way to incentivise ESPP participation is through direct recruitment which, until 2014, was only possible for the Job Centres. Since 2015, however, private providers are also allowed to recruit participants directly – though not people from the low-income group, who no longer fall under their responsibility. A potential recruit of a private provider would first have to go to the Job Centre, for clearance of eligibility, before being referred back to the private provider. In other cases, when a participant is recruited by the Job Centre or comes to the Job Centre on a voluntary basis, the client can choose a private provider – unless it is a low-income or any other type I client, in which case they have to stay with the Job Centre.

Towards a Korean-style unemployment assistance scheme

Because it targets people neither entitled to EI nor receiving BLSP, ESPP through the various incentive payments also to some extent bridges a gap in income support – even though the amounts paid are probably too low to qualify as unemployment benefits, in a true sense. Currently, the total maximum payment over a period of around 12-18 months is KRW 4.15 million – less than two times the monthly median wage or four times the monthly minimum wage. Because of the target group of the programme, it seems logical to explore the potential of ESPP in bridging current benefit gaps.

Recent research by the Korean Labour Institute (KLI) has done exactly this: explore how far one could go in, and what one could achieve by, expanding ESPP to such a degree that it closes some of the wide distance between EI and BLSP. Lee (2013[18]) concluded that an expansion of ESPP into a Korean-style unemployment assistance scheme could cost around KRW 850 billion annually (roughly 5-6 times the current cost of ESPP) and offer employment and income support to another 260 000 people (roughly double the current number of ESPP recipients). This exercise assumed that the scheme would pay a monthly benefit worth around 20% of the average wage for a period of up to 12 months (i.e. the duration of the programme) – which is similar to the current value of ESPP and also the value of unemployment assistance schemes in some OECD countries (see Chapter 3).

After the publication of the KLI report, a discussion has been started regarding whether Korea should introduce an unemployment assistance scheme of some form – building on the strong activation and employment support features already established under ESPP. The proposed KLI version of unemployment assistance would be affordable as the necessary spending would be less than 20% of current EI spending, for example. However, just doubling the number of recipients as assumed in this exercise would imply that also with the new scheme many jobseekers would fall between the cracks.

In 2017, the new government has decided to introduce an unemployment assistance scheme of some sort in gradual steps and has assigned KRW 1.2 trillion over the next five years for this purpose. In a first step better benefits will be provided to youth participating in ESPP and at a later stage, from 2020 onwards, also to other groups. The assigned amount is not enough to fully implement the KLI proposal, however.

Guaranteeing reasonable work incomes: Earned Income Tax Credit

Korea not only has to decide how to support more of its vulnerable jobseekers. It also needs to find ways to better support the large number of people not able to earn a decent living despite being in employment. Again, the Korean government is well aware of this problem and has introduced a special EITC scheme to address it. Like with other programmes, however, the system suffers from limited effectiveness driven by its tight eligibility criteria and low take-up. In any case EITC alone will not sufficiently reduce the high level of in-work poverty in Korea; other systems will have to play a role, too.

Increasing eligibility and take-up of EITC

Income tax credit schemes are used in many OECD countries to address in-work poverty. By reducing the income tax bill or providing cash refunds when the resulting tax deduction is larger than the actual tax to be paid, such schemes raise the take-home pay for working families with low incomes. Tax credits of this kind were shown to contribute to poverty reduction and have positive employment effects (OECD, 2005[19]). Empirical evidence also suggests that effectiveness of such tax credits is greatest in countries with low income tax rates, low social benefits for the non-employed and low minimum wages (Bassanini, Rasmussen and Scarpetta, 1999[20]) – conditions which all characterise Korea (at least until recently; see the minimum wage discussion below).

Korea introduced its EITC scheme in 2008 and, since then, expanded its scope and coverage continuously to include more and more workers. EITC initially targeted families with children only but was expanded to childless couples and, finally, also single-member households aged 50 and over. Initially special rates applied for families with children whereas today, since 2014, a special Child Tax Credit (CTC) is paid for up to three children in addition to EITC while the level of EITC itself only depends on the number of earners in the household. Income and asset thresholds and the maximum pay-out were also augmented repeatedly and varied with the composition of the household.

The tax credit granted by Korea's EITC, not including any CTC entitlement, ranges from 1.8% of the average wage for singles to 4.3% for single income and 5.3% for dual income families. Together with CTC, this can go up to 8-9% for eligible couples with three children (although the majority of EITC recipients do not qualify for CTC). The level of EITC is comparable to what is offered by similar schemes in other OECD countries. Only the systems in the United Kingdom (for all family types) and in the United States (only for families with two or more children) allow significantly higher maximum credits. However, EITC in Korea is phased out at relatively low levels of income. While EITC credits in Korea are phased out at the level of between one-third (for a single person) and one-half (for a single-income family) of the average wage, corresponding rates are around 100% of the average wage in France and the United States and much higher than this in New Zealand and Finland. This suggests that EITC in Korea is more tightly targeted to the lowest-income earners. Only Canada and the United Kingdom have phase-out ranges quite similar to those in Korea. Any additional CTC entitlements, however, are only phased out at income levels close to the average wage.[24]

Through various changes over the past few years, the number of EITC recipients has increased and the composition of recipients changed somewhat. The total number of EITC recipients increased from 0.5-0.6 million in 2008-10 to 0.8 million in 2011-13 and around 1.3 million in 2014-15. Total spending on EITC has increased in line with the increase in recipiency numbers. More families with higher incomes became eligible for EITC and people could receive slightly higher payments. The average payment, however, has changed little over time: it fluctuated around KRW 850 000 or 2% of the average wage per year, with 30-40% of all recipients receiving less than KRW 500 000. Similarly, today more people fall into the highest threshold group but still one-third of all recipients are families with annual incomes of less than KRW 5 million, i.e. families with incomes below one-third of the minimum wage (Table 2.7).

Table 2.7. EITC entitlement in Korea is gradually spreading to higher wage levels but the average payment remains relatively low

	2010	2011	2012	2013	2014	2015	2016
	Percentage distribution of EITC recipients by wage level, 2010 16 (EITC only)						
Total	100.0	100.0	100.0	100.0	100.0	100.0	100.0
Under KRW 5 million	30.3	30.3	32.0	40.3	34.5	30.4	32.9
KRW 5 to less than 10 million	30.1	29.2	28.4	26.6	21.7	21.4	24.1
KRW 10 to less than 15 million	30.9	31.7	26.3	22.3	22.9	22.1	21.4
KRW 15 to less than 20 million	8.7	8.9	11.2	9.0	15.9	18.9	15.8
KRW 20 to 25 million	0.0	0.0	2.1	1.7	5.1	7.1	5.8
	Percentage distribution of EITC recipients by benefit amount received, 2010 16 (EITC only)						
Total	100.0	100.0	100.0	100.0	100.0	100.0	100.0
Under KRW 500 000	29.3	29.6	33.5	41.7	31.9	31.9	36.2
KRW 0.5 to less than 1 million	30.9	30.7	30.2	29.1	23.4	24.2	27.9
KRW 1 to less than 1.5 million	39.7	39.8	24.0	19.5	20.9	21.5	18.1
KRW 1.5 to 2.1 million	0.0	0.0	12.2	9.7	23.8	22.4	17.8

Source: Administrative data from the National Tax Service.

StatLink http://dx.doi.org/10.1787/888933645478

Korea has not only expanded the scope of EITC by increasing the eligibility thresholds to cover more family types but, as of 2015, has also made self-employed families eligible. Since then, about one in three receiving families are regular workers, one-third daily workers and one-third families with business incomes (Table 2.8). EITC entitlement for self-employed families is complex, with special adjustment rates for the type of industry: the higher the adjustment rate, the lower the chances are that a family would be entitled to EITC. For instance, the adjustment rate is 20% for self-employed beneficiaries in the wholesale business sector; 45% in restaurants, manufacturing and construction; 75% in the service industry; and 90% for leasing services.

Table 2.8. Today, around one-third of all EITC recipients in Korea are families with business incomes

EITC recipients by type of employment, 2009-16

	2009	2010	2011	2012	2013	2014	2015	2016
Total	100.0	100.0	100.0	100.0	100.0	100.0	100.0	100.0
Regular workers	39.7	40.3	40.6	38.8	34.5	40.6	31.1	28.7
Daily workers	45.2	43.7	42.4	41.4	46.1	42.4	28.1	29.2
Income from regular and daily work	15.1	12.7	13.1	11.4	10.2	8.2	7.4	7.5
Self-employed	0.0	0.0	0.0	6.0	5.9	5.3	31.5	32.9
Others	0.0	3.3	3.9	2.4	3.3	3.6	2.0	1.8

Source: Administrative data from the National Tax Service.

StatLink http://dx.doi.org/10.1787/888933645497

For the future, the Korean government is planning to gradually expand EITC further to eventually reach an estimated number of 3.6 million households in 2030, a 2.5-fold increase from today in both recipiency numbers and total spending (Kim, 2016[21]).

Because of the relatively short history of EITC in Korea, evaluation studies are still rare. Available findings are mixed but, overall, point to a positive impact on labour supply – in terms of both participation and working hours – especially of households at the phase-in range of EITC, the range within which EITC benefits increase as earnings increase and therefore the range when work incentives are strongest (Song and Bahng, 2014[22]; Lee, Kwon and Moon, 2015[23]). Jeong and Kim (2015[24]) also found positive effects on the poverty rate for couple families but not for single parents and elderly single-member households. None of the studies, however, appear to have looked at the impact and implications of the inclusion of self-employed people. On the whole, these findings suggest that the planned further expansion of EITC could help some people, and more people than is currently the case, but for a fuller judgement the expansion to the self-employed population would need to be evaluated. Because of the low average payment, however, EITC and its expansion can only be one element in a broader strategy to tackle in-work poverty.

The role of other labour market institutions in tackling in-work poverty

A second main safeguard to ascertain that work provides sufficient income for working households is Korea's statutory Minimum Wage (MW) which, as of January 2017, corresponds to KRW 16.2 million per year for a full-time worker. At around 48% of the median wage, Korea's MW is in the lower half of OECD countries which have a statutory MW. However, the MW is presumably more important than in other countries because around 15% of all workers in Korea (17.4% in 2017, according to Korea's Minimum Wage Commission[25]) earn at or below the minimum wage – this is much higher a share than in most other OECD countries where typically only around 5% or less earn at or below the MW (Figure 2.12).[26]

The current government of Korea plans to increase the MW substantially over the next three years, from KRW 6 470 per hour today to KRW 10 000 per hour in 2020, implying a 15.6% compound increase every year for three successive years.[27] This change will lift Korea to the top quarter of OECD countries with regard to the MW level, and the share of workers receiving the MW would explode. Estimates by the government suggest that 20% of all workers would be affected by this change. A change to the MW of such a magnitude and in such a short period is unparalleled in OECD countries and implications could be considerable, also because Korea does not differentiate the MW as much as other countries which often apply lower minima, for example, for the youth population or less frequently also for people with disability.[28] A recent paper suggests that an increase in the hourly MW to KRW 10 000 would increase the number of MW earners 4-fold and have dramatic implications for certain low-wage industries and certain groups of workers, especially low-skilled and older workers (Wook, 2016[25]).

Figure 2.12. The share of workers earning at or below the minimum wage is very high in Korea

Minimum-wage workers as a share of all workers (left-hand scale) and minimum-wage levels as a share of the median wage (right-hand scale), latest available year

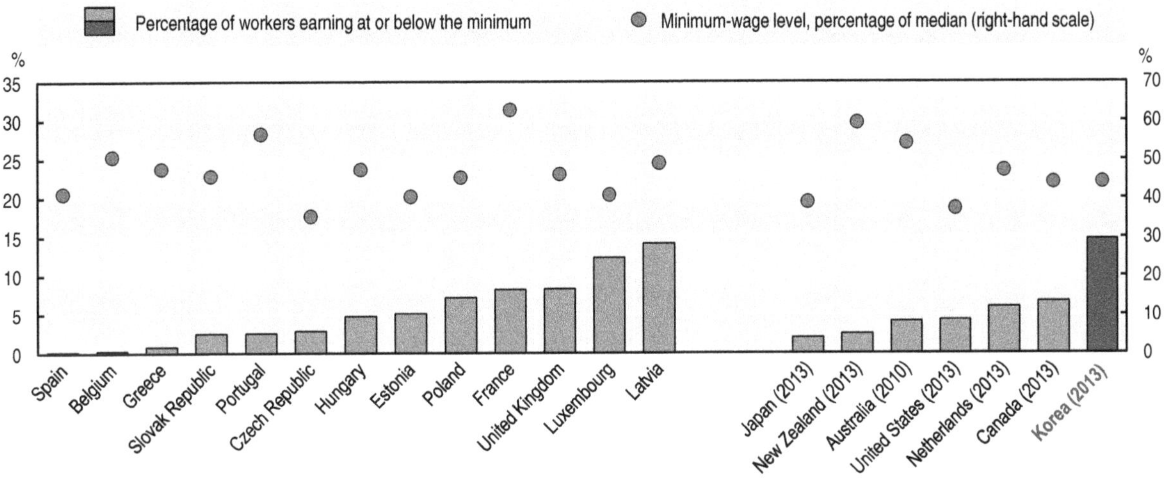

Note: The number of minimum-wage workers cannot usually be established with certainty and can vary between data sources. Because survey data counts are affected by measurement error, both in earnings and in working hours, it is common to include those with wages below the minimum and slightly above. As far as possible, data estimated for this figure refer to those earning less than 105% of the legal minimum applicable to each worker's age group. However, some data exclude workers in small firms in which minimum-wage workers tend to be overrepresented. Estimates therefore represent a lower boundary.

Source: OECD (2015), "Minimum wages after the crisis: Making them pay", p. 8, OECD Publishing, Paris, www.oecd.org/social/Focus-on-Minimum-wages-after-the-crisis-2015.pdf.

StatLink http://dx.doi.org/10.1787/888933645098

Considering the high level of in-work poverty and the large number of MW workers, the Korean government projects a number of positive effects from the drastic increase in the MW, including a boost in consumption and an expansion in employment and economic growth. To maximise such effects, considerable financial support will be provided (approximately KRW 3 trillion) to strengthen the payment capability of micro businesses. A thorough evaluation of the large MW increase will be important in consideration of its potentially large impact on the economy. Comparative OECD analysis shows that, because of the very low income tax burden in Korea, even a more modest increase in the MW would have a strong impact on workers' take-home pay – contrary to many other OECD countries in which the net effect of a MW increase is much smaller (Figure 2.13). Hence, even smaller MW increments could be effective.

An evaluation of labour demand effects of such a sharp MW increase goes beyond the scope of this report but the planned increase also has strong implications on other labour market institutions in Korea – such as the functioning of EITC, the functioning of EI (since the minimum EI benefit is set in proportion to the respective MW), and the functioning of BLSP. These institutions interact and mutually depend on each other. Any evaluation of the MW increase should, therefore, also look at the interplay with other labour market institutions. Generally, tax credits have been shown to be more effective than a MW in tackling in-work poverty (Pearson and Scarpetta, 2000[26]). But more research would be needed to establish the evidence on these relationships for Korea.

Figure 2.13. Minimum wage increases in Korea translate into large net income gains

Share of a minimum-wage increase that adds to net income, after accounting for income taxes, social security contributions and applicable benefit reductions: Example of a lone-parent family, 2013[a]

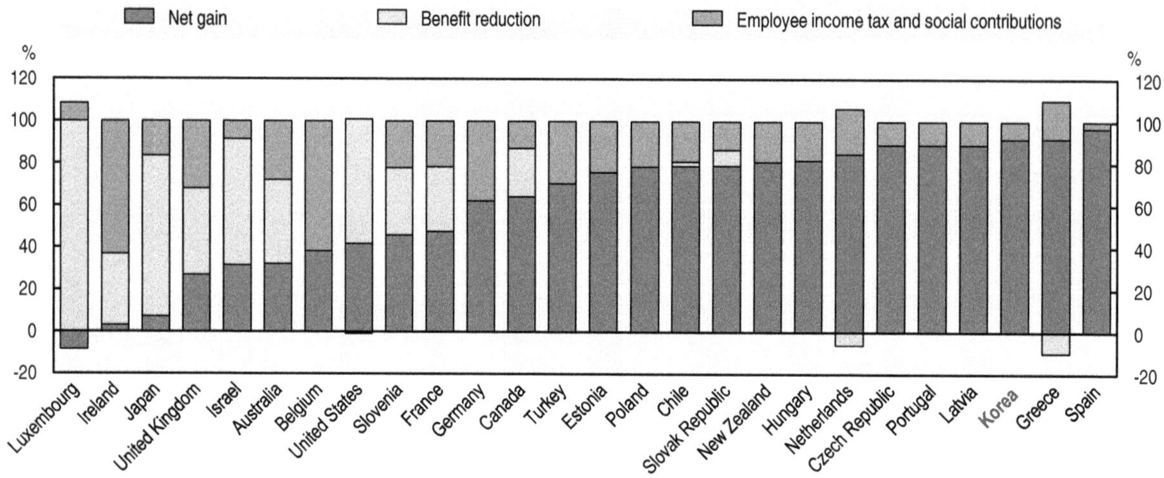

Note: The number of minimum-wage workers cannot usually be established with certainty and can vary between data sources. Because survey data counts are affected by measurement error, both in earnings and in working hours, it is common to include those with wages below the minimum and slightly above. As far as possible, data estimated for this figure refer to those earning less than 105% of the legal minimum applicable to each worker's age group. However, some data exclude workers in small firms in which minimum-wage workers tend to be overrepresented. Estimates therefore represent a lower boundary.

a) Minimum-wage levels in Germany refer to 2015.

Source: OECD (2015), "Minimum wages after the crisis: Making them pay", p. 6, OECD Publishing, Paris, www.oecd.org/social/Focus-on-Minimum-wages-after-the-crisis-2015.pdf.

StatLink http://dx.doi.org/10.1787/888933645117

Social assistance schemes also sometimes play a role in tackling in-work poverty by covering the difference between low earnings and families' income needs. In a number of OECD countries, receipt of social assistance is frequent for low-income workers and their families. This is not the case in Korea. More than 90% of all BLSP recipients are inactive. Of the 7% who are in the labour force, about half are unemployed and almost all others are daily workers (Table 2.9).

Table 2.9. Very few BLSP recipients in Korea are in employment

Distribution of BLSP recipients by labour force status and type of employment, 2015

	Total	Economically active						Inactive
		Regular employment	Temporary employment	Daily employment	Self-employ ment	Agriculture	Unemployed	
Number of recipients	1 554 484	3 748	6 965	37 631	8 570	3 758	50 737	1 443 075
Distribution (%)	*100.0*	*0.2*	*0.5*	*2.4*	*0.6*	*0.2*	*3.3*	*92.8*

Source: Ministry of Health and Welfare (2016), Annual statistics on BLSP recipients in 2015.

StatLink http://dx.doi.org/10.1787/888933645516

The limited role of Korea's BLSP as an instrument to support low-wage earners is surprising insofar as BLSP in principle can be received in addition to low income from work. It also appears that currently many families earning an income at the level at or below the MW could be entitled to a small top-up from BLSP. Any future strategy to tackle in-work poverty should look into the possible role and interaction of the three different institutions – EITC, MW and BLSP – and how these roles would change with increases in the level of payment provided through any of the three programmes.

Conclusion

Korea has developed its social protection system later than most OECD countries and in designing it has taken on board many of the lessons learned in other countries. Korea introduced strong activation and active labour market policies alongside better social protection and thereby avoided introducing undesirable benefit dependence or strong disincentives to work. However, because it is a relatively young system and because of a number of peculiarities in the labour market, which are also discussed in Chapter 1, there are still many gaps and loopholes in the system.

There is strong awareness in Korea, among researchers and policy makers alike, of the problems arising from the country's immature welfare system. A series of reforms have been put in place, affecting all relevant measures (EI, ESPP, BLSP, EITC), to increase the take-up and coverage of social protection and to improve labour market performance. These reforms, however, have had only limited impact. Large gaps and blind spots in social security persist, both *institutional* gaps (although legislation is quite advanced by now in most fields) and *effective* gaps (because people choose not to be covered or work in circumstances under which coverage is the exception).

Korea will have to make a real leap forward if it wants to close the stubbornly persistent gaps in social security to ensure that all people can benefit from public support and to promote good quality employment and, thereby, higher and more inclusive growth. Part of the solution will be better enforcement of existing legislation as it was shown that lack of enforcement is maybe a bigger problem than weak legislation. Better enforcement will require clearer obligations especially for employers and a strengthened enforcement role for various government bodies, with stricter monitoring and transparent sanctions.

But the system itself also needs further reform. Decisions will have to be taken in the coming years on how much to invest and where to invest to build a robust welfare state coupled with an effective labour market policy. This raises a general question: Is the Korean government and the Korean population ready for the corresponding necessary increase in taxes or social insurance contributions? There are clear limits in achieving more or better outcomes with the current amount of public spending.

Notes

1. Incapacity benefits include sickness benefits, disability benefits and allowances and workers' compensation payments. Last-resort benefits are means-tested payments which people can receive in most countries if they cannot generate enough income to assure a decent living through work and/or social benefits.

2. The estimated share is 9.6% for the period 2007-2014, obtained by classifying all those people as unemployment benefit recipients who have received unemployment benefit according to either the individual data file of KLIPS or the work history data file. The estimate should be treated with caution. While KLIPS is a high-quality panel survey often used for international comparisons, it is rarely used in Korea for analyses related to unemployment benefits because of possible sampling errors (sampling criteria include age and household size, for instance, but not benefit receipt). However, population survey data generally underestimate benefit receipt, not only in Korea. Comparing KLIPS results with administrative data records suggests over the period 2007-2014 KLIPS underestimates the number of unemployed people as well as the number of EI recipients by around 20%. This is a considerable degree of underestimation but not unusual.

3. Going back in time by another four or five years, the total recipiency number was only around 1.5 million because EITC and ESPP were only introduced in 2008 and 2009, respectively, and EI recipiency was around half a million lower before the global financial crisis in 2008/09.

4. To receive unemployment benefits, a self-employed person must sign up for EI within one year after the business opening date specified on the business registration certificate. There are seven insurance premium levels depending on the announced standard remuneration (Level 1: KRW 1 540 000, Level 7: KRW 2 690 000 in 2016), as specified by the self-employed person. The premium rate is 2.25% of the selected standard remuneration. The person must be insured for at least one year to be eligible for job-seeking benefits. In case of involuntary business closure, he/she can receive unemployment benefits amounting to 50% of the standard remuneration for a period of 90 to 180 days depending on the contribution period.

5. People who are employed or start up their own business after the age of 65 are not entitled to EI benefits but can still participate in employment security and vocational skills development programmes. Also not covered by Employment Insurance are public officials, private school teachers and special post office workers who, however, face a low unemployment risk and have their own occupational systems

6. In 2015, three years after the introduction of the opt-in option, only 1 290 self-employed received an EI benefit. No data is available on the number of self-employed who have opted into the system.

7. The Duru-Nuri programmes subsidises EI premiums but also premiums to the national pension scheme. The number of recipients of the latter is larger (over 900 000 workers in 2016 and over 490 000 employers) because not all of these workers fall under the EI programme. Health insurance contributions are not currently subsidised although this possibility is discussed.

8. There are also rational behavioural effects that explain the low effectiveness of the subsidy. Workers not contributing to EI are nevertheless covered by health insurance without paying contributions, through regional enrolment or as dependent household members. If subscribing to EI, health insurance premiums will be imposed on them because the different forms of social insurance are linked to some extent. The subsidy to the premium for both EI and the national pension insurance is lower than the additional health insurance premium they would have to pay.

9. According to the Employment Insurance Act, an employer shall make that report no later than the 15th of the month following the date on which the employee was hired. Until 2016

employers had to report to the corresponding Job Centre and from 2017 onwards, they must report to the Korea Workers' Compensation and Welfare Service (see also below).

10. The average unemployment benefit duration in Korea was very stable in the past decade, at around 85-90 days.

11. Before implementing BLSP, Korea operated the more restrictive Livelihood Protection System with the aim of providing protection mainly for those people who are unable to work because of their age or a disability.

12. BLSP is financed from general taxation. Costs are shared between the local and national administration: 20% of the total cost is covered by the local government and 80% by the Ministry of Health and Welfare.

13. Among the total number of BLSP recipients only about 56% are of working age and therefore of particular interest in this report. Other recipients are, in roughly equal shares, people younger than 20 years (typically receiving education benefit) and people older than 65 years. The latter number in particular could be much larger if the family support obligation rule would be relaxed further.

14. In these countries, in the past social assistance claimants may have been expected to seek support from parents or grandparents or, in the case of older claimants, children or grandchildren. How these rules work in practice varied considerably and social welfare workers generally had the discretion not to apply them. In some countries, these rules were formally abolished and in others they are no longer applied.

15. The seven benefits paid under BLSP are: a) living benefit (covering the gap between the benefit threshold and the recipient's income; sometimes referred to as the main benefit); b) housing benefit (providing mostly cash assistance with rent costs); c) medical care benefit (almost free-of-charge in-patient care and a subsidy for out-patient care); d) education benefit (covering enrolment and tuition fees for primary, middle and high school); e) child-birth benefit (a lump-sum payment); f) funeral benefit (a lump-sum payment); and g) self-supporting benefit (a loan for self-sufficiency).

16. It should be noted, however, that BLSP recipients who study or work three or more days per week, or are registered as self-employed or as a family carer are exempt from the conditionality requirement.

17. As mentioned in Box 2.1, an EI beneficiary who falls ill can receive 100% of the EI entitlement until being well enough to resume job search. But very few people benefit from this regulation and there is no special benefit option for Koreans who are sick and not receiving EI (because they are not covered, not eligible e.g. due to a voluntary quit, or still employed).

18. Conditional BLSP participants join a self-reliance work programme of their choice (market entry type, social service type, or work maintenance type), with the aim to establish a self-reliance business. There are 251 regional self-reliance centres across the country. The self-reliance programme is also open on a voluntary basis to non-conditional BLSP recipients.

19. Effectively, other previously existing subsidised job programmes for vulnerable target groups – such as the new start project for youth or the new start project for the aged – were integrated into ESPP.

20. The 2015 change came simultaneously with a massive expansion of ESPP for the youth population (aged 15-34), in turn implying a very sudden increase in the number of clients to be served by private employment service providers. The reform thereby led to a complete overhaul in the role of the private providers which until then used to have clients from the vulnerable, low-income group only. Critique was voiced that this (unexpected) shift in the

composition of the clientele has partly destroyed the existing private market as providers had to develop new competences.

21. The Job Centre selects about 3% of the private agencies on a random basis (previously it was 5%) and inspects their service twice a year. In case of doubts about the correct legal operation of services, inspection can be expanded.

22. A "better job" is a job of 30 hours per week or more, with a wage above KRW 1.5 million per month, and with employment insurance.

23. All public Job Centres have their regional area to provide services. If a private service provider is located in that area, the provider is controlled by the corresponding Job Centre. In practice, the Job Centre requests among other things data on performance and participants, ideas on improving the performance of the service operation and, if necessary, the participation in meetings held at the Job Centre.

24. Korea's CTC is an interesting hybrid programme which was born out of EITC. CTC now provides up to KRW 500 000 per child per year, for up to three children, to families earning less than the average wage. The actual amount paid declines between the level of half the average wage and the average wage. Families with no declared income are not entitled to CTC. Such, the programme combines a number of features: it is an in-work poverty measure for families with low incomes, provides work incentives for non-working families and reduces the cost of children for families with some income from work.

25. The most recent figure, according to data from Korea's Minimum Wage Commission, is 17.4% for 2017. In the 1990s this share fluctuated around 2%, then it gradually increased to about 12% after the worldwide financial crisis and since then it slowly increased to its current level.

26. According to results from the latest establishment survey in 2016 which provides statistics on wages actually paid, 7.3% of all workers in Korea earn less than the minimum wage.

27. For 2018, Korea's Minimum Wage Commission has approved a 16.4% increase of the statutory minimum wage. Further increases in 2019 and 2020 will depend on the impact of that increase on the labour market.

28. People with very low ability to work due to a mental or physical handicap can be excluded from MW application in Korea and during an apprenticeship period workers can receive 90% of the MW.

References

Bassanini, A., J. Rasmussen and S. Scarpetta (1999), *The Economic Effects of Employment-Conditional Income Support Schemes for the Low-Paid*, http://dx.doi.org/10.1787/083815484206. [20]

Borland, J. and Y. Tseng (2007), "Does a Minimum Job Search Requirement Reduce Time on Unemployment Payments? Evidence from the Jobseeker Diary in Australia", *ILR Review*, Vol. 60/3, pp. 357-378, http://dx.doi.org/10.1177/001979390706000303. [6]

Crépon, B., M. Dejemeppe and M. Gurgand (2005), "Counseling the unemployed: does it lower unemployment duration and recurrence?", https://halshs.archives-ouvertes.fr/halshs-00590769 (accessed on 31 July 2017). [3]

Hainmueller, J. et al. (2011), "Do Lower Caseloads Improve the Effectiveness of Active Labor Market Policies? New Evidence from German Employment Offices", *SSRN Electronic Journal*, http://dx.doi.org/10.2139/ssrn.1926683. [8]

Hofmann, B. et al. (2012), "Wirkung und Wirkmechanismen zusätzlicher Vermittlungsfachkräfte auf die Arbeitslosigkeitsdauer – Analysen auf Basis eines Modellprojektes", *Zeitschrift für Evaluation*, Vol. 11/1, http://www.zfev.de/fruehereAusgabe/ausgabe2012-1/abstracts/Abstract_Hofmann%20et%20al._dt.pdf (accessed on 31 July 2017), pp. 7-38. [9]

Hwang, T. (2013), *Unemployment insurance in Asia*, KLI, Seoul, http://catalogue.nla.gov.au/Record/6491153 (accessed on 31 July 2017). [13]

Jeong, C. and J. Kim (2015), "The redistributive effects of EITC and of CTC on one-earner and dual-earner household", *Korean Social Security Studies*, Vol. 31/1. [24]

Kim, D. (2016), *Evaluating the Social Security Subsidy Program in Korea*, https://papers.ssrn.com/sol3/papers.cfm?abstract_id=2845211 (accessed on 31 July 2017). [11]

Kim, M. (2016), "The Current Status of the Earned Income Tax Credit in South Korea and the Implication to Japan—Earned Income Tax Credit or Reduced Tax Rate?", NLI Research Institute, Seoul, http://www.nli-research.co.jp/files/topics/52502_ext_18_en_0.pdf?site=nli (accessed on 31 July 2017). [21]

Klepinger, D. et al. (2002), "Effects of Unemployment Insurance Work-Search Requirements: The Maryland Experiment", *ILR Review*, Vol. 56/1, http://econpapers.repec.org/article/saeilrrev/v_3a56_3ay_3a2002_3ai_3a1_3ap_3a3-22.htm (accessed on 31 July 2017), pp. 3-22. [5]

Lee, B. (2012), "Informal work in Korea: Non-regulation or Non-compliance?", Korea Labour Institute, Seoul. [12]

Lee, B. (2013), *Plan for introducing a Korean-style unemployment assistance*, KLI, Seoul. [18]

Lee, B. (2016), *An evaluation of the employment impact of the Employemnt Success Package Program*, KLI, Seoul. [15]

Lee, D., G. Kwon and S. Moon (2015), "Studies on policy effects of the EITC", *The Korean Association for Policy Studies*, Vol. 24/2. [23]

McVicar, D. (2008), *Labour economics.*, North Holland, http://econpapers.repec.org/article/eeelabeco/v_3a15_3ay_3a2008_3ai_3a6_3ap_3a1451-1468.htm (accessed on 31 July 2017). [7]

OECD (2005), *OECD Employment Outlook 2005*, OECD Publishing, http://dx.doi.org/10.1787/empl_outlook-2005-en. [19]

OECD (2013), *Strengthening Social Cohesion in Korea*, OECD Publishing, http://dx.doi.org/10.1787/9789264188945-en. [2]

OECD (2013), "Activating jobseekers: Lessons from seven OECD countries", in *OECD Employment Outlook 2013*, OECD Publishing, Paris, http://dx.doi.org/10.1787/empl_outlook-2013-7-en. [16]

OECD (2015), "Activation policies for more inclusive labour markets", in *OECD Employment Outlook 2015*, OECD Publishing, Paris, http://dx.doi.org/10.1787/empl_outlook-2015-7-en. [17]

Pearson, M. and S. Scarpetta (2000), "An overview: What do we know about policies to make work pay?", *OECD Economic Studies*, Vol. 31/2, https://www.oecd.org/eco/growth/2676194.pdf (accessed on 31 July 2017). [26]

Pedersen, J., M. Rosholm and M. Svarer (2012), "Experimental Evidence on the Effects of Early Meetings and Activation", http://ftp.iza.org/dp6970.pdf (accessed on 31 July 2017). [4]

Song, H. and H. Bahng (2014), "The Effect of EITC on Job Creation in Korea", *The Korean Economic Review*, Vol. 62/4. [22]

Wan, K. (2016), "A Financial Assessment and Development of Estimation Model for the Basic Livelihood Security System", KIHASA, Seoul, https://www.kihasa.re.kr/english/publications/eng_research/view.do?menuId=68&tid=34&bid=30&ano=473 (accessed on 31 July 2017). [14]

Won, J. and T. Kim (2013), "Projecting Social Expenditure and Total Tax Burden in Korea -A Study on Forecasting Social Expenditure for OECD Countries and Corresponding Total Tax Revenue for Korea", http://repository.kihasa.re.kr:8080/handle/201002/10893 (accessed on 27 April 2017). [1]

Wook, H. (2016), *KERI Brief 16-24*, Policy brief, https://www.keri.org/web/www/issue_02;jsessionid=81076D22CCF18AFB13ECF047CFB745CD?p_p_id=EXT_BBS&p_p_lifecycle=0&p_p_state=normal&p_p_mode=view&p_p_col_id=column-1&p_p_col_count=1&_EXT_BBS_struts_action=%2Fext%2Fbbs%2Fview_message&_EXT_BBS_sCategory=&_EXT (accessed on 31 July 2017). [25]

Yoo, G. (2013), "Institutional Blind Spots in the South Korean Employment Safety Net and Policy Solutions", *KDI FOCUS*, https://www.kdi.re.kr/kdi_eng/publication/publication_view.jsp?pub_no=13273 (accessed on 27 July 2017). [10]

Chapter 3. Peer-learning for bolder social protection in Korea

This chapter looks at the social protection measures applied in OECD countries. The analysis benchmarks common types of income support and activation measures for unemployment, temporary work incapacity and other types of poverty risk. It highlights lessons for Korea based on the commonalities and differences among the measures implemented across the OECD, focusing on several of their operational features. The discussion, in particular, looks at the coverage conditions such measures entail; the duration and scope of the support they provide; the active features they embody; and the supporting policies through which they are implemented.

The statistical data for Israel are supplied by and under the responsibility of the relevant Israeli authorities. The use of such data by the OECD is without prejudice to the status of the Golan Heights, East Jerusalem and Israeli settlements in the West Bank under the terms of international law.

Learning from international experience

The Korean approach to social protection policy

Korea's social protection measures are considerably young compared with those in many other OECD countries. Policy makers have an incredibly rich pool of international experience from which to draw ideas, insights and warnings. Lessons of this kind have already helped Korea to introduce effective social protection measures and deliver on many of its economic, social and labour market goals.

Social protection measures in Korea have consistently been introduced with a characteristic "cautiousness" on the part of policy makers. With each new measure put in place, both formal coverage and the level of support have tended to start from a very modest base. Afterwards – once any behavioural effects were observed and the necessary implementation channels established – incremental reforms to each measure created new coverage opportunities and expanded the support on offer.

Korea's cautiousness in this area has probably contributed much to its strong activation climate; sustained employment outcomes; and unprecedentedly low levels of long-term unemployment. Nevertheless, Korea's cautious approach to social policy-making also underpins its biggest remaining weaknesses. Three leading challenges stand out in this respect: large pockets of jobseekers still remain outside the coverage of income and employment support measures; workers undergoing sickness have no guarantee of support and are commonly dismissed from their jobs, impeding their recovery and rehabilitation; while other needy groups – including low-income workers – often gain too little support or miss out on it altogether. Bolder policy actions may be necessary to address the issues on each of these remaining fronts.

The lessons developed among Korea's peers within the OECD offer key solutions and guidance to embolden policy makers. The purpose of this chapter is to explore such lessons for the enrichment of Korea's social protection environment. The analysis outlines a range of assertive, innovative and bold policy actions Korea might consider to decisively address its remaining social protection challenges.

Benchmarking OECD countries' approaches

The present chapter's analysis establishes a number of benchmarks relating to OECD countries' social protection measures and supporting institutions. Drawing on the diverse array of approaches, measures and conditions developed, the analysis highlights the potential merits, drawbacks and pitfalls they represent for Korea.

The discussion targets the central themes already developed in Chapter 2:

- Addressing the remaining coverage gaps of Korea's *Employment Insurance* (EI), the analysis looks at the equivalent eligibility, entitlement and behavioural conditions other countries use. The discussion points out viable ways of tackling some of EI's most prominent omissions.
- Addressing the relatively narrow scope of the income support offered under EI, the analysis compares how other OECD countries calculate unemployment benefits. The discussion highlights the positive role non-contributory measures can play as a secondary "tier" of income support and the future part Korea's *Employment Success Package Programme* (ESPP) might choose to play.

- Addressing the current lack of social protection for workers undergoing sickness in Korea, the analysis looks into the types of policies and measures used elsewhere. It points out potential avenues for Korea.
- Addressing poverty and in-work poverty, the analysis compares Korea's *Basic Livelihood Security Programme* (BLSP) and *Earned Income Tax Credit* (EITC) with parallel measures used in other OECD countries. The discussion looks into the relevant coverage conditions in each case and, in particular, the different features making up the means tests they apply.

The following three sections of this chapter compare and review OECD countries' social protection measures targeting the working-age population under three specific circumstances: in unemployment; through a temporary period of work incapacity; and otherwise under a risk of poverty. Each discussion compares the *coverage conditions* such measures entail; the *scope of support* they provide; the *active features* they involve; and the *supporting policies* integral to their implementation, drawing out potential best practices for Korea. A short concluding section reiterates the main messages.

Protections for unemployed persons in OECD countries

Unemployment insurance and unemployment assistance

Social protection measures for unemployment commonly seek to balance two competing objectives. On the one hand, they seek to compensate unemployed persons for all or part of their previous earnings. For individual jobseekers, this enables a degree of support in maintaining work capacity and providing for dependents during the unemployment spell. For the broader economy, it entails an automatic stabilising effect on earnings volatility to help smooth consumption, on aggregate (Rejda, 1966[1]; OECD, 2011[2]; Di Maggio and Kermani, 2016[3]). On the other hand, social protection measures for unemployed persons seek to promote jobseekers' transitions into work. For individual jobseekers, this enables a livelihood, self-sufficiency and fulfilment through work. For the broader economy, achieving such transitions both swiftly and robustly enlarges the workforce, bolsters skills development and increases fiscal gains.

Functioning labour markets rely, to a considerable degree, on the fine balance achieved between these two competing goals. Changes in the coverage or calculation of unemployment benefits must thus be careful always to consider how they might alter the balance and, hence, work incentives.

Every OECD country targets support towards unemployed persons under certain circumstances. Two types of measures stand out in particular:

- *Unemployment insurance benefits* offer income support to jobseekers on a contributory basis. Most are conditional on evidence of jobseekers' work history and, in any case, on their job-seeking behaviour. Virtually all are limited over a fixed period of time. Coverage is compulsory for most salaried workers in virtually every OECD country and increasingly open to others. Korea's EI belongs to this category of measures.
- *Unemployment assistance benefits* offer income support to jobseekers who either exhaust their entitlement under an insurance-type measure or never contribute to one in the first place (including, in many cases, new labour market entrants). Entitlement is usually restricted through a means test. Such measures exist in a number of OECD countries as second-tier unemployment benefits and, in some cases and for most non-salaried workers, as the first or only tier. Korea's ESPP broadly falls into this category of measures.

The discussion below elaborates on the many ways in which OECD countries currently apply such measures: the conditions of coverage they entail; the scope of support they provide; and their active features.

Eligibility, entitlement and job-seeking behaviour

Unemployment benefit measures in OECD countries typically restrict coverage through conditions applied at three distinct stages: they determine who is *eligible* to contribute into the common fund, while still in work (if the measure is contributory); who is *entitled* to start claiming its benefits, in case of unemployment; and whose job-seeking *behaviour* is adequate, once the claim period is underway. Conditions applied at these three respective stages are referred to throughout this chapter as "eligibility conditions", "entitlement conditions" and "behavioural conditions".[1]

Coverage is restricted for a variety of groups under Korea's EI benefit (Yoo, 2013[4]). "Blind spots" of this kind exist, to some extent, in every OECD country. Most countries limit unemployment insurance coverage for two main groups of workers in particular: *non-salaried workers* (own-account workers, employers and contributing family workers) and some categories of *non-regular salaried workers* (including certain groups of non-typical workers and part-time workers with short or irregular time commitments).

While many OECD countries maintain common blind spots for these groups, the impact this has on Korea's labour market is greater, since both groups feature more in Korea's labour market than elsewhere. Korea has among the highest rates of self-employment and contributing family work in the OECD (Figure 3.1) and an elevated share of non-regular workers among salaried employees.

Figure 3.1. Self-employment and contributing family work are prominent in Korea

Employment by status in OECD countries, 2016 (percentage of total employment)

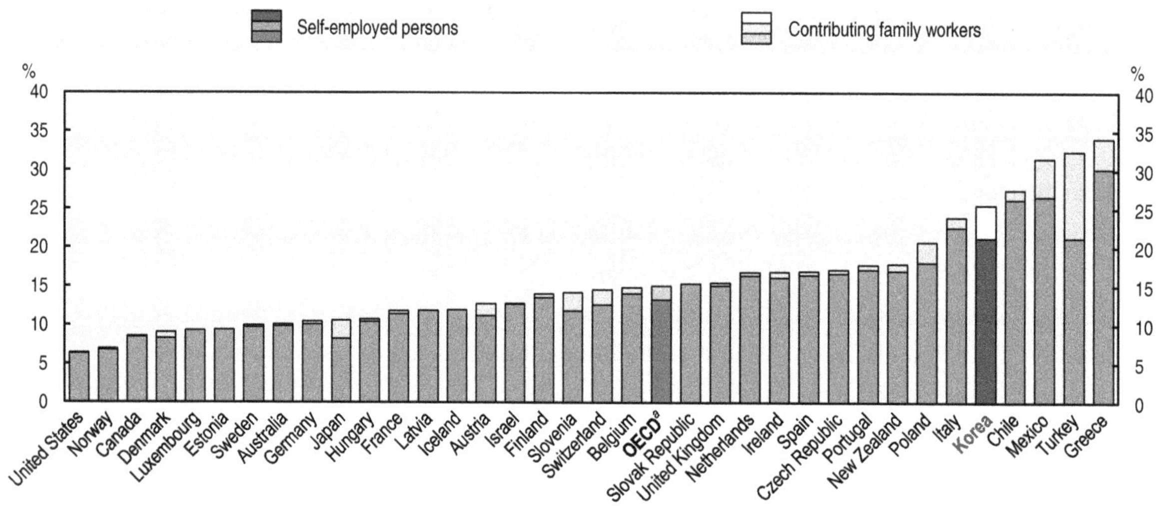

Note: All data are for 2016 except Latvia (2015).

a) Weighted average of the 35 OECD countries.

Source: *Employment by activities and status* (ALFS), a subset of the *OECD Annual Labour Force Statistics* (ALFS) *Database*, http://stats.oecd.org//Index.aspx?QueryId=81036 (accessed on 7 November 2017).

StatLink http://dx.doi.org/10.1787/888933645136

Some 5.6 million Koreans were self-employed in 2016 (4.0 million of them own-account workers and 1.6 million employers), accounting for 21.2% of total employment. The weighted share for the OECD as a whole was 13.3%. There were also 1.1 million contributing family workers in Korea in 2016, accounting for an additional 4.3% of total employment. The equivalent share in a majority of OECD countries is lower than 1%.[2]

Of Korea's 19.6 million salaried workers in August 2016, 3.7 million were employed on a non-permanent basis; 2.5 million on a part-time basis (meaning they had fewer than 36 regular work-hours per week); and 2.2 million through non-typical work contracts (as, for example, daily workers, contractors, temporary agency workers or domestic workers) (Statistics Korea, 2017[5]). With some overlaps, these three groups – collectively called non-regular workers – accounted for 32.8% of all salaried employees in Korea.

While Korea discounts self-employed persons, contributing family workers and some non-regular employees from mandatory unemployment insurance coverage, a number of OECD countries have designed innovative rules to encompass them. The following sub-section reviews the coverage conditions other OECD countries apply, focusing on self-employed persons. With minor variations, many of the same solutions discussed can equally apply to contributing family workers and the categories of non-regular salaried employees currently omitted from the scope of EI's coverage.

Extending coverage to self-employed persons

Countries exclude self-employed persons from the coverage of their unemployment insurance measures for a number of justifiable reasons. Income from self-employment can fluctuate much from month to month, making it difficult to establish usual earnings. The time devoted to self-employment and its tenure may be unclear, making it tricky to benchmark with salaried employment. Self-employed persons are self-accountable for maintaining their labour output, which introduces a moral hazard of defaulting on work in favour of benefits. Once a self-employed person starts claiming benefits, there might also be a temptation to carry out some own-account work covertly should the opportunity arise in parallel. In any case, it may be difficult to establish whether self-employment has fully stopped and to what extent unemployment is involuntary.

In light of these obstacles, a number of OECD countries opt to provide no unemployment insurance coverage at all for self-employed persons (although many do, however, routinely cover them for other contributory measures including national pensions, work-related injury, sickness and parental benefits). Under such circumstances, self-employed persons entering unemployment have to make do with what private support might be on offer or resort to lower-tier social assistance measures (typically pending a means test).[3]

Countries deviating from this approach either offer *voluntary* affiliation for self-employed persons on an opt-in basis or make coverage *mandatory* under similar conditions as for regular salaried workers (Table 3.1).

Voluntary unemployment insurance affiliation for self-employed persons is emerging in more and more OECD countries: Germany first introduced it in 2006; Austria in 2009; Spain in 2010; and Korea, under EI, in 2012. Denmark, Finland and Sweden provide unemployment insurance coverage on a voluntary basis to all workers, in any case, under their so-called "Ghent system" measures. Self-employed persons there are largely undistinguished from regular salaried workers, choosing in the same way whether or not to opt in for unemployment protection.

Table 3.1. Three types of unemployment insurance coverage for self-employed persons

Type of unemployment insurance coverage provided for self-employed persons in OECD countries, 2016

No coverage	Voluntary affiliation	Mandatory affiliation
Belgium	Austria	Czech Republic
Canada[a]	Denmark[b]	Greece
Chile	Finland[b]	Hungary
Estonia	Germany	Iceland
France	Korea	Luxembourg
Ireland[a]	Slovak Republic	Poland
Israel	Spain	Portugal[c]
Italy	Sweden[b]	Slovenia
Japan		
Latvia		
Mexico		
Netherlands		
Norway[a]		
Switzerland		
Turkey		
United Kingdom		
United States		

Note: Australia and New Zealand are excluded since they have no statutory unemployment insurance measure (only unemployment assistance, which applies, in any case, to self-employed persons).

a) Canada, Ireland and Norway: Coverage is possible only for self-employed fishermen.

b) Denmark, Finland and Sweden: Coverage is voluntary for all working persons (non-salaried and salaried alike) in any case.

c) Portugal: Coverage is mandatory for employers and "dependent" own-account workers (defined as those for whom at least 80% of revenues come from a single market source); dependent own-account workers earning below EUR 2 528 per year may opt in of coverage, voluntarily; own-account workers whose revenues come from a broader mix of market sources have no coverage.

Source: Compiled using MISSOC (2017), *Social protection of the self-employed*; SSA and ISSA (2016, 2017) *Social Security Programs throughout the World*; and OECD (2017) *Benefits and Wages: Country Specific Information.*

Voluntary affiliation is not always truly open insofar as some of the above-named countries restrict the option through certain key caveats. Germany, for example, limits affiliation only to former salaried employees who transition into self-employment and desire to maintain the regular coverage they had up until then. Germany's option is thus more of a *continuation* of coverage than a true opt-in and, in any case, expires following one year of detachment from salaried employment (MISSOC, 2017[6]; Bäcker, 2017[7]). Austria limits the option of registering for coverage to a 12-month window occurring once every nine years: those who fail to register during their first year of self-employment must wait eight years before they can do so again; those failing in the ninth year must wait another eight years; and so on (ILO, 2013[8]; Lee et al., 2016[9]). Korea's EI limits the option insofar as own-account workers may only opt in during their initial year of self-employment and employers with 50 workers or more are forbidden.

Voluntary affiliation may be worthwhile in allowing individuals to choose their own exposure to the risk of unemployment. In reality, however, the risk is not the same for everybody. Voluntary insurance measures of any kind embody a problem of "adverse selection": the least successful entrepreneurs have the greatest incentive to opt in although they run the highest risk of becoming unemployed. In practice, moreover, numerous countries have found that voluntary affiliation results in extremely low levels of participation among self-employed individuals (European Commission, 2011[10];

Fondeville et al., 2015[11]; Lee et al., 2016[9]). Even in Finland, where all unemployment insurance participation is voluntary, survey findings reveal that only 21.4% of own-account workers and just 10.3% of employers opted in during 2015, compared with 85.9% among regular salaried employees (Kalliomaa-Puha and Kangas, 2017[12]).

Mandatory unemployment insurance affiliation offers less choice to self-employed persons but entails at least two key advantages over voluntary affiliation: it escapes the problem of adverse selection and it spreads the benefits of protection to a greater number within society. Seven OECD countries currently operate mandatory affiliation to unemployment insurance measures for all self-employed persons: the Czech Republic, Greece, Hungary, Iceland, Luxembourg, Poland and Slovenia (Table 3.1).

Most of these countries implemented mandatory coverage for self-employed persons at a nascent stage in the development of their measures. The Czech Republic, Hungary and Poland, for example, embraced mandatory coverage for self-employed persons when they first introduced insurance-based financing for unemployment benefits in the early-1990s (Dervis, 1994[13]; MISSOC, 2017[6]). Iceland and Luxembourg have implemented it since at least the 1980s (OECD, 2008[14]; MISSOC, 2017[6]). Slovenia previously had voluntary affiliation for self-employed persons but made it mandatory in 2011 under its Labour Market Regulation Act – primarily in response to a perceived coverage gap among "dependent" own-account workers (Ignjatović, 2013[15]). Greece introduced mandatory affiliation for most self-employed persons in 2011 as well – primarily in response to its unfolding economic and labour market crisis – although entitlement to the benefit is means-tested (OECD, 2013[16]; Theodoroulakis, Sakellis and Ziomas, 2017[17]).

Portugal represents something of a peculiar case among the OECD countries since four separate groups of self-employed persons there are subjected to very different kinds of coverage rules (MISSOC, 2017[6]; Perista and Baptista, 2017[18]). Employers all gain coverage on a mandatory basis in the same way the regular salaried workers they employ do. Own-account workers plus contributing family workers also gain mandatory coverage provided they meet two key conditions:

1. Their annual earnings are higher than six times the national Social Support Index (*indexante dos apoios sociais*; set at EUR 421.32 in 2017) – a threshold equivalent to roughly one seventh of Portugal's average wage or a third of its statutory minimum wage.
2. They are in a situation of "dependent" self-employment – defined, in Portugal's case, as gaining 80% or more of their earnings from an individual source.

Own-account workers who fail to meet only the first of these conditions can opt in for coverage voluntarily, if they so wish. Own-account workers who fail in the second condition, however, are excluded from unemployment insurance coverage altogether.

The result for Portugal is that all employers and virtually all persons in dependent self-employment (including contributing family workers) gain unemployment insurance coverage on a mandatory basis. Conversely, genuinely independent own-account workers – those with a more diverse client portfolio – gain no coverage opportunity at all.

Portugal introduced its instrument fairly recently under key reforms enacted in 2012 in response to a tangible rise in dependent self-employment, similar to Slovenia (Perista and Baptista, 2017[18]). Spain introduced a similar measure in 2010 – called the *Régimen de Trabajadores Autónomos de la Seguridad Social* (RETA) – although affiliation relating to unemployment protection is voluntary (Rodríguez-Cabrero et al., 2017[19]). Italy also introduced a similar measure in 2015 – called the *Indennità di Disoccupazione per i*

Collaborator (DIS-COLL) – covering only non-typical workers under a particular type of work-contract (Iudicone and Arca Sedda, 2015[20]; Jessoula, Pavolini and Strati, 2017[21]).

Unlike regular salaried employment, self-employment gives rise to a number of idiosyncrasies among workers that result in a host of practical questions unemployment insurance measures must resolve: How precisely to define self-employment for social insurance purposes? How to assess earnings from self-employment? What insurance premium to adopt? And how to combat the moral hazards that might arise?

The remainder of this sub-section identifies some of the practical solutions selected OECD countries apply, taking each of the four questions in turn.

Defining self-employment

Countries may differ in the precise legal definitions they give to self-employment. In most cases, the distinction between regular salaried employment and self-employment is relatively clear: the former subordinates workers to a particular role within the employing organisation while the latter enables them a tangible degree of autonomy over executive business decisions around investment, hiring and other such matters. While this much may be clear in a majority of countries, many encounter a certain grey area when it comes to dependent self-employment (sometimes called "bogus", "fake", "quasi-" or "contingent" self-employment or, in certain modern contexts, "gig economy work").

Dependent self-employment may satisfy neither the legal conditions of employment nor conform reasonably to a common understanding of what self-employment ought to look like. For social protection purposes, such grey areas can create loopholes for participation under which employers or individuals might renege on their social insurance duties by maintaining informal employment relationships or disguising otherwise regular ones as a form of self-employment.

Well-established legal definitions can go a long way towards tightening such loopholes and, at the very least, clarifying who is entitled to which protections and under what specific circumstances. In countries such as Korea where some social insurance measures cover self-employed persons while others do not, such clarity might be all the more necessary in enforcing existing rules and limiting abuse.

The European Union's *European Working Conditions Survey* provides a statistical definition of dependent self-employment as encompassing own-account workers who satisfy two or more of three conditions: they have only a single employer or client; they cannot hire employees, even if their workload is heavy; and they cannot autonomously take important decisions regarding their business (Oostveen et al., 2013[22]). While statistical definitions of this kind are useful, they can be cumbersome to establish for legal purposes. Efforts may be complicated further by the sheer diversity of work arrangements modern labour markets encompass, with grey areas not only around own-account work but also non-typical salaried work that can include daily workers, contractors, temporary agency workers, domestic workers, plus a whole range of private individuals earning their income through technologically-driven on-demand services delivery platforms.

In light of such challenges, OECD countries that offer unemployment insurance coverage to workers in dependent self-employment tend to opt for more pragmatic definitions. One key difference is between definitions founded on a *relative* threshold or an *absolute* one:

- Some OECD countries have recently introduced definitions of dependent self-employment based on how concentrated an own-account or non-typical worker's earnings might be on their biggest client, relative to the rest of their income. For Portugal and Slovenia, the line is drawn at 80% of the worker's total earnings; Spain uses 75% (Perista and Baptista, 2017[18]; Stropnik, Majcen and Prevolnik Rupel, 2017[23]; Rodríguez-Cabrero et al., 2017[19]). Regardless of how much an individual might earn in total, any instance where their total earnings are concentrated on a single employer in excess of the threshold amount constitutes a relationship of dependent self-employment. This typically covers workers engaged on non-typical contracts; those subcontracted as own-account workers; and, in some cases, contributing family workers. In all three countries, the definition underpins a range of labour rights and labour market regulations applicable – not least of which regard who can (or must) be covered for which branches of social insurance.

- Other OECD countries define own-account workers' dependence through absolute threshold values such as a nominal amount of income a worker may gain at one time from a particular client or the time they might devote to such work. The Czech Republic, for example, identifies dependent self-employment when the commitment a non-typical workers devotes exceeds either an income threshold of CZK 10 000 per month (about KRW 520 000 per month) for a specific output (or one quarter of that if the work is of a more general nature) or a time threshold of 300 hours per year for a specific output (or 20 hours per week for work of a more general nature) (Sirovátka, Jahoda and Malý, 2017[24]). Other countries rely on similar absolute thresholds of this nature (MISSOC, 2017[6]).

Transparent formulas of either of these kinds engender a legal definition of dependent self-employment that can underpin the rights and obligations such workers (and their clients) must adhere to around social insurance. Once dependent self-employment is identified in one such clear way, it becomes easier to design appropriate coverage rules.

Assessing earnings from self-employment

Social insurance measures assess people's usual earnings for two elementary purposes: as a basis for the premiums they charge and as a function of which the income support they could receive is calculated (except in the case of flat-rate benefits). A higher assessment of earnings may thus be a drawback for participants in terms of costlier social contributions but an advantage in terms of higher-value benefits.

The earnings regular salaried employees make are relatively easy to assess: they tend to be more-or-less uniform across the year; received at timely intervals; and transparently documented by the employer. The earnings self-employed persons make, on the other hand, are often none of these things, raising questions over how to assess them. Moreover, the taxable income self-employed persons gain from their work is justifiably a mix of two separate things – *earnings* (related to what labour the individual expends through their self-employment) and *profits* (related to their overall business performance, investments and holdings) – that might be difficult to separate out.

Countries that provide some social insurance to self-employed persons overcome these issues in a large variety of ways. Some take a fixed, formulaic approach while others offer more flexibility for individuals to draw their own line between earnings and profits.

The Czech Republic, Luxembourg, the Slovak Republic, Slovenia and Sweden exemplify the most rudimentary formulaic approaches conceivable: all of them assess self-employed participants' earnings on the basis of a simple ratio that determines how much of their taxable income (i.e. their total revenues minus business expenses) should be taxed as earnings and how much as profits – the former being subject to social contributions and the latter not. In the Czech Republic, social contributions are charged on only half a self-employed person's taxable income (Sirovátka, Jahoda and Malý, 2017[24]); in the Slovak Republic on roughly two thirds (Gerbery and Bednárik, 2017[25]); in Slovenia, on three quarters (Stropnik, Majcen and Prevolnik Rupel, 2017[23]); and in Luxembourg and Sweden, on all of it (Pacolet and Op de Beeck, 2017[26]; Nelson et al., 2017[27]).

The ease with which such rules can be administered represents a key advantage over other approaches. Nevertheless, it might be unsatisfactory to apply the same rigid, simplistic and, ultimately, rather arbitrary formula to all participants alike.

Iceland has a formulaic approach as well, though one that is significantly more nuanced. Each year, the government issues a centralised list of reference earnings for every occupational category, representing the amount of money a self-employed person could expect to earn carrying out the same work in a regular salaried position (Ríkisskattstjóri, 2017[28]). These so-called "presumptive" earnings (*reiknað endurgjald*) establish the sole basis on which self-employed persons in Iceland make social contributions: regardless of their *actual* earnings, it is solely the presumptive amount for each occupation that sets the basis for social insurance (Ólafsson, 2017[29]; KPMG, 2017[30]). Deviations from this benchmark are only possible under extenuating circumstances and, in any case, require approval from the Directorate on Internal Revenue (Ólafsson, 2017[29]). Presumptive earnings likewise underpin the way all contributing family workers in Iceland make social contributions.

Iceland's unique approach offers an intuitive formula for establishing the earnings of self-employed persons. Those with incomes above the presumptive amount gain the full benefits of social protection alongside the profits they keep. Those with income far below the presumptive amount ultimately pay a disproportionate amount for social insurance and may well feel encouraged to opt for a salaried position instead.

Most other OECD countries take a more flexible approach, though not without certain boundaries. Korea, Portugal and Spain, for example, allow self-employed individuals a considerable degree of freedom in assessing their own earnings (MISSOC, 2017[6]). In Korea, self-employed persons volunteering for EI coverage unilaterally choose one of seven separate earnings assessment levels defined, in 2016, between thresholds of KRW 1 540 000 and KRW 2 690 000 per month. Portugal and Spain likewise allow participants to choose their own protection level, constrained by two such threshold amounts (SSA and ISSA, 2016[31]). Hungary and Poland offer a similar choice, constrained only by a minimum threshold amount: fixed at 150% of the statutory minimum wage in Hungary (Albert and Gal, 2017[32]) and at 60% of the previous year's national average wage in Poland (Chłoń-Domińczak, Sowa and Topińska, 2017[33]). Austria, finally, allows self-employed persons to declare their covered earnings freely but, as a constraint, fixes the level they choose so it cannot be altered except once during every eight-year period (Lee et al., 2016[9]).

The flexible choice approach is worthwhile insofar as it allows individuals a significant freedom over the degree of support to insure for, within certain bounds. It amounts, in practice, to choosing one's own exposure to the risk of unemployment. The main drawback, however, is that individuals largely tend to take a somewhat short-sighted approach by opting for the lowest amount of coverage possible: this has been the experience in Hungary, Poland and elsewhere, where a majority of self-employed persons simply opt for the minimum possible earnings assessment (Albert and Gal, 2017[32]; Chłoń-Domińczak, Sowa and Topińska, 2017[33]). While this thus results in relatively low levels of income support, it helps to maximise entitlement to employment support.

Setting insurance premiums for self-employed persons

Regular salaried employees in most OECD countries gain their social insurance coverage based on two separate payments: an *employee's contribution* is deducted along with other taxes from their regular earnings (usually at the end of each month) and an *employer's contribution* is made by the employing institution, as a compulsory part of their broader legal labour costs. Self-employed persons eligible for social insurance benefits usually make payments equivalent to the employee's and employer's contribution combined. This is the case, for example, in Hungary, Iceland and Slovenia.

Under Korea's EI, regular salaried workers currently contribute a premium worth 0.7% of their earnings to the measure, while employers' pay an additional 0.9-1.5%, depending on their size. Self-employed persons opting in for EI affiliation pay a premium of 2.3%.

Other OECD countries collect smaller-value social contributions from self-employed persons. Spain, for example, collects a voluntary premium of 2.2% to cover the risk of unemployment under RETA, compared to the 1.6% and 5.5% premiums a regular salaried employee and their employer pay under the general scheme (Rodríguez-Cabrero et al., 2017[19]). Germany and Poland both have a phased-in approach whereby self-employed persons are insured for only half of their reference earnings during the first two years of voluntary coverage and the full amount thereafter (SSA and ISSA, 2016[31]). Greece collects a flat-rate contribution of EUR 10 per month from the self-employed persons it covers on a mandatory basis, although entitlement to the benefit is means-tested (Theodoroulakis, Sakellis and Ziomas, 2017[17]).

Reducing the premium for self-employed persons might offer an incentive for more to opt in (Davies, 2013[34]; Hombert et al., 2017[35]). But preferential treatment for self-employed persons might also distort labour market incentives towards self-employment, potentially encouraging tax evasion and bogus self-employment (OECD, 2008[36]).

Addressing potential moral hazards

The economic activity of self-employed persons might be more difficult to monitor or account for, given its overall independent nature. While this may not present a problem among most beneficiaries, it does highlight some potential moral hazards for misusing unemployment benefits that measures covering self-employed persons should take care to guard against. One moral hazard for self-employed persons might be to default on work during a quiet period in the business cycle, in favour of claiming benefits. Another might be to carry on with self-employment despite claiming unemployment benefits.

There are countless examples among the OECD countries of potential ways to mitigate this problem. Some compelling illustrative examples may be grouped as follows:

- *Stricter entitlement conditions* for self-employed claimants to fulfil before being able to claim benefits can offer an effective tool against possible misuse. Contribution conditions exceeding 12 months, for example, can prevent short-term defaults into unemployment during the business cycle. Several countries impose longer contribution conditions for self-employment. Finland, for example, requires self-employed participants to collect at least 15 months of social contributions within a four-year period, compared with just 6 months within a 28-month period for regular salaried employees (Kalliomaa-Puha and Kangas, 2017[12]). Portugal requires a minimum of 720 days within a 4-year period, compared with only 369 days within a two-year period for regular salaried workers (Perista and Baptista, 2017[18]). Luxembourg, finally, requires at least two years of social contributions, compared with just 26 weeks out of one year for regular salaried workers (Pacolet and Op de Beeck, 2017[26]).

- *Minimum earnings thresholds* may be used in a similar way to discount self-employed persons with limited commitment or little success in their business. The Czech Republic, for example, has an earnings threshold for self-employed persons equivalent to 25% of the national average wage (or 10% if they work part-time) but imposes no such threshold on regular salaried workers (SSA and ISSA, 2016[31]). Spain, likewise, sets its minimum earnings threshold roughly one sixth higher for self-employed persons than it does for regular salaried workers (SSA and ISSA, 2016[31]).
- *Activation measures* can be used to channel formerly self-employed jobseekers exclusively into regular salaried employment to avert potential flip-flopping in and out of self-employment. Luxembourg, for example, grants unemployment benefits to formerly self-employed claimants exclusively on the behavioural condition that they seek *salaried* employment. Reactivation into self-employment is therefore not an option (MISSOC, 2017[6]).
- *Delaying the start of the benefit period* might also be effective for discouraging voluntary unemployment. Poland, for example, imposes a waiting period of 90 days on all formerly self-employed jobseekers starting on the day they register as unemployed (Chłoń-Domińczak, Sowa and Topińska, 2017[33]).
- *Mandating evidence of cessation of business operations* can be an effective way to ensure benefit claimants do not undertake self-employment activity covertly. Most OECD countries with coverage for self-employer persons thus place at least *some* formal burden of evidence on jobseekers to certify that they are no longer active in their self-employment. Iceland, for example, mandates a double layer of evidence from any self-employed person registering as unemployed: a written declaration stating that all business operations have been discontinued, giving the reasons; and a formal letter from the Directorate of Internal Revenue certifying the claimant's business has been removed from the employers' register or their name deleted from a register of own-account taxpayers (Ólafsson, 2017[29]). Sweden requires a similar burden of proof but goes one step further to impose a strict ban from unemployment benefits for a period of five years on anyone found abusing the system or guilty of fraud (Nelson et al., 2017[27]).

What may or may not work, in any case, will be the result of various social and cultural factors plus how well-equipped public employment services may be at spotting potential wrong-doers. Given this complexity, a solution developed in one country might not work in another. The right mix of conditions, penalties and other countervailing measures can probably only be achieved through an extended period of experimentation.

Entitlement conditions for unemployment insurance benefits

Unemployment insurance measures in every country limit their coverage further through an additional set of entitlement conditions. Three kinds of conditions are in particularly common use among the OECD countries:

- *Minimum contribution conditions* set a threshold of insurance affiliation or employment below which eligible workers are not entitled to claim benefits. Such conditions exist under every unemployment insurance measure and are virtually always expressed as a function of time: a set number of hours, days, weeks or months of prior work that entitle jobseekers to a given contributory benefit.[4]

- *Maximum cut-off conditions* establish an expiry date at which past contributions effectively cease to count. Such conditions are usually expressed as the timeframe within which a worker must complete their minimum contribution condition: for example, 180 days of contributions *within the past 18 months* (as under Korea's EI). Conditions of this kind effectively amount to a maximum period of time a worker can disengage from the labour market before forfeiting their entitlement to unemployment benefits. They thus inhibit long periods of inactivity.
- *Conditions on the nature of unemployment* are commonly imposed as penalties for jobseekers leaving their previous employment under circumstances that were, in some way, reasonably avoidable or of their own choosing. Virtually all OECD countries have some legal criteria or an official guideline to differentiate "involuntary" unemployment situations from "voluntary" ones and, hence, to permit or restrict jobseekers' entitlement to unemployment benefits.[5]

Figure 3.2 shows the minimum contribution and maximum cut-off conditions applied to unemployment insurance measures across the OECD. The periods of time under both conditions differ considerably from one country to another.

Minimum contribution conditions range from less than six months in Canada, Iceland and France to two years or more in Ireland, Mexico, the Slovak Republic, Slovenia and Turkey. The median and mode contribution periods among the OECD countries are both 12 months. Korea's minimum contribution period of 180 days – roughly 8½ months (calculated as 180 ÷ 5 ÷ 52 x 12) – is slightly lower than in most OECD countries.

Maximum cut-off conditions differ more significantly. Turkey requires jobseekers to have worked continuously during the entire 24 weeks prior to the start of their benefit claim, resulting in an effective maximum cut-off period of zero. Spain, at the opposite extreme, requires only 360 days of contribution within a 6-year period, resulting in a potential cut-off period of over 4½ years. The median and mode cut-off periods among the OECD countries are both 12 months. Korea's maximum cut-off period of 9½ months (18 months minus the roughly 8½ months required to fulfil 180 working days) is broadly in line with the OECD median.

Regarding voluntary unemployment, countries generally enforce one of three types of penalties on such jobseekers: a *suspension*, a *sanction* or a *disqualification*. Suspensions impose a fixed-term waiting period on the claimant, simply delaying the start of their benefit claim. Sanctions also impose a fixed-term waiting period but subtract from the overall entitlement period (effectively consuming the benefit, instead of just delaying it). Disqualifications, finally, eliminate the claimant's entitlement to benefits altogether, thus excluding them for the entire duration of unemployment (Langenbucher, 2015[37]).

Table 3.2 summarises the types and scope of the penalties applied under the unemployment insurance measures found in OECD countries (plus the unemployment assistance measures of Australia and New Zealand, which make up their primary tier of income support for jobseekers in both countries).

Among the OECD countries, only Hungary and the Slovak Republic decline to impose any kind of a formal penalty on voluntary jobseekers for unemployment insurance benefits (though they penalise those fired for misconduct under certain circumstances).

Figure 3.2. OECD countries differ in the contribution and cut-off conditions they set for entitlement to unemployment insurance benefits

Conditions on the minimum period of insurance affiliation and the maximum cut-off period for entitlement to unemployment insurance benefits in OECD countries, 2016

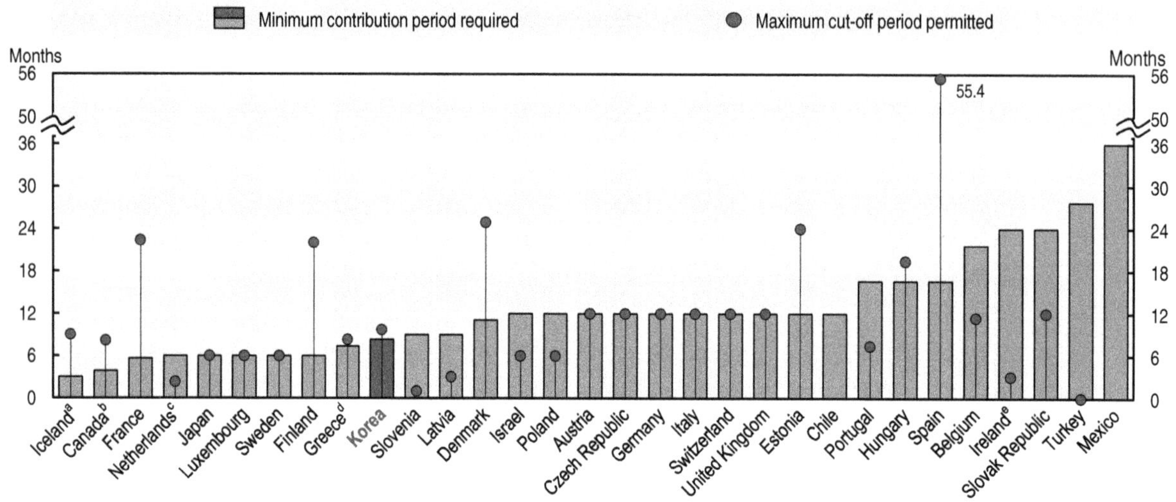

Note: Where variable conditions apply, data assume the jobseeker is 40-years-old, single and without any dependents. Conditions defined in days were converted into months assuming a 5-day working week, with 52 weeks divisible into 12 equal months for every year. Conditions defined in hours were converted in the same way, assuming a 40-hour working week. Australia and New Zealand are not shown since they have no statutory unemployment insurance benefits. Norway is not shown since the minimum period of contribution for unemployment insurance is calculated from cumulative earnings. Mexico does not define a maximum cut-off condition (entitlement is conditioned by cumulative insurance contributions).

a) The minimum contribution period shown (10 weeks in the preceding year) enables entitlement for some benefits. Full entitlement requires 12 months out of the preceding year.

b) The minimum contribution period is lower in provinces with higher levels of unemployment. The figure presented assumes an unemployment rate of 6-7%.

c) The minimum contribution period shown (26 weeks in the preceding 36 weeks) applies to the short-term benefit. Longer-term benefits require affiliation during 4 of the preceding 5 years.

d) The minimum contribution period shown (80 days per year in each of the previous 2 years) is for first-time claimants. Those claiming unemployment insurance benefits for a second time or more must either contribute for 125 days in the previous 14 months or 200 days in the previous 24 months.

e) There are two minimum contribution conditions – *first*, to have made at least 104 weekly contributions at any point in time and, *second*, to have made at least 39 weekly contributions within the preceding calendar year or 26 within each of the previous 2 years. The periods shown represent both.

Source: Compiled using OECD (2017), "Benefits and Wages: Country Specific Information", www.oecd.org/els/soc/benefits-and-wages-country-specific-information.htm (accessed on 3 November 2017).

StatLink http://dx.doi.org/10.1787/888933645155

Most countries apply a suspensions or sanction period of some set length. These are enforced by the public employment services, in each case, based on either a pre-defined guideline or a discretionary approach. Suspension and sanction periods vary in duration from between three and four weeks in Austria and Denmark to upwards of three months in Finland, France, Israel, Japan and Poland.

Korea's EI penalises voluntary jobseekers through disqualification. Thirteen other OECD countries take the same approach including Canada, Italy, Spain and the United States.

Table 3.2. Penalties for voluntary unemployment differ among OECD countries

Penalties issued for voluntary unemployment in OECD countries, 2014

Country	Type and duration of penalty for voluntary quit
A. Countries where voluntary quit has no impact on entitlement to benefits	
Hungary	None
Slovak Republic	None
B. Countries where voluntary quit involves a penalty on entitlement to benefits (but does not revoke them completely)	
Australia	Sanction of 8-12 weeks
Austria	Suspension of 4 weeks
Belgium	Sanction of 5-13 weeks in most cases (but may result in disqualification)
Czech Republic	Reduction of claimable benefit amount to 45% of usual net income
Denmark	Suspension of 3 weeks
Finland	Sanction of 90 days
France	Sanction of 4 months
Germany	Suspension of 12 weeks plus at least ¼ shortening of entitlement period
Iceland	Sanction of 2 months in first instance (otherwise 3)
Ireland	Sanction of up to 9 weeks
Israel	Sanction of 90 days
Japan	Sanction of 3 months
Latvia	Suspension of 2 months
New Zealand	Sanction of 13 weeks
Norway	Suspension of at least 8 weeks
Poland	Suspension of 90-180 days (depending on whether due notice was given before the quit)
Switzerland	Suspension of 31-60 benefit days (6-12 weeks)
Sweden	Suspension of 45 benefit days (9 weeks) in first and second instance; disqualification thereafter
United Kingdom	Sanction of 13 weeks; 26 weeks in second instance (within one year of first); 156 weeks in third instance (within one year of second)
C. Countries where voluntary quit results in disqualification from entitlement to benefits	
Canada	Disqualification
Chile	Disqualification
Estonia	Disqualification
Greece	Disqualification
Italy	Disqualification
Korea	Disqualification
Luxembourg	Disqualification
Mexico	Disqualification
Netherlands	Disqualification
Portugal	Disqualification
Slovenia	Disqualification
Spain	Disqualification
Turkey	Disqualification
United States	Disqualification (though some states have sanctions or suspensions)

Source: Adapted from Langenbucher, K (2015) “How demanding are eligibility criteria for unemployment benefits, quantitative indicators for OECD and EU countries”, *OECD Social, Employment and Migration Working Papers*, No. 166, OECD Publishing, Paris, http://dx.doi.org/10.1787/5jrxtk1zw8f2-en.

Penalties are usually justified on the grounds that they discourage workers from defaulting on employment in favour of benefits, thereby strengthening labour market outcomes and combatting a moral hazard among some to misuse the system. In practice, however, such a strict penalty as disqualification can encourage a different kind of moral hazard – for employers and employees to *negotiate* the terms of their dismissals to ensure the worker will retain their unemployment benefit entitlements. Such practices are apparently widespread in a number of countries (OECD, 2016[38]).

Somewhat lighter penalties might therefore be preferable. Most OECD countries see benefit sanctions or suspensions of a certain period as a viable enough solution for encouraging job mobility (and, thus, labour market dynamism) while ensuring income and employment support reached those who may need it.

Entitlement conditions for unemployment assistance benefits

Unemployment assistance benefits usually entail entitlement conditions distinct from those applied under contributory measures. Where unemployment assistance benefits are the secondary tier of income support for jobseekers, alternative entitlement rules can help to maximise the overall coverage. For example, unemployment assistance measures can provide employment support and help to activate new labour market entrants in a way that insurance-type measures inherently cannot. Such measures may therefore be of specific benefit to school-leavers who might otherwise fall into a so-called "NEET" situation (being neither in employment, education, or training). Unemployment assistance measures can also ensure that employment support reaches the poorest, most vulnerable or hardest-to-place jobseekers in a way insurance-type measures seldom do. This may be of particular use in activating those who might otherwise exit the labour market.

The coverage of unemployment assistance measures is usually restricted via three separate sets of entitlement conditions: those related to a jobseeker's *age*; those related to the *means* that they possess (including individual or household income, savings, assets and so on); and those related, in some way, to their recent *labour market activity*.

Table 3.3, below, details the entitlement conditions that apply under 15 unemployment assistance measures identified among the OECD countries, including Korea's ESPP.[6]

Entitlement conditions related to age typically span the entire working-age population. Most unemployment assistance measures welcome participants from early adulthood – starting at ages 15-20 – up to the legal retirement age – around age 65. Only Chile and New Zealand appear not to have a legal maximum age: entitlement to unemployment benefits ends, instead, upon the formal start of an individual's retirement.

Entitlement conditions related to means testing are applied under virtually all unemployment assistance measures. Among the OECD countries, only Chile and Sweden are exceptions to this rule: neither of their unemployment assistance measures involves a means test, though both offer only relatively low-value benefits and over a limited period of time.[7] Finland's flat-rate unemployment assistance benefit is generally means-tested, though not for jobseekers aged 55 and above. Korea's ESPP is also generally means-tested, though not for young participants (aged 18-34) *plus* certain categories of jobseekers deemed as "vulnerable".[8]

Means-test waivers of the kind used in Finland and Korea offer an effective way to ensure that employment support, training and other activation-oriented services reach particular groups that might require them more. Reducing means-testing requirements can also simplify the application procedure for support and may reduce administrative costs.

Table 3.3. Entitlement to unemployment assistance benefits in OECD countries

Selected benchmarks on entitlement for unemployment assistance benefits in OECD countries, 2016

Country	Benefit calculation and maximum duration	Entitlement conditional on age (range in years)	Entitlement conditional on means	Entitlement conditional on recent labour market activity	Relationship with UI (primary-tier) benefits		
					Payable to those who have exhausted UI benefits	Payable to those eligible for but not entitled to UI	Payable to those not eligible for UI
A. Countries where UA is the primary-tier unemployment benefit							
Australia	Flat rate for an unlimited period	16-65	•	None	n/a	n/a	n/a
New Zealand	Flat rate for an unlimited period	18 until retirement	•	None	n/a	n/a	n/a
B. Countries where UA operates as a secondary-tier unemployment benefit (alongside primary-tier UI benefits)							
Chile	Flat rates for 360 days (decreasing over time)	18 until retirement	-	12 months of pension contributions in prior 2 years (the last 3 being continuous and with one employer); NLMEs are not entitled	•	•	-
Estonia	Flat rate for up to 270 days (renewable in some cases)	16-63	•	UI exhausted or 180 days of employment, self-emp., education; childcare; sickness; military service or detention in prior 12 months; NLMEs other than these are not entitled	•	•	•
Finland	Flat rate for an unlimited period	17-67	• (except if aged 55+)	6 months of employment in prior 28 months (or 15 months of self-employment in prior 4 years); NLMEs aged 17-24 must complete vocational training or wait for 5 months	•	•	•
Germany	Flat rate for an unlimited period	15-64	•	None	•	•	•
Ireland	Flat rate for an unlimited period	18-65	•	None	•	•	•
Korea[a]	Flat rate for up to 12 months (renewable after 3-30 months)	18-64	• (except youth and vulnerable groups)	None	•	•	•
Portugal	Flat rate for up to 540 days (for initial claim)	18-64	•	UI exhausted or 180 days of employment in prior year; alternatively, 720 days of self-employment in prior 4 years; NLMEs are not entitled	•	•	Self-employed and dependent non-regular
Sweden	Flat rate for up to 60 weeks	20-65	-	UI exhausted or 6 months of employment in prior 12 months; NLMEs are not entitled unless recovering from an illness, completing full-time study or are returning from parental leave	•	•	•
United Kingdom	Flat rate for an unlimited period	16-65	•	None	•	•	•

Country	Benefit calculation and maximum duration	Entitlement conditional on age (range in years)	Entitlement conditional on means	Entitlement conditional on recent labour market activity	Relationship with UI (primary-tier) benefits		
					Payable to those who have exhausted UI benefits	Payable to those eligible for but not entitled to UI	Payable to those not eligible for UI
C. Countries where UA predominantly extends support only to those exhausting primary-tier UI benefits							
Austria	92-95% of UI amount renewable annually	19-65	•	Only if UI exhausted; NLMEs are not entitled	•	-	-
France	Flat rate renewable every 6 months	16-65	•	5 years of employment (including any training) in prior 10 years; NLMEs are not entitled	•	-	Only some groups of self-employed
Greece	Flat rate for up to 12 months	20-66	•	UI exhausted and 60 days of employment during the calendar year prior to registration	•	Only NLMEs after a 12-month wait	Only NLMEs after a 12-month wait
Spain	Flat rate for up to 6 months (renewable only twice)	16-65	•	Generally only if UI exhausted (return migrants are entitled with 12 months of employment in prior 6 years; self-employed covered under UI are excluded)	Only if responsible for family or aged 45+	Only if contribution condition is unmet and job loss is involuntary	Only those recovering from illness and ex-prisoners

Note: "UA" refers to unemployment assistance benefits. "UI" refers to unemployment insurance benefits. "NLMEs" refers to new labour market entrants. "•" indicates entitlement is conditional on a means test or (in the right-hand columns) that benefits are payable, in a majority of circumstances, to the specified group. "-" indicates entitlement is not conditional on a means test or (in the right-hand columns) that the specified group is generally not covered by the measure.

a) The row for Korea refers to ESPP. Two broad groups are exempted from a means test for participation under ESPP – certain "vulnerable groups" under type-1 programmes and jobseekers aged 18-34 under type-2 programmes. Vulnerable groups, in this case, include disabled persons; low-income self-employed persons; low-income non-regular workers; female heads of households; unmarried mothers; lone parents; former soldiers with technical skills; bankrupts; ex-prisoners; homeless people; international migrants by marriage; and defectors from the Democratic People's Republic of Korea.

Source: Compiled using OECD (2017), "Benefits and Wages: Country Specific Information", www.oecd.org/els/soc/benefits-and-wages-country-specific-information.htm, cross-checked and updated using SSA and ISSA (2016, 2017), *Social Security Programs throughout the World.*

Entitlement conditions related to jobseekers' recent labour market activity vary the most significantly across the OECD countries. Several of them include no such particular conditions: entitlement to unemployment assistance benefits is determined independently of previous labour market activity and, instead, may solely rely on the age restrictions imposed; a means test (if one is applied); and any additional behavioural conditions that may apply afterwards. This is the case for Korea's ESPP and under the unemployment assistance measures applied in Australia, Germany, Ireland, New Zealand and the United Kingdom. These countries' measures embrace new labour market entrants.

Other countries set specific conditions on previous labour market activity, usually expressed as a minimum length of employment within a recent period of time. Such conditions usually exclude new labour market entrants but may offer special conditions for them. Finland's unemployment assistance measure, for example, exempts new labour market entrants aged 17-24 from its labour market activity condition (of having at least six months of employment within the preceding 28 months) provided they complete a programme of vocational training or, otherwise, undergo a five-month "qualifying period" during which the benefit is suspended.

Unemployment assistance measures in Estonia and Sweden take an alternative approach: both have labour market activity conditions but include, under this, not only employment and self-employment but also periods of time spent in full-time education, caring for children, sickness, military service, imprisonment and other such justified activities.

Conditions like these open up the possibility of participation for new labour market entrants (and returners) as a crucial step towards activation. Young people, inactive housewives, those regaining their work capacity after sickness, and ex-prisoners might all be in need of the additional help and support unemployment assistance measures can offer. The alternative, for many, might otherwise be a default to inactivity. In the same spirit, the vulnerable groups exempted from means testing under Korea's ESPP offer an exemplary policy for others to follow.[9]

Behavioural conditions and activation

Unemployment benefit measures can encourage activation by restricting the income support they offer to ensure it is tangibly less than work. Another way is to impose a maximum duration on benefits, beyond which they are "exhausted" and cease to be paid. Perhaps the main way that unemployment benefit measures ensure activation, however, is through the behavioural conditions they enforce. Such conditions may variously require beneficiaries of unemployment protection measures to register as unemployed; to consult with public employment services for advice and oversight at regular intervals; to ensure they are readily contactable; to ensure they are capable of work; to ensure they are available for work (sometimes imminently); to actively search for work and provide evidence of this; to accept any reasonable job offer the public employment service might identify; and to accept participation in any active labour market programme or training the public employment service might deem necessary, among other such conditions.

Behavioural conditions play an important role in the activation of jobseekers, once a benefit claim is underway, apportioning penalties on those who do not comply.

Shortcomings around activation are generally evidenced by high rates of unemployment and, in particular, long-term unemployment. Korea, on the other hand, has among the lowest rates of both among the OECD countries (Figure 3.3).

Korea's formal unemployment rate was 3.8% in 2016. The share of those unemployed for 12 months or more was a mere 0.9% among the total unemployed – the lowest of any OECD country. The Czech Republic, Germany, Hungary, Japan and Switzerland had similarly low unemployment rates as Korea but significantly higher shares of long-term unemployment of some 40% or more. Greece, Italy, Portugal and Spain currently perform outstandingly poorly on both variables. For the OECD as a whole, unemployment stood at 6.5% and long-term unemployment at 30.5% in 2016.

The time it takes from becoming a jobseeker to exiting unemployment was just 3.0 months in Korea in 2016, according to the *Economically Active Population Survey* (Statistics Korea, 2017[5]). Comparable data for other OECD countries from 2014-15 show significantly longer durations: 4.6 months in Canada; 6-7 months in Norway and the United States; 10-12 months in Australia, Finland and Poland; 16½ months in Switzerland; and upwards of 18 months in the Czech Republic, Hungary and the Slovak Republic (OECD, 2017[39]).

Assuming that the majority of unemployed people genuinely find work under such circumstances – and are not merely exiting the labour force in large numbers – the indicators noted above signal a healthy (and even exemplary) activation climate in Korea.

Figure 3.3. Korea has among the lowest unemployment and long-term unemployment rates

Unemployment rate and incidence of long-term unemployment in OECD countries, 2016 (percentages)

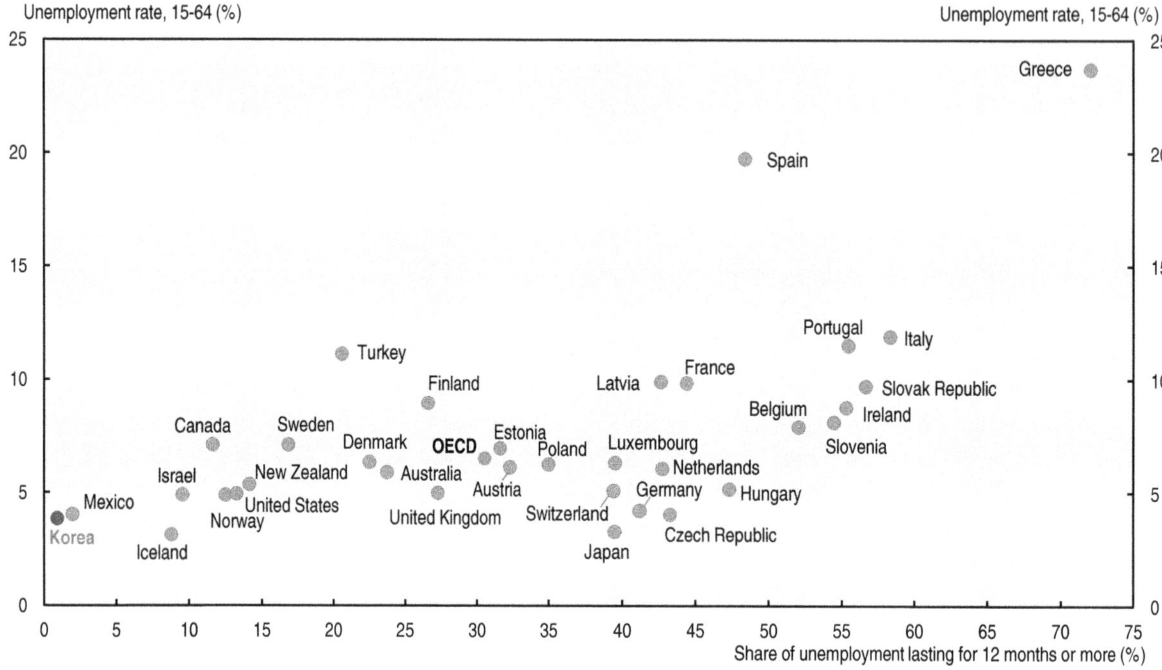

Note: Data include all persons aged 15-64. Unemployment duration is based on ongoing (incomplete) spells. The figure ncludes all OECD countries except Chile, for which comparable data were unavailable.
Source: *OECD Employment Database*, www.oecd.org/employment/database (accessed on 4 May 2017).

StatLink http://dx.doi.org/10.1787/888933645174

Duration and value of income support

The income support unemployment benefit measures offer differs much among the OECD countries. This can be said of both the maximum *duration* benefit claims can last for and of the *value* of the income support they offer. Table 3.4 pinpoints these two features for the various unemployment insurance and unemployment assistance measures implemented among the OECD countries.

In terms of the duration, income support under Korea's EI can last for a maximum of 90-240 days, depending on the jobseeker's total contribution period and their age.[10] This is relatively short compared with most other OECD countries' unemployment insurance measures, among which the median and mode duration are both 12 months. In some countries, the duration can last for considerably longer still: upwards of three years for some workers in France, Iceland and the Netherlands and for a potentially unlimited time in Belgium (though the benefit amount gradually declines towards a flat rate over time). Unemployment assistance benefits, on the other hand, can potentially be claimed for much longer durations since most are unlimited, in principle, or renewable for most participants.

In terms of the value, income support under Korea's EI is technically supposed to replace 50% of jobseekers' previous gross earnings although is more resembles a "flat-rate" benefit, in practice, given its very narrow range between a minimum benefit value of KRW 46 584 and a maximum of KRW 50 000 per day, as of April 2017.

Table 3.4. Scope of income support for unemployment in OECD countries

Selected benchmarks on the income support offered for unemployment in OECD countries, 2016

	Type of measure	Measure is means-tested	Maximum claim period	Formula calculation for the benefit amount (replacement share of previous gross earnings)
A. Countries with only assistance-type protection for unemployment				
Australia	Assistance	•	No limit	Flat rate ^
New Zealand	Assistance	•	No limit	Flat rate ^
B. Countries with both assistance-type and insurance-type protections for unemployment				
Austria	Insurance	-	9 months	55% (of previous net earnings)
	Assistance	•	12 months (renewable)	92-95% of previous insurance benefit
Chile	Insurance	-	10 months within any 5-year period	70% for 1 month; 55%, 45%, 40% and 35% in the following 4 months, respectively; 30% thereafter
	Assistance	-	360 days	Flat rate for 90 days; ¾ of this rate for 90 days; ½ of the original rate thereafter
Estonia	Insurance	-	360 days * (360 daily instalments paid on every day of the week)	50% for 100 days; 40% thereafter
	Assistance	•	270 days (renewable in some cases)	Flat rate
Finland	Insurance	-	100 weeks * (500 daily instalments paid only on 5 days in every week)	Flat rate *plus* 45% of daily earnings of EUR 33-160 *plus* 20% of daily earnings above EUR 160
	Assistance	• (except those aged 55+)	No limit	Flat rate
France	Insurance	-	36 months ^	57-75% (higher percentages for low earners)
	Assistance	•	6 months (renewable)	Flat rate
Germany	Insurance	-	24 months *^	60% (of previous net earnings)
	Assistance	•	No limit	Flat rates (variable by family composition)
Greece	Insurance	-	12 months * for former employees and 9 months * for former self-employed	Flat rate
	Assistance	•	12 months	Flat rate
Ireland	Insurance	-	234 days *	Flat rate
	Assistance	•	No limit	Flat rate ^
Korea[a]	Insurance	-	240 days *^ (240 daily instalments paid on every day of the week)	50%, formally, but effectively a flat-rate benefit (capped at 90% of the daily minimum wage), given tight margin between floor and ceiling amounts
	Assistance	• (except youth and vulnerable groups)	4 weeks counselling at stage 1; up to 8 months training, start-up support or internship at stage 2; 3 months job-placement support at stage 3 (renewable after 3-30 months)	Flat rates per day of participation at each stage, capped at a maximum monthly amount
Portugal	Insurance	-	540 days *^	65% for 180 days; 55% thereafter
	Assistance	•	540 days for initial claim; 270 thereafter	Flat rate (equivalent to 80% of the UI floor amount)
Spain	Insurance	-	24 months *	70% for 6 months; 60% thereafter
	Assistance	•	6 months (renewable up to 2 times)	Flat rate ^
Sweden	Insurance	-	60 weeks (300 daily instalments paid only on 5 days in every week)	80% for 40 weeks; 70% thereafter
	Assistance	-	60 weeks	Flat rate
United Kingdom	Insurance	-	6 months	Flat rate
	Assistance	•	No limit	Flat rate
C. Countries with only insurance-type protection for unemployment				
Belgium	Insurance	-	No limit	65% for 3 months; 60% for 9 months; 40-60% for up to 36 additional months; gradual decrease to a flat rate
Canada	Insurance	-	45 weeks (or lower, depending on local unemployment rate) *	55%

	Type of measure	Measure is means-tested	Maximum claim period	Formula calculation for the benefit amount (replacement share of previous gross earnings)
Czech Republic	Insurance	-	11 months	65% (of previous net earnings) for 2 months; 50% for 2 months; 45% thereafter
Denmark	Insurance	-	104 weeks	90%
Hungary	Insurance	-	90 days *	60%
Iceland	Insurance	-	36 months	70% for 3 months; flat rate thereafter
Israel	Insurance	-	175 days	36-80% ^ (higher percentages for lower earners) for 5 months up to a ceiling; ceiling reduced thereafter
Italy	Insurance	-	18 months (under 2017 rules)	75% of monthly earnings up to EUR 1 195 *plus* 25% of those above that for 3 months; reduced by 3% in each month thereafter
Japan	Insurance	-	330 days *^ (330 daily instalments paid on every day of the week)	50-80% (higher percentages for lower earners)
Latvia	Insurance	-	9 months	50-65% * for 3 months; discounting ¼ for 3 months; discounting ⅓ for the final 3 months
Luxembourg	Insurance	-	12 months (renewable for some)	80% for 6 months; ceiling reduced thereafter
Mexico	Insurance	-	90 days *	100%
Netherlands	Insurance	-	38 months *	75% for 2 months; 70% thereafter
Norway	Insurance	-	104 weeks (or 52 weeks below a certain income threshold)	62.4%
Poland	Insurance	-	18 months (or lower, depending on local unemployment rate)	Flat rate *
Slovak Republic	Insurance	-	6 months	50%
Slovenia	Insurance	-	25 months *^	80% for 3 months; 60% for 9 months; 50% thereafter
Switzerland	Insurance	-	520 days *^	70%
Turkey	Insurance	-	300 days *	40%
United States	Insurance	-	26-46 weeks (in most states)	50% (in most states)

Note: "•" indicates entitlement is determined based on a means test. "-" indicates entitlement does not entail a means test. "*" indicates the amount is typically reduced for jobseekers with shorter contribution periods (only the maximum amount is stated above). "^" indicates the amount may be reduced for jobseekers among younger cohorts (only the maximum amount is stated above). Longer claim periods or higher-value benefits that may apply on the basis of family composition or targeting co-habiting dependents are discounted.

a) Insurance-type measure refers to EI and assistance-type measure refers to ESPP. Two broad groups are exempted from a means test for participation under ESPP – certain "vulnerable groups" under type-1 programmes and jobseekers aged 18-34 under type-2 programmes. Vulnerable groups, in this case, include disabled persons; low-income self-employed persons; low-income non-regular workers; female heads of households; unmarried mothers; lone parents; former soldiers with technical skills; bankrupts; ex-prisoners; homeless people; international migrants by marriage; and defectors from the Democratic People's Republic of Korea.

Source: Compiled using OECD (2017), "Benefits and Wages: Country Specific Information", www.oecd.org/els/soc/benefits-and-wages-country-specific-information.htm, cross-checked and updated using SSA and ISSA (2016, 2017), *Social Security Programs throughout the World.*

Genuine flat-rate unemployment insurance measures transfer the same benefit amount to all entitled claimants, regardless of their previous earnings. Such benefits are paid for the entire claim period in Greece, Ireland, Poland and the United Kingdom and in the later stages of those in Belgium and Iceland. Unemployment assistance benefits also virtually always take on a flat-rate value.

Variable-rate unemployment insurance benefits, on the other hand, retain a close link with beneficiaries' previous earnings. During the initial stage of the claim period, such benefits replace up to 80% of previous earnings in Israel, Japan, Luxembourg, Slovenia and Sweden; 90% in Denmark; and even 100% in Mexico.

In practice, even variable-rate unemployment benefits are "flattened", to some degree, at either extreme of the earnings distribution by "floor" and "ceiling" amounts that define the range of benefit values any measure can deliver. Benefit floor and ceiling amounts can be defined in various ways, including both *explicit* and *de facto* thresholds:

- *Explicit benefit thresholds* are set at a particular value, defined by policy makers, and typically adjusted over time. Some are officially pegged to certain labour market variables like the statutory minimum wage or the national average wage or simply set to change in line with inflation. The explicit floor for Korea's EI is officially capped at 90% of the daily minimum wage. Estonia has an explicit floor-cap of 50% of the previous year's full-time minimum wage. In Hungary and Turkey, the benefit *ceiling* is pegged to the full-time minimum wage: at 100% and 80% of its level, respectively. In Luxembourg, the floor and ceiling amounts are both pegged at 80% and 250% of the minimum wage, respectively. In Israel, the ceiling amount is fixed at 100% of the national average wage.
- *De facto benefit thresholds* operate somewhat differently and can supplant explicit thresholds under certain circumstances. The standard formula replacement rate for a minimum wage earner, for example, can function as a de facto floor amount: a benefit that reimburses, say, 60% of usual earnings cannot fall below a value of 60% of the minimum wage for any entitled jobseeker leaving a formal full-time job. The standard replacement rate for the minimum wage may thus count as a de facto floor for unemployment benefits – at least for formal, full-time workers. De facto ceiling amounts may exist where the covered earnings used to calculate social contributions are capped at some maximum threshold. Such thresholds effectively set a de facto ceiling on the benefit amount a jobseeker can receive, since only their covered earnings count towards insurance. Many countries employ such caps including Canada, France, Germany, Norway and Switzerland.

Putting together the information on all such thresholds, it is possible to compare OECD countries' unemployment benefit measures regarding the range of values their income support can offer. Figure 3.4 shows the range of possible values for both unemployment insurance and unemployment assistance measures in OECD countries relative to the average wage (Panel A) and (where applicable) the statutory minimum wage (Panel B).[11]

Based on this analysis, Korea emerges as an outlier among the OECD countries in two main ways. First, the tight margin between EI's explicit floor and ceiling amounts represent the smallest range of any OECD country (apart from those with explicitly flat-rate benefits). EI thus effectively functions more like a flat-rate benefit than any other countries' measures do. Second, EI's floor is especially high compared with other countries' measures. Such a high floor makes Korea the only OECD country that brings all primary-tier unemployment benefit recipients above the relative poverty threshold of 50% of the average wage (albeit for only the relatively short duration of 90-240 days that EI benefits can last) (Figure 3.4, Panel A). EI's high explicit floor also makes Korea the only OECD country where all such beneficiaries gain more than the minimum wage (Figure 3.4, Panel B). Although the EI floor is officially capped at 90% of Korea's daily minimum wage, the minimum amount a claimant can receive is actually greater than the minimum wage, in practice, since the benefit is claimed on seven days per week.[12]

EI's explicit ceiling is less of an outlier: broadly equivalent to those established in Denmark, Italy and Sweden (relative to their average wages) or Belgium, Canada and Spain (relative to their statutory minimum wages) but significantly lower than those of Finland, France, Germany, Latvia, Luxembourg, the Netherlands, the Slovak Republic and Switzerland, for example, where benefits may far exceed 100% of the average wage and 250% of the statutory minimum wage (Figure 3.4).

Figure 3.4. Unemployment benefit ranges differ much across OECD countries, relative to their average wage and (where applicable) statutory minimum wage

A. Floor, ceiling and flat-rate amounts of unemployment benefits in selected OECD countries as a share of the average wage for a full-time regular salaried employee, 2016 (percentages)

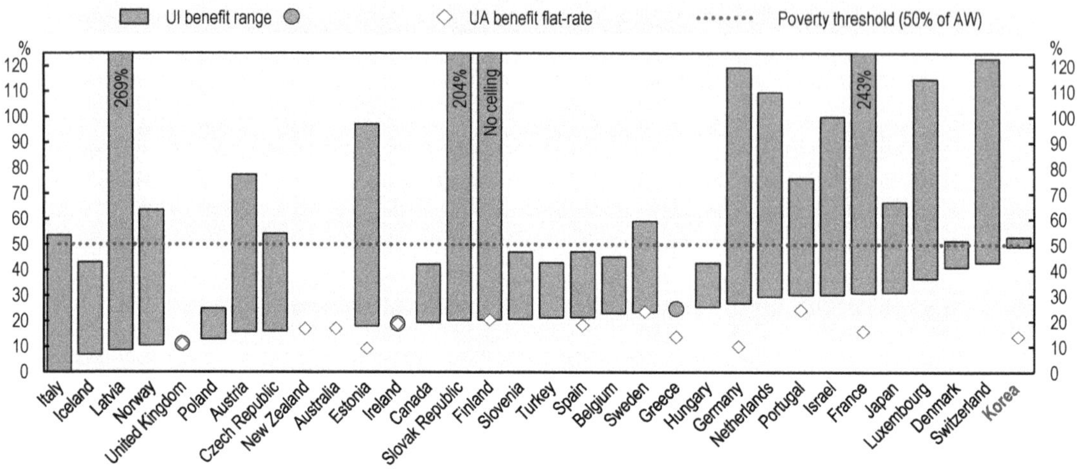

B. Floor, ceiling and flat-rate amounts of unemployment benefits in selected OECD countries as a share of the statutory minimum wage for a full-time regular salaried employee, 2016 (percentages)

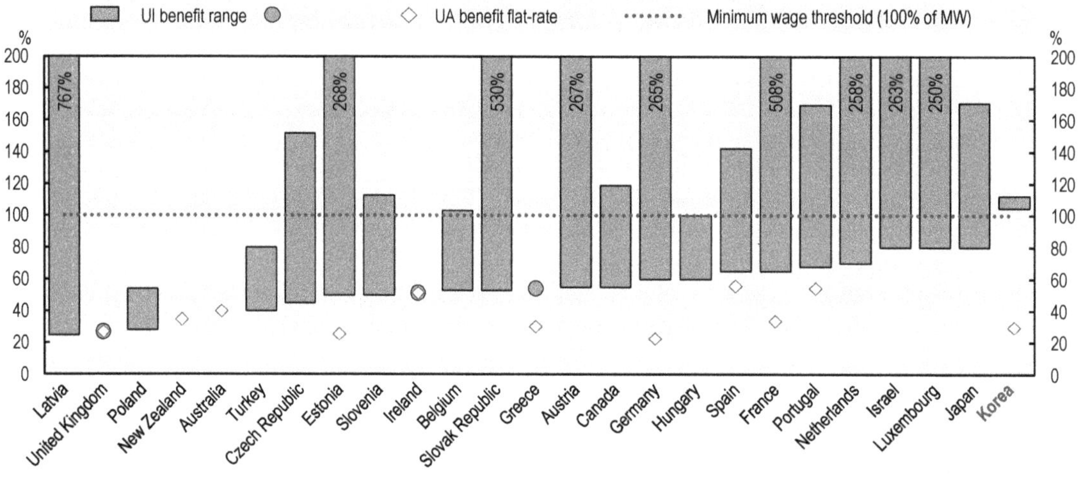

Note: UA: Unemployment assistance benefits; UI: Unemployment insurance benefits; AW: Full-time average wage of a regular employee, estimated by dividing the national-accounts-based total wage bill by the average number of employees in the total economy and multiplying by the ratio of average usual weekly hours per full-time employee to average usual weekly hours for all employees; MW: Statutory minimum wages.

Information on benefit amounts is valid for circa 2015-16 and information on average wages and minimum wages for 2016, except for Korea, whose data have been updated using the latest parameters, valid for 2017. Benefit amounts are relevant for jobseekers who meet all applicable eligibility, entitlement and behavioural conditions; are aged 40; and are single and without dependents. Floor amounts shown are whichever is highest between: i) the explicit minimum benefit amount, and ii) the de facto minimum benefit amount a jobseeker would gain after stopping full-time employment in which they earned the minimum wage. Original amounts stated in annual, weekly, daily or hourly terms were converted to monthly figures assuming either a 40-hour or a 5-day working week, with 52 weeks divisible into 12 equal months in every year. Chile, Mexico and the United States are not included due to insufficient data.

Source: Average wages and statutory minimum wages data are from the *OECD Employment Database*, www.oecd.org/employment/database (accessed on 04 May 2017), series on "average annual wages" and "minimum wages at current prices in NCU"; benefit ranges compiled using OECD (2017), "Benefits and Wages: Country Specific Information", www.oecd.org/els/soc/benefits-and-wages-country-specific-information.htm, cross-checked and updated using SSA and ISSA (2016, 2017), *Social Security Programs throughout the World*.

StatLink http://dx.doi.org/10.1787/888933645193

Under Korea's ESPP, the maximum transfer of KRW 400 000 per month under stage 2 (including a training allowance of up to KRW 284 000 plus a training incentive of KRW 116 000) is currently equivalent to 14.0% of the monthly average wage. This is broadly in line with the flat-rate amounts paid by secondary-tier unemployment benefits in France, Greece and the United Kingdom. It is rather lower, however, than the amounts provided in Finland, Portugal and Sweden, where the equivalent is 20-25% of the average wage (Figure 3.4).

Figure 3.5, below, shows the floor and ceiling amounts for primary-tier unemployment benefits in OECD countries relative to their standard formula replacement rate: the share of an entitled jobseeker's previous earnings that unemployment benefits compensate. The formula replacement rate is calculated for the first month of the unemployment claim (though it may reduce in subsequent months), as specified in Table 3.4 above.

Based on this analysis, most OECD countries fall into one of three general groups:

A. Some determine benefit amounts according to the same fixed-rate benefit for all jobseekers. In practice, such measures replace relatively low amounts of around 10-25% of the average wage. Countries with such measures include Australia, Greece, Ireland, New Zealand, Poland and the United Kingdom.

B. Some set the benefit range above and below the average formula replacement rate. Floors and ceilings defined in this way limit extreme benefit outcomes at either end of the income distribution while retaining the formula replacement rate for jobseekers with previously average earnings. This group of countries includes Japan, France, Germany and others.

C. Some set the entire benefit range below the average formula replacement rate. Floors and ceilings defined in this way result in relatively low-cost unemployment benefit measures and reduce, in any case, the value of entitlements for jobseekers around the middle of the income distribution. This group of countries includes Canada, Spain, Sweden and others.

Korea's EI does not conform neatly to any of these three models.

When EI was first established in 1995, the benefit floor and ceiling amounts closely resembled those of present-day Austria, Estonia or Japan: a relatively modest formula replacement rate of 50% of usual earnings was contained, on either side, by floor and ceiling amounts equivalent to 17.9% and 79.6% of the average wage.[13] At EI's inception, Korea would thus have neatly fit in among the group-B countries shown in Figure 3.5.

As Korea's benefit floor increased from 70% to 90% of the minimum wage after 1999; and as the minimum wage itself increased rapidly over time; the EI floor converged closer to the formula replacement rate and to the ceiling amount. Between 2011 and 2016, the EI ceiling was slightly lower than the formula replacement rate of the average wage, thus resembling the group-C countries' measures shown in Figure 3.5.[14]

By 2017, the EI benefit range has become so narrow it is virtually a flat-rate benefit. Korea today thus resembles the group-A countries shown in Figure 3.5, except that the implied replacement rate – at around 50% of the average wage – is much higher than the 10-25% provided by the genuine flat-rate unemployment insurance measures like those of Ireland, Poland or the United Kingdom.

Figure 3.5. Unemployment benefit ranges differ much across OECD countries, relative to their formula replacement rate

Floor and ceiling amounts of unemployment benefits in selected OECD countries relative to the actual replacement rate for a full-time, average-wage employee within the first month of unemployment, 2016 (percentages)

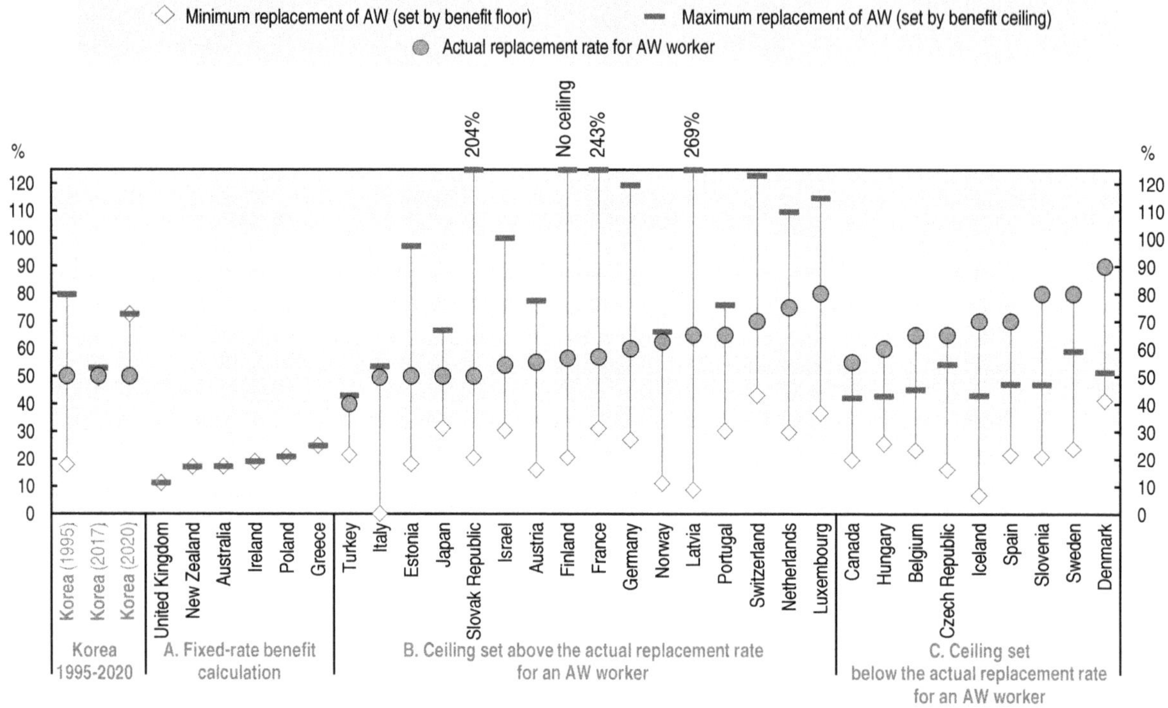

Note: AW refers to the full-time average wage of a regular employee, estimated by dividing the national-accounts-based total wage bill by the average number of employees in the total economy and multiplying by the ratio of average usual weekly hours per full-time employee to average usual weekly hours for all employees. Information on benefit amounts is valid for circa 2015-16 and information on average wages for 2016, unless stated otherwise. Benefit amounts are relevant for jobseekers who meet all applicable eligibility, entitlement and behavioural conditions; are aged 40; and are single and without dependents. Floor amounts shown are whichever is highest between: a) the explicit minimum benefit amount, and b) the de facto minimum benefit amount a jobseeker would gain after stopping formal full-time employment in which they earned the minimum wage.

Source: Average wages data obtained from the *OECD Employment Database*, www.oecd.org/employment/database (accessed on 04 May 2017), series on "average annual wages"; benefit ranges compiled using OECD (2017), "Benefits and Wages: Country Specific Information", www.oecd.org/els/soc/benefits-and-wages-country-specific-information.htm; cross-checked and updated using SSA and ISSA (2016, 2017) *Social Security Programs throughout the World*.

StatLink http://dx.doi.org/10.1787/888933645212

Looking ahead, political leaders in Korea have announced a goal to increase the statutory minimum wage to KRW 10 000 per hour, perhaps by the year 2020. The current EI floor of 90% of the minimum wage would thus result in a minimum benefit of KRW 72 000 – roughly equivalent to 72.6% of what the average wage might be by then.[15]

Korea already has the highest unemployment benefit floor of any OECD country, relative to its average wage. Maintaining the current EI floor at 90% of the minimum wage by 2020 would make Korea the only OECD country whose floor amount is greater than the formula replacement rate for an average worker. Even the already confirmed increase of the minimum wage to KRW 7 530 per hour from January 2018 implies an EI benefit floor of KRW 54 216 per day (calculated as 7 530 x 8 x 0.9), which will replace 56.5% of the average daily wage by then – a much higher floor than anywhere else in the OECD.

To restore a balance to this situation, policy makers should ultimately decide what kind of an EI Korea wants. There are several potential avenues forward:

- Korea could decisively merge the EI floor and ceiling amounts together to offer a genuine flat-rate benefit like those of the group-A countries, mentioned above.[16]
- Korea could reduce the EI floor amount to a lower share of the minimum wage (such as, for example, the 70% it originally was before 1999 or to something lower like the 40% currently set in Turkey or the 50% in Estonia) and raise the ceiling (to, e.g. Luxembourg's 250% of the minimum wage or Israel's 100% of the average wage) to resemble more the group-B countries, mentioned above.
- Korea could maintain its current floor and ceiling amounts as they are but offer EI benefits on five days per week (as both Finland and Sweden do), instead of on seven, within the current total maximum total claim period of 90-240 benefit-days. This would effectively lower the weekly and monthly floor and ceiling amounts EI claimants can receive by 28.6% (calculated as 2 ÷ 7) without, on the face of it, affecting the total amounts jobseekers are entitled to nor, necessarily, the insurance premiums required to finance such an EI. This approach offers perhaps the quickest and simplest solution for EI to resemble more the group-C countries' measures, mentioned above.
- Finally, Korea could maintain its current floor amount as it is but raise the formula replacement rate from its current 50% of usual earnings to 80% (as in Luxembourg, Slovenia and Sweden) or 90% (as in Denmark) and increase the ceiling accordingly. This would somewhat rationalise the uncommonly high floor amount EI currently has but result in more costly transfers.

Providing a detailed costing for these different options is, unfortunately, beyond the scope of this report. Any adjustments, however, should certainly be careful to consider their fiscal impacts on the sustainability of EI plus any knock-on effects on work-incentives.

In any case, returning EI to the relative floor and ceiling levels it originally launched with in 1995 (i.e. those equivalent to roughly 18% and 80% of the average wage, respectively, as shown in Figure 3.5) would today require a floor amount of KRW 16 900 per day – roughly 33% of today's daily minimum wage – and a ceiling of KRW 75 100 – roughly 150% of the current ceiling level.

Choosing a slightly narrower range like that of Japan's current unemployment insurance measure (with thresholds of roughly 30% and 65% of the average wage, as shown in Figure 3.5) would require an EI floor amount of KRW 28 300 per day – roughly 55% of today's daily minimum wage – and a ceiling of KRW 61 400 – roughly 125% of the current ceiling level.

All of these options are within the scope of what policy makers can achieve. Maintaining the current high floor and tight ceiling amounts of EI deviates from its original design and almost completely eliminates the link between the benefit amount and regular earnings.

Protections for sickness in OECD countries

Common support measures

The majority of OECD countries implement income support measures for employees undergoing temporary absences from work. Such benefits commonly seek to compensate workers whose capacity to perform their work (and, thus, to earn an income) is restricted in some justifiable way over a limited period of time.

Temporary work incapacity can commonly arise from sickness or an injury. Two key types of policy measures are commonly applied under such circumstances:

- *Employers' liability for sickness* places a burden of duty on employers to provide for eligible workers during a period of ill-health. Employers may thus be obliged to pay part (or all) their worker's salary, over a period of their absence. In some cases, employers must also rehabilitate the worker within a separate role or secure for them a different job elsewhere. In Korea, employers face no such liabilities for their workers at the statutory level.[17]
- *Cash sickness benefits* can provide more extensive income support for workers in case of sickness beyond a period of employers' liability. Most such benefits operate as contributory measures though some countries complement them with assistance-type benefits. Korea has neither, beyond the limited scope of support that delaying EI entitlement can offer to workers who relinquish their jobs.

The discussion below elaborates on the many ways in which OECD countries currently apply such measures, elaborating on the potential best practices for Korea.[18]

Employers' liability for sickness

Employers in most OECD countries are liable for at least part of the risk associated with their employees' absences in case of sickness. Most OECD countries mandate employers to continue paying an absent worker (in full or in part) over a period of 5-15 working days. In several cases, employers' liability covers a much longer potential period of time: extending to around six weeks in Germany and Poland; 11-12 weeks in Austria and Luxembourg; 18 weeks for some workers in France; 36 weeks in Italy; and up to two years in the Netherlands (Spasova, Bouget and Vanhercke, 2016[40]).[19]

Employers in Korea have no such statutory obligations. Among the OECD countries, this is likewise the case in Canada, Denmark, Greece, Ireland, Japan, Portugal and the United States. Under such circumstances, it is predominantly at employers' own discretion to decide what support to offer a worker. In practice, this can lead to a polarisation in the support different groups within the labour market might receive, potentially excluding many elderly workers; workers with pre-existing health conditions; non-regular workers; and employees in smaller firms. It also enables discrimination.

Employers in some countries may be bound to equivalent obligations under the terms of their workers' employment contracts or via a collective agreement. Indeed, collective agreements sometimes set the norm for determining sickness pay and leave allowances. Switzerland, for example, regulates sickness protection predominantly through collective agreements, linking the employers' liability very closely to workers' tenure (lasting three weeks for new staff and upwards of six months for decades-tenured employees) (OECD, 2014[41]). Israel, likewise, determines sickness protection predominantly on the basis of collective agreements (SSA and ISSA, 2017[42]). Finland has statutory provisions for employers covering nine days of a worker's absence due to sickness, while collective agreements increase it to 30 days for most manual workers and upwards of 90 days for professional and government employees (Spasova, Bouget and Vanhercke, 2016[40]).

In France, most collective agreements oblige employers to make up the difference between cash sickness benefits and their workers' full usual earnings over a period of several weeks (Spasova, Bouget and Vanhercke, 2016[40]).

Collective agreements offer a purposeful alternative to statutory provisions but may leave out large segments of the workforce. Statutory employers' liability distributes the risks associated with sickness more equitably by holding all employers to a common standard of protection. Statutory employers' liability also ensures that a minimum baseline of coverage is provided for all employees alike – indiscriminately of their sector, age or working time – thus helping to reduce the associated duality in support that can arise among different groups within a labour market.

Coverage of cash sickness benefits

Almost all OECD countries implement some social protection measure providing income support to workers under a period of temporary work incapacity. Such measures usually extend far beyond the limited provisions of employers' liability for sickness.

Table 3.5 gives an overview of the coverage entailed by cash sickness benefits in OECD countries. Most provide income support through contributory measures. Australia, Finland, New Zealand and the United Kingdom also provide non-contributory income support, pending a means test. Korea has no equivalent measure in place.

In Korea, EI benefits may offer limited support to workers undergoing sickness under two specific sets of circumstances: those who are *employed* at the time they fall ill and forced to leave their jobs may choose to postpone the start of their EI benefit claim until they regain the capacity to seek work up to a maximum period of four years (though they gain no income support during this time); and those who are *unemployed* and already claiming EI benefits at the time they fall ill are exempted from behavioural conditions during what remains of their regular entitlement period (of 90-240 days). In either case, however, anyone still formally attached to an employer is ineligible for income support.

Given this circumstance, the best option for many workers undergoing sickness in Korea is simply to be fired. Such outcomes lead to indefinite breaks in employment relationships that are inefficient for workers and employers alike. Such outcomes also remove all liability from employers, opening the way for discrimination and potentially prolonging workers' rehabilitation. Such outcomes, finally, can increase social exclusion for those who do not find their way easily back into work.

While EI may thus offer a limited degree of support for *unemployed persons* following a period of sickness, cash sickness benefit measures in other countries support *existing employees* during an absence from work due to sickness. The difference is crucial since one central goal among the latter kinds of measures is ultimately to preserve the employment relationship – something altogether neglected in Korea. Meeting this goal strengthens the positive role employers can play in their workers' recovery and can significantly ease transitions back to work. Failing to meet this goal may add to the burdens workers face, resulting in longer periods of time spent on social benefits.

Among the remaining OECD countries, only Israel, Switzerland and the United States likewise have no statutory cash sickness benefit measures in place. Nevertheless, workers in Israel and Switzerland are generally relatively well protected: those in Israel through extensive sickness provisions common to practically all collective agreements and those in Switzerland through far-reaching employers' liability laws. Only Korea and some parts of the United Sates thus have no equivalent policy in place.

Table 3.5. Coverage of cash sickness benefits in OECD countries

Selected benchmarks on the coverage of cash sickness benefit measures in OECD countries, 2016

	Regular coverage includes			Coverage of unemployed persons	Voluntary coverage available
	Regular salaried employees	Self-employed persons	Non-regular salaried workers		
A. Countries with only non-contributory, means-tested cash sickness benefits					
Australia	•	•	•	•	n/a
New Zealand	•	•	•	•	n/a
B. Countries with both contributory and non-contributory cash sickness benefits					
Finland	•	•	•	•	n/a
United Kingdom	•	•	•	•	n/a
C. Countries with only contributory cash sickness benefits					
Austria	•	•	• (apprentices)	•	-
Belgium	•	•	•	•	n/a
Canada	•	-	...	•	• (for self-employed)
Chile	•	•	• (contractors)	-	•
Czech Republic	•	-	-	-	• (for self-emp. and foreign-owned firms)
Denmark	•	•	•	•	•
Estonia	•	•	•	•	n/a
France	•	•	• (trainees)	•	•
Germany	•	-	• (apprentices)	•	• (for self-employed)
Greece	•	-	•	-	-
Hungary	•	•	•	•	n/a
Iceland	•	•	•	-	n/a
Ireland	•	-	-	-	-
Italy	•	-	• (contractors)	•	-
Japan	•	-	...	•	• (for SMEs and agricultural workers)
Latvia	•	•	-	•	•
Luxembourg	•	•	•	•	n/a
Mexico	•	-	-	...	•
Netherlands	Mainly through EL	-	•	•	• (for self-employed)
Norway	•	•	•	•	n/a
Poland	•	• (after a 90-day wait)	-	•	• (for non-regular)
Portugal	•	• (after a 30-day wait)	•	-	n/a
Slovak Republic	•	•	-	•	•
Slovenia	•	•	•	•	n/a
Spain	•	•	•	•	n/a
Sweden	•	•	-	•	-
Turkey	•	•	• (domestic workers)	-	•
D. Countries without statutory cash sickness benefits					
Israel	No, but widely found in collective agreements	-	-	-	n/a
Korea	-	-	-	• (through EI)	-
Switzerland	Voluntary only plus EL	-	-	•	•
United States	Only in some states	-	-	-	-

Note: "•" indicates relevant coverage is provided, as standard. "-" indicates relevant coverage is not provided. "..." indicates there is insufficient information available. "EL" refers to employers' liability for workers' sickness. All information is valid for 2016 except Canada, Chile, Mexico and the United States, which are valid for 2015.
Source: Compiled using SSA and ISSA (2016, 2017), *Social Security Programs throughout the World.*

Scope of income support for sickness

Beyond coverage, three key dimensions determine the scope of the income support cash sickness benefits may provide:

- The maximum *duration* of cash sickness benefits differs greatly across countries. Some offer support for relatively limited periods of time (such as 15 weeks in Canada and 22 weeks in Denmark), while others do so for up to 18 months or longer (such as Germany, Japan, Portugal, Sweden and elsewhere) or for theoretically indefinite periods of time in case a recovery is expected (as in Slovenia, Turkey and the United Kingdom) (SSA and ISSA, 2016[31]).
- The *value* of the income support cash sickness benefits provide also varies much across countries. As with unemployment benefits, most cash sickness benefits are calculated as a share of the claimants' usual work-related income. Cash sickness benefits commonly compensate anything from 50-55% of this amount (as in Canada, Greece and the Slovak Republic) to all of it (as in Denmark, Ireland and Norway), subject to floor and ceiling amounts (SSA and ISSA, 2016[31]).
- The *interaction between cash sickness benefits and employers' liability* also differs much between countries. Some rely exclusively on employers' liability (such as the Netherlands and Switzerland) while others have only social insurance (such as Canada, Japan, Portugal and others). Most, however, rely to some extent on both (Spasova, Bouget and Vanhercke, 2016[40]).

Figure 3.6 illustrates the income support provided for sickness in six OECD countries, taking account of the three dimensions of differences noted above.

Germany illustrates perhaps the most common combination of support applied among the OECD countries: following the start of a worker's sickness, their employer is liable to compensate all (or most) of their earnings over a limited period of time, after which cash sickness benefits provide income support over a longer period. Except for minor differences in duration, value and eligibility criteria, the general approach illustrated by Germany is observed in a majority of OECD countries (SSA and ISSA, 2016[31]).

Luxembourg has a similar mix of measures as Germany, though its employers pool their own risks together through a mutual insurance fund operated at the national level. Employers who opt in to this fund are reimbursed 80% of the cost of their liability for workers' sickness for up to 77 days per worker, beyond which point the worker gains entitlement for cash sickness benefits.[20] Employers in France, Switzerland and elsewhere also make use of such collective insurance practices – sometimes provided privately (Spasova, Bouget and Vanhercke, 2016[40]). Where such insurance may be mandatory, it usually entails opt-out clauses for government departments bound by separate liabilities or very large firms big enough to manage their own risks unilaterally (OECD, 2014[43]).

The Netherlands places a uniquely weighty statutory liability for sickness upon employers, covering 70% of a sick employee's wage (or 100% under most collective agreements) up to a ceiling amount during absences lasting up to two years.[21] Workers who have no regular employer (including most non-regular workers plus unemployed persons) are entitled to social benefits of an equivalent amount and duration. Among the other OECD countries, only Switzerland has broadly similar employers' liability provisions, covering 100% of a sick employee's pay for up to a period of 3-46 weeks, depending on their tenure (OECD, 2014[41]; SSA and ISSA, 2016[31]).

Figure 3.6. OECD countries offer very different levels of income support for sickness

Maximum duration, value and type of income support for sickness in selected OECD countries, 2016

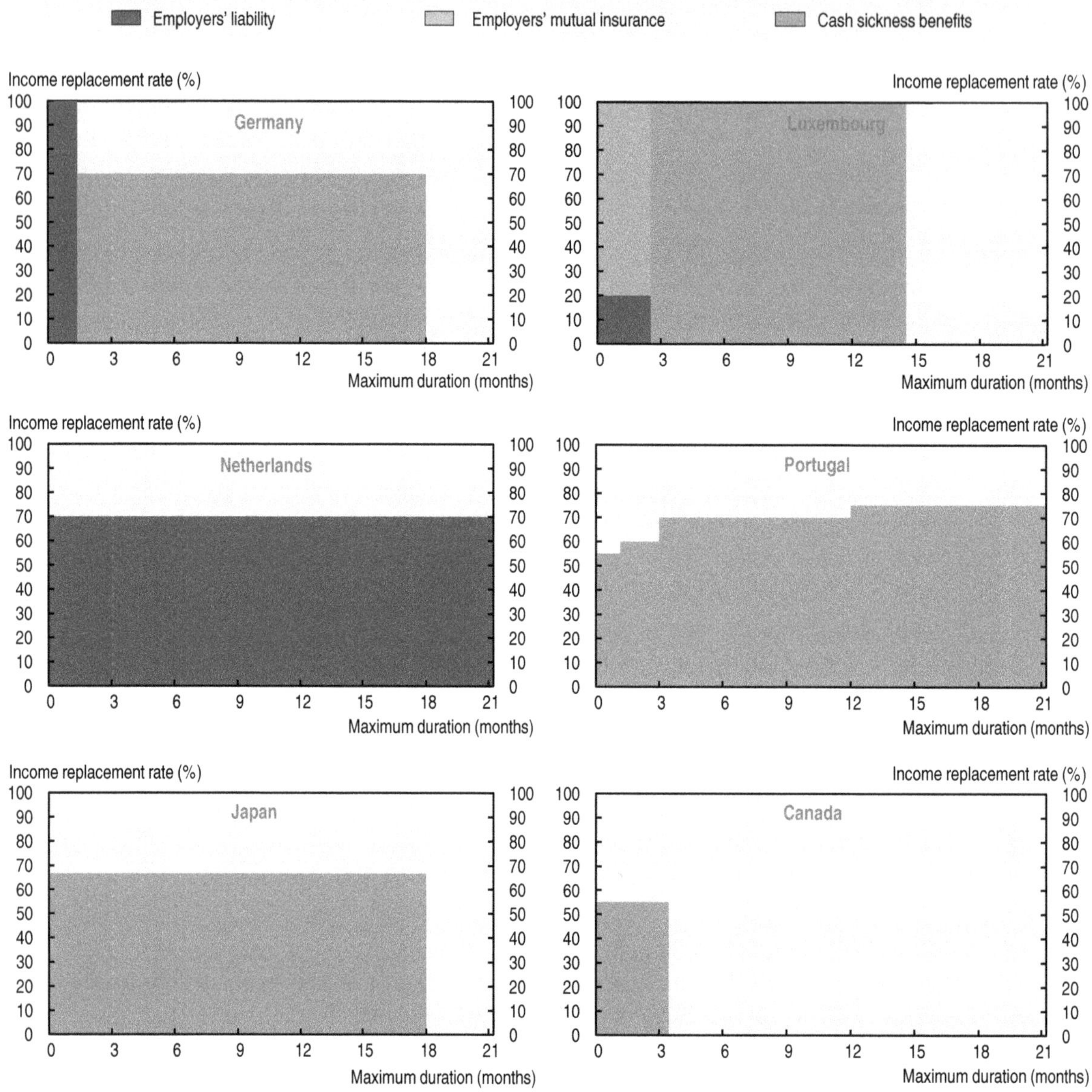

Source: Compiled using SSA and ISSA (2016, 2017), *Social Security Programs throughout the World.*

StatLink http://dx.doi.org/10.1787/888933645231

Canada, Japan, Portugal and other OECD countries impose no statutory employers' liability for sickness but ensure support through sickness insurance measures alone. In Portugal, the benefit amount rises at one, three and 12 months, continuing for up to three years in total or for a potentially unlimited duration for cases of tuberculosis (SSA and ISSA, 2016[31]). Cash sickness benefits in Slovenia and Spain have a similar design by which the benefit amounts increase at a certain point in the claim period. In Japan, on the other hand, the Injury and Sickness Allowance maintains a uniform replacement rate of two-thirds of usual income throughout the benefit claim period of up to 18 months (SSA and ISSA, 2017[42]). Japan's measure is financed through contributions made under the broader health insurance system. In Canada, finally, cash sickness benefits have a relatively low value and duration, replacing only 55% of a worker's usual income for up to a maximum period of 15 weeks (SSA and ISSA, 2016[44]). Canada's cash sickness benefits operate and are financed under the same *Employment Insurance* measure that provides unemployment benefits.

The six cases thus outlined illustrate a variety of possible approaches to providing social protection for sickness, although they are by no means exhaustive. The fact that Korea has neither employers' liability nor income support for workers undergoing absences from work due to sickness highlights an important shortcoming for the social protection system. Introducing a degree of statutory liability for employers would be a positive step within this context. Korea could also implement an effective insurance-based income support measure through its existing national health insurance infrastructure (as Japan and other countries do) or via its EI infrastructure (as Canada and other countries do), tailoring somewhat the social contributions collected from workers and employers while broadening the remit and entitlement criteria these measures might entail.

The key importance of rehabilitation strategies

Whatever future pathway Korea might take on this question, social protection for sickness requires a sound strategy for rehabilitation. Rehabilitation measures can be seen as the "activation component" of employers' liability for sickness and cash sickness benefits, through which to ensure that workers with adequate capacity return to work.

Rehabilitation strategies aim to provide those with at least some work capacity with the motivation and means to fulfil it. Such strategies seek to reintegrate beneficiaries within their former workplace or (if unemployed) into the labour market more generally. Such strategies are of the utmost importance for avoiding unnecessarily long absences from work or permanent exits from the workforce. Such strategies are fundamental for fighting the "benefit traps" sickness protection measures may encounter when beneficiaries regain their capacity but relinquish the will to work. Failure to rehabilitate sick workers swiftly and effectively can easily prolong unemployment or inactivity, stagnating workers' skills; increasing time they spend on benefits, and resulting in potential social exclusion.

OECD countries approach rehabilitation in a variety of different ways. For example, Austria, Denmark, Ireland and others provide "partial capacity benefits" as a follow-up form of income support for beneficiaries who return to work upon regaining all or part of their work capacity (Spasova, Bouget and Vanhercke, 2016[40]). Such approaches can help decrease benefit dependency and improve incentives for work.

Some countries build rehabilitation conditions directly into the entitlement rules of their benefit measures. Cash sickness benefits in Sweden, for example, apply a "rehabilitation chain" to ensure beneficiaries gain employment if they can do so: claimants receive benefits for up to 90 days if they cannot carry out their regular job for their regular employer; for up to 90 days more if they cannot carry out *any* job for the same employer; and beyond 180 days only if they cannot carry out *any* job for *any* formal employer (Försäkringskassan, 2016[45]).[22] Beneficiaries undergo a medical assessment at each stage in the chain to determine their work capacity. Those deemed to be capable of working are then moved onto unemployment benefits and obliged to fulfil the behavioural conditions and various other steps usually required around activation. Such an approach presents workers with very clear choices at clearly-defined intervals. It directs those who can work into the kinds of jobs they can do, demanding they explore broader work opportunities at each progressive step in the chain to ensure their rehabilitation.

Some countries, finally, target rehabilitation primarily through the supporting services they provide under the health service, public employment service or some specialised entity dealing specifically with rehabilitation. The United Kingdom, for example, launched its *Fit for Work* service in September 2015 to provide specialised advice and support through an online one-stop-shop. The service is publically-funded, optional and free to access. It consists of an online domain and telephone service offering official occupational health advice on managing sickness absences tailored towards three distinct groups of stakeholders: employers, workers and medical practitioners. It also provides a streamlined referral service for work capacity tests. Similar services operate in Austria, Ireland, the Netherlands and elsewhere.

Beyond the approaches briefly outlined here are a multitude of other possible solutions for achieving rehabilitation. Whatever the outcome for Korea, any future sickness protection measure should give careful consideration to such strategies.

Protection for other groups at risk of poverty in OECD countries

Common support measures

Beyond the specific poverty risks related to unemployment and incapacity discussed in the preceding two sections, social protection measures can also alleviate a variety of more general poverty risks. For example, some social protection measures seek to ensure all households can secure at least a given minimum standard of living by delivering cash or in-kind support. Other social protection measures focus more on children's welfare to ensure they all have access to, at least, a certain threshold of means. Still other measures aim chiefly to boost earnings (i.e. work-related income) to secure strong work incentives and secure a minimum livelihood for households with working members.

Across a diverse range, social protection measures implemented across the OECD tend to target one or more of these separate goals. Many of them, indeed, combine all three. Several distinct types of measures can be identified:

- *Social assistance benefits* are paid in cash to individuals or households below a given poverty threshold, as determined through means testing. Such measures are almost always non-contributory as the very lowest tier of income support. Some such measures benefit inactive household members, under certain circumstances, though most retain strong activation principles for those capable of working. In Korea, the *living benefit* under BLSP belongs to this category of measures.
- *Housing benefits* are often an integral component of broader social assistance measures that cover, specifically, beneficiaries' costs of accommodation. Some such benefits may vary their amounts by family-type and from locality to locality. Particular housing benefits, such as rental subsidies, can also operate as stand-alone social protection measures. In Korea, the *housing benefit* component of BLSP belongs to this category of measures.
- *Family benefits* usually also form part of broader social assistance measures but vary according to household composition. Under certain circumstances, such benefits may cover children of different ages; non-employed spouses; elderly relatives; and, sometimes, other co-habitants. Particular family benefits, such as lone-parent benefits, may operate as stand-alone social protection measures, though most exist as components of broader social assistance or in-work benefit measures. Three of Korea's social protection measures fall under this broad category: the *living benefit* component of BLSP provides a regular, recurring family benefit; the *child-birth benefit* under BLSP provides a one-off, lump-sum

family benefit; and the stand-alone Child Tax Credit (CTC) provides a form of family benefit for working households.

- *In-work benefits* (or *employment-conditional benefits*) commonly aim to encourage poor households into productive activity by making work more rewarding. Such measures are central for tackling in-work poverty. Some in-work benefit measures offer direct cash transfers as top-ups to low-wage work: "wage subsidies", "income supplements" and other direct in-work benefits operate in this way, topping up the otherwise low earnings of eligible workers. Other in-work benefits essentially achieve the same end indirectly through fiscal incentives instead: "tax credits", "tax allowances" and "earnings' disregards" thus reduce workers' tax burden. Korea's EITC as well as the Duru Nuri Social Insurance Subsidy Programme belong to these categories of measures.[23]

The discussion below elaborates on the coverage conditions OECD countries apply under such measures; the scope of the income support that they offer; and how successful they are at reaching the poorest in society. A closing sub-section follows up with a brief look at ongoing debates around the "basic income" idea.

Coverage conditions

Most social assistance measures are means-tested: they support only those households with the least access to capital *flows* (i.e. earnings and other income) and *stocks* (i.e. savings, real estate and other assets). Most means tests encompass only the capital flows and stocks that belong directly to the direct inhabitants of the applying household. The means of relatives belonging to other households thus tend not to count into the equation.

Korea's BLSP, however, employs the so-called "family support obligation" whereby the means test encompasses not only members of the benefitting household but also their spouses, parents and offspring (although it excludes siblings and other family members) whether or not they live in the same place. The policy is arguably founded in Confucian family values, rooted in a time when Korea had no welfare state to speak of. Historical parallels exist in other OECD countries, underpinned in western ones by Catholic social principles of subsidiarity: the idea that state support should come as a complement, rather than a substitute, to family support (Fleckenstein and Lee, 2017[46]). The subsidiarity principle still commonly applies among family members *within* an individual household but rarely encompasses those outside of it (MISSOC, 2013[47]).

By and large, most OECD countries have gradually abandoned their reliance on family support over time in favour of more direct state intervention. In some cases, this trend was coupled with the emergence of less stable families over time – evidenced by falling fertility and rising divorce rates – and their becoming more nuclear – evidenced by falls in the share of multi-generational households – alongside new social risks arising from family conflicts over care duties and resources allocation (Fleckenstein and Lee, 2017[46]).

Family support obligations thus seldom apply in OECD countries to such an explicit extent as under Korea's BLSP. Most countries' family laws and precedents under case law can amount to family care obligations under certain circumstances, though these rarely affect entitlements to social protection explicitly. Germany considers family support under the means test its social assistance measure applies, although this regards only the support relatives *actually* provide, on a regular basis, as opposed to the *potential* support they could deliver, according to their means, as under BLSP (MISSOC, 2017[48]).

Insofar as BLSP relies on such estimates of the potential support family members might offer, it may be unreliable: while many families will adhere to the Confucian values, there will always be some who do not. Under such circumstances, a struggling household may doubly lose out: first from their own family's neglect and second under the BLSP's rigid family support conditions. The diversity of family relationships in any society and at any time may always lead to such cases, highlighting a clear role for government action.

One concern around the BLSP's family support obligation might be that weakening it could precipitate a breakdown of traditional family norms. One could argue that public support may tamper with the complex incentives involved around the altruistic support family members confer to one another by their common practice. But public support need not necessarily trump traditional inter-family support if the two are considered as complements, rather than substitutes. Conceivably, a majority of caring families would go on supporting a vulnerable member irrespective of any BLSP allowances they might receive, posing no significant risk for Confucian values. Meanwhile, neglectful families could equally renege on supporting their relatives regardless of BLSP. Under both sets of circumstances, it makes sense to gradually relax the family support obligation, ensuring reliable support for all poor households alike.

Scope of protection for groups at risk of poverty

OECD countries differ very much around the overall amount of support they provide for poorer households. OECD countries also differ in the ways in which support is structured, relating to the composition of their different social protection measures.

The OECD Tax-Benefit Models offer a useful way to evaluate how such support measures sum together; how they interact with the tax system; and the ways in which they are affected by household characteristics (such as gross earnings, work-status, family composition and other such variables) in OECD countries (OECD, 2017[39]). The Models facilitate detailed estimates of the income different household-types might expect to gain (or lose) via applicable social protection measures, taxes and social contributions. The Models thus offer a variety of valuable insights into the ways OECD countries design their social protection measures and, ultimately, the scope of the income support they seek to provide for households under different circumstances.

The modelled estimates presented in this sub-section consider only one particular type of household: a married couple cohabiting with two children where one partner is employed and the other inactive. Each such household is assumed to have only modest assets and savings such that they can pass a relevant means test under each modelled measure. The country-level estimates shown below thus vary only by the gross household earnings (represented, in each figure below, along the horizontal-axis normalised to deciles of national average household earnings). The findings relate to the income such households in selected OECD countries can receive from each category of social benefit plus the *net amount* they actually gain after income taxes and social contributions (represented, in each figure below, by the solitary dot within each bar).[24]

Figure 3.7 shows the social protection measures such a family might have access to in Korea. BLSP social assistance benefits make up the biggest component for families earning below the minimum wage, bringing the lowest-income families up to a minimum living standard of around 30-35% of average household income. BLSP housing benefits provide additional support, though only (again) to those earning below the minimum wage. BLSP's modest family benefit applies equally to households of all income levels (from 1-100% of average household earnings and beyond). Finally, EITC and CTC in-work benefits from 2015 offer only very modest support for those earning up to 50% of the national household average. Net household income is only marginally below the bar-totals in each column, illustrating Korea's relatively low rates of income tax and social contributions.

Figure 3.7. Social protection measures in Korea bring entitled families to within 45% of average household income

Modelled estimates of household income in Korea by benefit type when a sole-earner supports a non-working spouse and two children, by gross household earnings (percentage of average earnings), 2015

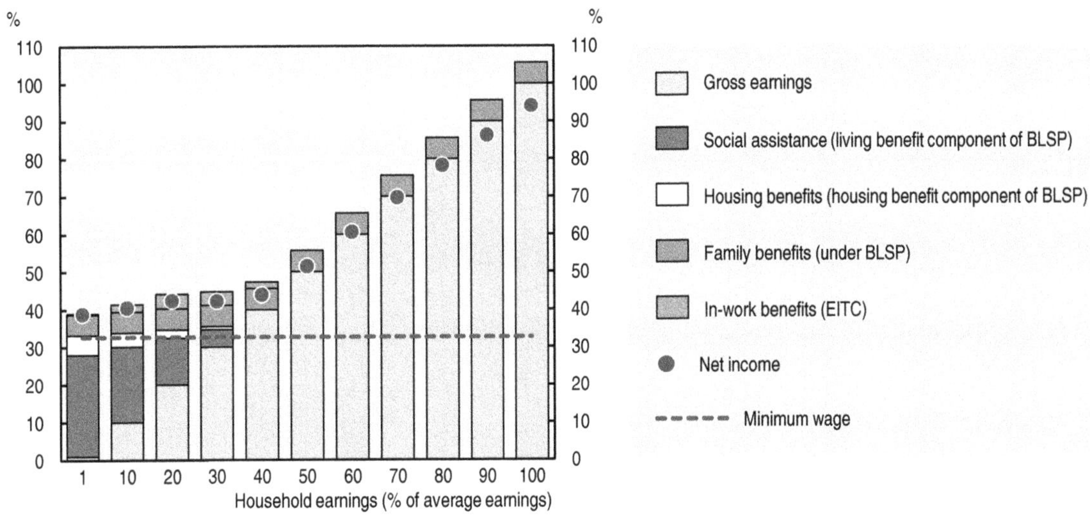

Note: Median net household incomes are before housing costs (or other forms of "committed" expenditure). Results are equivalised based on the square root of the household size and account for all relevant cash benefits, as indicated. Net income figure shows the final amount after deducting income taxes and social contributions. Two children are assumed to be aged 4 and 6.

Source: Modelled estimates from OECD (2017), *Social Protection and Well-being Database*.

StatLink http://dx.doi.org/10.1787/888933645250

Figure 3.8 illustrates how equivalent measures in other OECD countries combine for low-income families of the same type, revealing a genuine variety of approaches:

- Some countries predominantly provide income support through social assistance benefits (Figure 3.8, panels in row A). In Denmark, for example, social assistance benefits alone bring the income of low-earning households to within 45-60% of average income, while housing and family benefits add a further 15-20 percentage points on to of this. Japan has similar social protection, although housing benefits count more for those earning more than the minimum wage. Luxembourg has similar measures as well, bringing families with gross earnings of 10-70% of average earnings to a virtually flat level of net income worth 75% of the national average. Germany, France, Poland, Sweden and Switzerland also place a similar emphasis on social assistance benefits.[25]

Figure 3.8. Social benefits combine in many different ways across the OECD

Modelled estimates of household income in selected OECD countries by benefit type when a sole-earner supports a non-working spouse and two children, by gross household earnings (% of average earnings), 2015

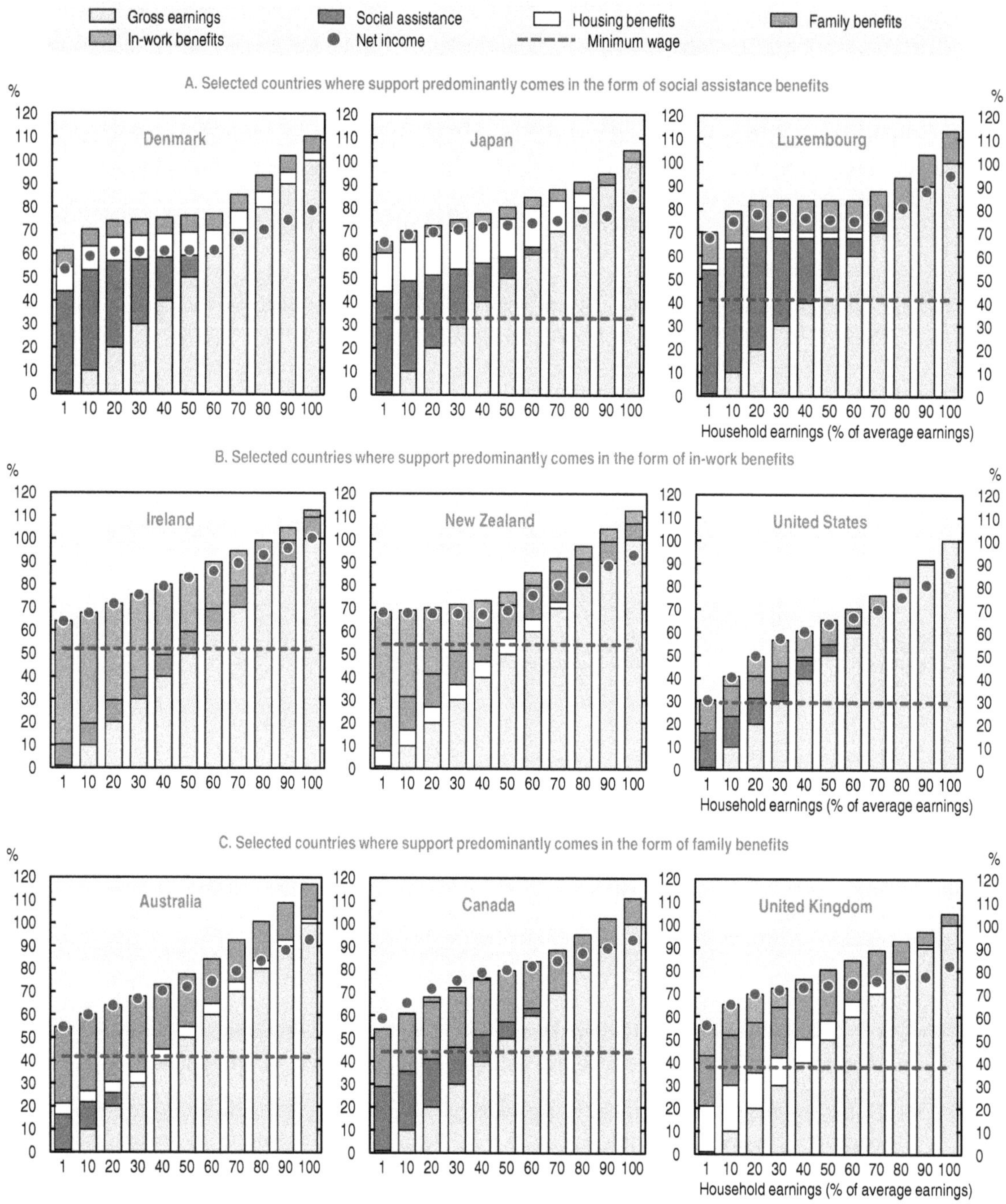

Note: Results are equivalised based on the square root of the household size and account for all relevant cash benefits, as indicated. Net income figure shows the final amount after deducting income taxes and social contributions. Where benefit rules are not determined on a national level but vary by region or municipality, results refer to a "typical" case (e.g. Michigan in the United States; the capital in some other countries). The two children in each scenario are assumed to be aged 4 and 6.

Source: Modelled estimates from OECD (2017), *Social Protection and Well-being Database*.

StatLink http://dx.doi.org/10.1787/888933645269

- Some countries predominantly provide income support through in-work benefits (Figure 3.8, panels in row B). Among the OECD countries, Ireland, New Zealand and parts of the United States place the most pronounced emphasis on in-work benefits. In all three countries, in-work benefits amount to significant sums and continue to apply on earnings far higher than the full-time minimum wage.
- Some countries predominantly provide income support through family benefits (Figure 3.8, panels in row C). For example, family benefits in Australia, Canada and the United Kingdom play the most pronounced role for the modelled family-type, relative to other measures. In all three countries, the benefit amount declines among households with higher earnings.

The Tax-Ben Models reveal the extent to which OECD countries place entirely different emphases on the social protection measures they use. For policy makers, however, the particular mix is conditioned by the leading social outcomes they desire. Social assistance benefits, for example, may be the best for ensuring that no individual household falls below a level of income necessary for a decent standard of living. In-work benefits may be preferential for making work pay and encouraging, in turn, poor households to gain or retain an active role within the labour market. Family benefits and housing benefits may be best for reducing unequal opportunities among children within society to ensure that all of them, at least, grow up within a certain standard of means.

Which of these particular goals Korea may want to emphasise, in turn, ought to shape its decisions about the future direction for structuring and further developing BLSP, EITC, CTC, Duru Nuri and other such income support measures.

Targeting support to society's poorest members

The mix of social protection measures any given country implements can be more or less adept at delivering support to the poorest in society. Some countries' measures comprehensively target social transfers towards the poorest households – with the most valuable benefits predominantly reaching those at the bottom of the income distribution. Other countries neglect to nurture such redistributive goals – with higher social transfers reaching richer households than poorer ones.

Figure 3.9 illustrates the average aggregate social transfer amounts that reach households in the top and bottom income quintiles (i.e. those in the poorest and richest 20% of the overall income distribution), relative to the value of the average social transfer. The figure gives a sense of how strongly these countries' social protection measures redistribute income towards the least well-off in society. Data refer to each country's working-age population and include all social cash transfers available for this group, including unemployment benefit and social assistance but also disability benefit, sickness benefit, family benefit, housing benefit and early retirement benefit, if applicable.

Countries that achieve the strongest redistributive outcomes tend to rely more heavily on non-contributory, means-tested assistance-type social protection measures rather than insurance-type ones or use flat-rate benefit payment rates more commonly rather than payments linked to an individual's previous earnings. Australia and New Zealand, for example, rely exclusively on far-reaching non-contributory, predominantly means-tested ones, paid for from general government expenditures. The Netherlands and the United Kingdom have mature social assistance measures in place with strict means-testing requirements geared towards achieving strong support for the poor and a general preference for flat-rate social insurance payments to enhance this goal. Denmark, Finland and Sweden also have significant flat-rate benefit components in place through which they achieve a high level of redistribution to the poorest.

Countries that achieve the weakest redistributive outcomes tend to have relatively limited or low-value non-contributory support in place or a strong focus on payments linked to individual earnings. Social assistance benefits in Greece and Spain, for example, offer no direct income support to working-age beneficiaries except as in-kind support for housing and health care. Italy has long relied on a decentralised system of social assistance that has only recently been harmonised and still has some way to go towards maturity.

Korea fits in between these two extremes – with roughly equal-value social transfers reaching society's richest and poorest working-age households alike (Figure 3.9). This places Korea close to the OECD average on this indicator. If policy makers in Korea desire more redistributive outcomes, there is significant scope to improve the status quo.

Figure 3.9. Social beneficiaries in Korea's top and bottom income quintiles gain transfers of a broadly equal value

Social transfers received by working-age individuals in low- and high-income groups, percentage of average transfers among the top and bottom quintiles, 2014 or latest year available

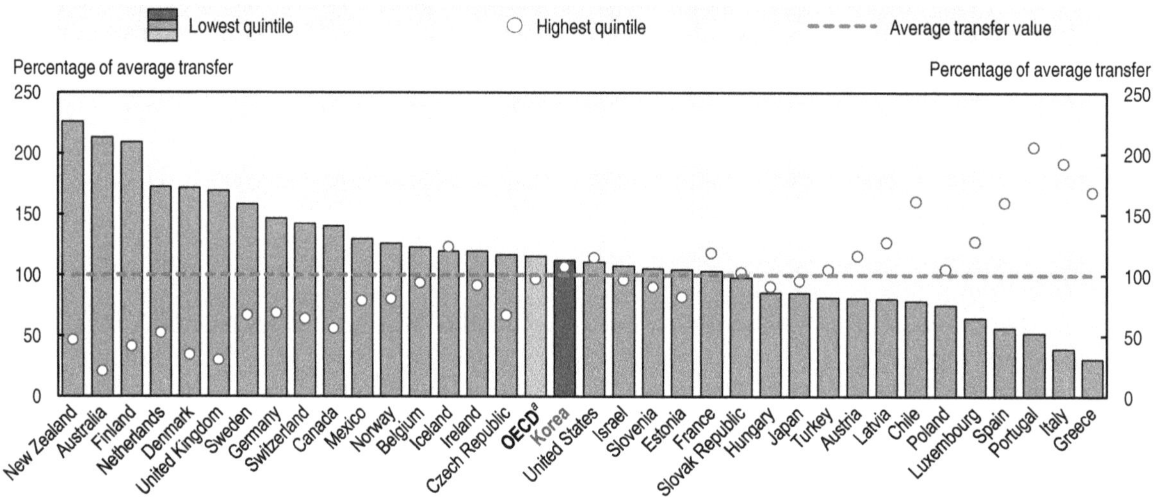

Note: Working-age refers to age group 18-65. Data refer to public social cash transfers at the household level, adjusted for household size. Income quintiles are calculated according to disposable income.

a) Unweighted average of the 35 OECD countries.

Source: Estimates based on the *OECD Income Distribution Database* (http://oe.cd/idd).

StatLink http://dx.doi.org/10.1787/888933645288

Korea's welfare system could achieve better support for its poorest members through policy actions in terms of both their *design* and *implementation*. In terms of design, BLSP could entail more explicit targets around poverty reduction, especially in-work poverty. BLSP could also improve support for low-income households by relaxing some of its entitlement conditions – first and foremost its family support obligation. Furthermore, expanding EI eligibility to cover self-employed persons and more categories of non-regular workers would have a disproportionate effect on those with lower earnings, thus assisting poorer households.

In terms of implementation, BLSP, EITC and CTC could make much more of an effort to reach households that fail (for whatever reason) to claim their entitlements. For BLSP, this could include awareness-raising activities aimed at de-stigmatising benefit receipt. For EITC and CTC, it could include bolder intervention from Korea's tax authorities in streamlining participation and, potentially, securing tax rebates for latecomers.

Most of the changes proposed under each measure would increase their overall costs. Increasing support for Korea's poorest households in a fiscally neutral way is potentially only achievable through a much broader realignment towards an altogether different social welfare paradigm. Entirely non-contributory, means-tested social welfare systems like Australia's or New Zealand's, for example, achieve strong outcomes for their poorest members at relatively small fiscal expenditures. In order to do so, they concentrate social protection expenditures on the least well-off within society. Such systems have the advantage of covering every sort of worker and jobseeker, irrespective of their past or present status in employment, thus achieving more equal treatment in a fragmented labour market. Such systems also bypass administrative challenges related to eligibility conditions; undocumented workers evading contributions; and complicated entitlement conditions. They do, however, remove most support for better-off households and require putting in place highly robust ways of determining applicants' means.

Ongoing debates around basic income

The concept of a basic income (sometimes also called a "guaranteed minimum income", a "guaranteed adequate income" or a "citizens' income") has featured prominently in recent public debates on social protection, gaining interest from across the political spectrum.

One common description equates the basic income idea to a social transfer capable of meeting the following four defining properties (BIEN, 2017[49]):

1. It is provided *periodically*, not as a one-off, lump-sum payment.
2. It is provided *in cash*, rather than in kind or as vouchers.
3. It is provided *to individuals*, rather than to groups or households.
4. It is *unconditional* on individuals' active search or availability for work.

A "universal basic income", in turn, would meet one additional key property:

5. It is *universal*, paid to all members of society regardless of their existing means.

Some advocates for the basic income idea promote using it to replace existing social protection systems, many of which currently rely on means-testing and other such costly administrative processes. Proponents primarily support the basic income idea as a powerful and elegant solution to end national poverty; lower income inequality; and otherwise empower society's individuals. Radical proponents for the idea argue that a genuine universal basic income could replace not only most social protection measures but most existing labour market institutions such as minimum wages; paid sickness and parental leave; and publicly-funded education, among other things. More moderate proponents argue that a more targeted (non-universal) basic income could valuably complement existing social protection measures, replacing only the lowest-tier social assistance programmes while retaining a strong activation focus.

Detractors of the basic income idea tend to focus on its potentially vast fiscal cost. Others argue a basic income would essentially create a publicly-funded subsidy for inactivity, reducing labour force participation and, hence, threatening economic stability and long-term economic performance. Both of these arguments deserve close attention as neither is easily dismissed (OECD, 2017[50]).

Public interest in the basic income idea has grown rapidly over the past two years or so. *Google* (2017[51]) provides an analytical tool for quantifying online searches related to individual themes or expressions over time. Figure 3.10 shows the weekly trends in *Google* searches, worldwide, on the topic of basic income.[26] The data are normalised at 100, relative to the top number of searches made within a given week (i.e. relative to the observation labelled "E" in the figure below). Online interest in the basic income topic gained particular traction around two key events in June 2016 and January 2017:

- The *first* major peak of interest in basic income coincided with a referendum in Switzerland held on 5 June 2016 regarding whether or not to make constitutional changes to guarantee a nation-wide universal basic income. The proposed level would enable all recipients "to live a dignified life and participate in public life", which campaigners suggested might have amounted to CHF 2 500 per month (roughly KRW 2.9 million) for every adult and CHF 625 (KRW 725 000) for every child. While the motion generated vast public interest, worldwide, voters rejected it in the final outcome by a majority of 76.9% on a turnout of 2.5 million (around 47% of those registered).
- The *second* major peak of interest in basic income is primarily attributable to a large-scale national trial of the idea Finland launched on 1 January 2017. The pilot measure guarantees a basic income of EUR 560 per month (KRW 730 000) over a two-year period to 2 000 residents aged 25-58, selected at random, who received unemployment benefits at the start of the trial. The transfer amount replaces any non-contributory benefits participants could otherwise have claimed (but does not affect their contributory benefits). Beneficiaries continue to receive the amount regardless of any transition into employment.

Figure 3.10 illustrates a number of similar decisions, experiments and events that have coincided with increased levels of online interest in basic income. The events and dates labelled are by no means exhaustive nor are they necessarily the true underlying causes of increased online interest in every case. They are labelled below simply in terms of their coincidence with the observed spikes within the *Google* (2017[51]) data.

Ongoing trials in various OECD countries and elsewhere contribute to a spirited ongoing debate around the basic income idea. Nevertheless, much uncertainty remains around the possible impact such a measure could have on recipients' behaviour (especially around labour force participation) and how to create the necessary fiscal space for it. Until an adequate evidence base emerges on questions such as these, political leaders will have every reason to approach the idea cautiously.

In Korea, too, an active public debate has emerged on basic income. During the presidential election of 2017, one ambitious proposal came about to provide a basic income of KRW 83 300 per month in the form of a "life-cycle dividend" for individuals aged 0-29 and those aged 65 and above. Under the proposal, a "special dividend" of up to an equal value would also be provided for certain categories of workers earning a low income and for disabled people. By excluding a majority of the working-age population outright, champions of the proposal argued it could have little impact for work incentives. Funding for the programme was closely discussed and proposed to come from tighter public spending in other areas and new taxes on land holdings. The policy has not been realised.

Figure 3.10. Online interest in the basic income idea has increased much over time

Worldwide Google searches per week related to the basic income topic in multiple languages, October 2012 to October 2017 (percentage relative to the peak week)

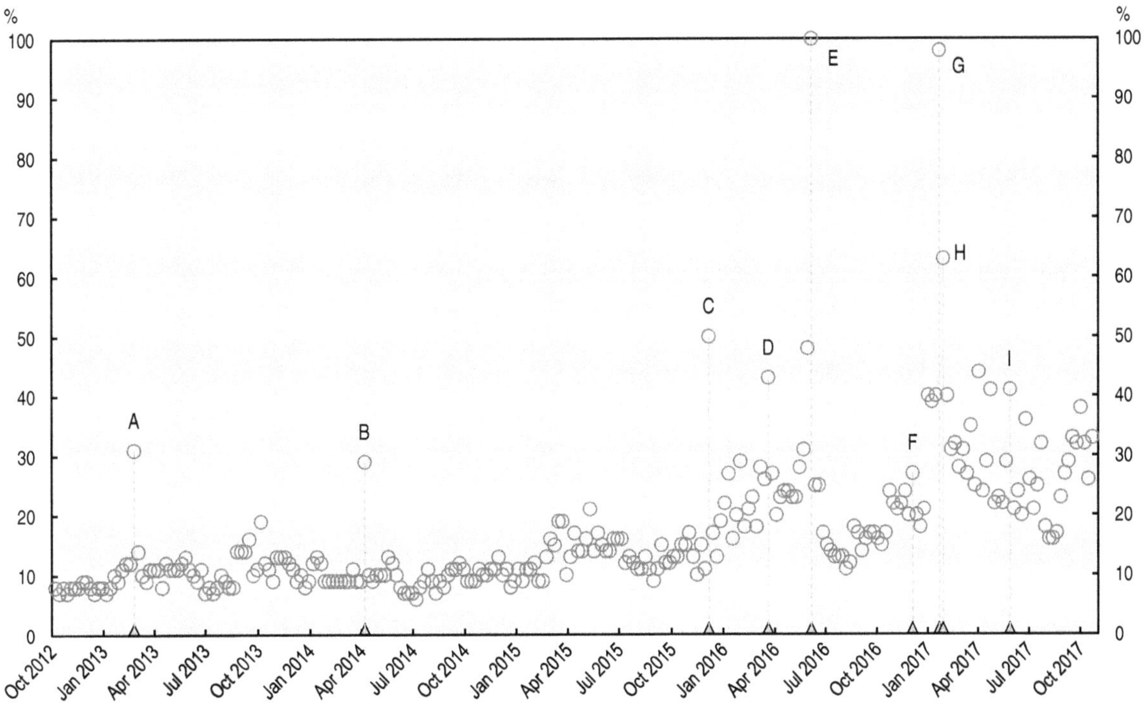

A **Italy**: General elections take place in which two political parties (*Movimento 5 Stelle* and *Sinistra Ecologia Libertà*) propose replacing existing social protection measures with a basic income.

B **European Union**: European Economic and Social Committee hosts a conference on "emancipating European welfare", bringing together leading thinkers on basic income.
United Kingdom: Charities launch a "campaign for a basic income for all", promoting the idea.

C **Finland**: Government announces it will draw up plans by November 2016 to replace its existing social protection system with a national basic income of EUR 800 per month for all adult citizens.

D **Canada**: Announcement of upcoming basic income pilot for residents in Ontario province.

E **Switzerland**: Referendum rejects introduction of a nation-wide basic income by a 77% majority.
United States: Group of business actors announce support for basic income as "the social vaccine of the 21st century", funding a high-profile experiment to take place in Oakland, California.
Italy: Basic income pilot is launched over six months in the city of Livorno.

F **Canada**: Ontario province finalises its plan to launch a large-scale pilot scheme in early-2017, offering a basic income to working-age adults below the poverty line.
United States: High-profile business leaders pledge USD 10 million to support research into the basic income idea under the Economic Security Project.

G **Finland**: National basic income trial is launched over two years for 2 000 unemployed adults.

H **United Kingdom**: Devolved government of Scotland announces plans for basic income trials.
European Union: European Parliament rejects a recommendation to "seriously consider" a basic income to address possible job-losses arising from technological advances by a 53% majority.

I **United States**: Mark Zuckerberg, the CEO of *Facebook*, delivers a speech publically endorsing the universal basic income idea and calling on governments, worldwide, to explore its option.

Note: Numbers represent search interest via Google relative to the highest point on the chart. A value of 100 thus represents the peak popularity for the topic within a given week; a value of 50 means the topic is half as popular as that; and a value of 0 means it was less than 1% as popular as in the peak week. The data represent worldwide Google searches, grouping all relevant search-terms using separate languages.

Source: Google (2017), *Google Trends*, https://trends.google.com/trends/ (accessed on 03 November 2017).

StatLink http://dx.doi.org/10.1787/888933645307

Municipal administrators in Seongnam – a city of 950 000 inhabitants located 26 km south east of Seoul in Korea's Gyeonggi province – implemented a form of basic income through their "youth dividend" programme (청년배당), launched in January 2016. The measure provides a transfer of KRW 250 000 per quarter (i.e. roughly KRW 83 300 per month) to young people who have lived in the city for at least three years. Originally intended to reach all of the city's inhabitants aged 19-24, the youth dividend is thus far only been implemented for those aged 24 due to budgetary constraints. The transfer amount is provided in a local currency called the "Love Seongnam Gift Certificate" (성남사랑상품권) accepted exclusively by selected retailers within the city limits. The transfer entails neither means-testing nor any explicit activation conditions.

There appears to be no methodical impact assessment of Seongnam city's youth dividend. Records reveal that the benefit was delivered to a total of 17 745 beneficiaries during 2016 and a further 14 822 and 10 639 respectively in the first and second quarters of 2017. It is unknown, however, what impact the transfer has had on beneficiaries' work activity and other behaviours. It is unknown, moreover, how the benefit influences expenditure: what proportion beneficiaries ultimately invest in education or training, for example, or incorporate, rather, into their regular disposable income.

Questions of this sort would be valuable to answer for the basic income debate to move forward in Korea. Numerous insights could be gained if the Seongnam city programme was monitored and studied as closely as, for example, Finland's ongoing basic income experiment. Despite the global attention it has received, the Finnish experiment has a sample of less than one eighth of Seongnam city's beneficiaries and a smaller total budget. The Finnish experiment has been billed, from the start, as a time-limited, one-off trial that might, as such, have only a limited or skewed influence on individuals' behaviour. Seongnam city's programme, by contrast, is a longer-lasting policy.

Failing to investigate the behavioural impacts of Seongnam city's youth dividend represents a wasted opportunity for Korea and, indeed, a drawback for the broader scientific community interested in the basic income policy option. Both supporters and opponents of the idea could benefit from stronger evidence of this kind.

Conclusion

This chapter compares the different ways in which social protection measures are applied in OECD countries, elaborating on the various conditions, features and objectives they involve. By illustrating the diversity of policy options, the discussion seeks to identify what might work best for Korea. The variety of policy options signals not one but multiple good solutions to address Korea's ongoing shortcomings in the labour market (discussed in Chapter 1) and gaps around social protection (discussed in Chapter 2).

Five key findings stand out from the analysis. *First*, the analysis evaluates a number of policy solutions other countries use to bridge some of EI's ongoing coverage gaps. It identifies numerous best practices for extending EI to self-employed persons (most of which apply equally well to unpaid family workers and non-regular salaried workers).

Second, the analysis compares the value of Korea's EI benefits with those found elsewhere. It calculates that EI's floor is the highest among its OECD equivalents (relative to their average wages) and its floor and ceiling the closest to one another of any such variable-rate measure. Policy makers could rationalise these amounts by treating EI as an explicitly flat-rate benefit; by altering certain key parameters; or by returning to the original broad benefit range EI had upon its launch in 1995.

Third, the analysis finds that ESPP fulfils many of the same functions and has similar design features with unemployment assistance measures in other OECD countries. Laudably, ESPP already embodies many of the best practices identified among these, delivering its employment services to the most vulnerable jobseekers within a highly effective activation framework.

Fourth, the analysis highlights a troubling lack of support for individuals undergoing a temporary incapacity to work due to sickness: Korea has neither statutory employers' liability for sickness nor a targeted cash sickness benefit measure. Such an apparent policy vacuum singles Korea out among the OECD countries, most of which ensure ample support through both employers' liability and comprehensive cash sickness benefits. Korea might follow their examples, offering more support than it currently does alongside a robust rehabilitation strategy.

Finally, the analysis finds no parallel among the OECD countries to Korea's rigid "family support obligation" applied under BLSP. The discussion argues that the rule is not only outmoded but potentially unreliable and unfair.

Notes

1. Jobseekers failing to meet eligibility conditions gain no coverage for unemployment insurance ex ante. Jobseekers failing on entitlement conditions effectively lose their coverage (in whole or in part), despite having made contributions. Only jobseekers meeting both of these sets of conditions can begin their claim, though they may be penalised if they fail to meet the behavioural conditions.

2. Note that women and men are relatively polarised among these two groups of workers in Korea: men accounted for 71.9% of self-employment in 2016, while women made up 86.5% of contributing family workers.

3. Note that the general approach these countries take is consistent with the relevant ILO conventions regarding social protection for unemployment – the Social Security (Minimum Standards) Convention, 1952 (No. 102) and the Employment Promotion and Protection against Unemployment Convention, 1988 (No. 168) – neither of which explicitly mentions coverage for self-employed persons owing to the practical difficulties of assessing their work situation (ILO, 2013[8]).

4. Among the OECD countries, only Norway expresses its minimum contribution condition not as a function of working time but, rather, on the basis of earnings. Jobseekers in Norway are eligible to claim unemployment insurance benefits so long as they have earned NOK 140 451 (valid as of May 2017) during the preceding calendar year – equivalent to roughly one quarter of Norway's national average wage – or twice that amount within the preceding three years.

5. Note that most such penalties also encompass jobseekers who were fired from their job because of serious misconduct or some other such infraction. The language countries use to draw the distinction between voluntary and involuntary unemployment differs, in some cases, although the central aim is the same: some measures thus refer to voluntary unemployment as being without "good reason", without "legitimate" or "just cause", "self-inflicted" or otherwise arising from a person's "own fault", among other such expressions.

6. Strictly speaking, Korea's ESPP is not an unemployment assistance benefit although it shares many of the same features insofar as it offers non-contributory, means-tested income support to jobseekers alongside employability services and training. ESPP is discussed throughout this section as an unemployment assistance measure.

7. Chile's unemployment assistance benefit was worth less than 2% of the average wage in 2015 (roughly 3-8% of the statutory minimum wage) and claimable for only up to 360 days; Sweden's unemployment assistance benefit was worth less than one quarter of the average wage in 2016 and offered for up to 60 weeks (OECD, 2017[52]).

8. The vulnerable groups exempted from means testing under Korea's ESPP include disabled persons; low-income self-employed persons; low-income non-regular workers; female heads of households; unmarried mothers; lone parents; former soldiers with technical skills; bankrupts; ex-prisoners; homeless people; international migrants by marriage; and defectors from the Democratic People's Republic of Korea.

9. Note that the converse is true in some countries: new labour market entrants in Austria, Chile, France, Greece, Portugal and Spain gain no coverage from either tier of unemployment benefits and, hence, neither have access to the income nor employment support these measures can offer. Such unemployment assistance measures tend, at the very most, only to extend support to jobseekers exhausting their unemployment insurance benefits (pending a means test), thus predominantly affecting those in long term unemployment. While the highly restricted coverage of such measures can ensure a low cost, they may fail to bring employment services to some of those in most need of them.

10. The maximum period of 240 days applies to workers who have made insurance contributions for upwards of 10 years and are either disabled or above the age of 50. Shorter periods apply to younger workers and those with fewer contributions.

11. Note that the calculations for Korea assume a monthly average wage of KRW 2 862 410 for 2017. This figure is based on the "average annual wage" estimate published on OECD.Stat; divided by 12 to give a monthly figure of KRW 2 815 114 for 2016; and multiplied by 1.017, based on the 1.7% compound annual growth rate achieved over the past five years (2011-16) according to the time-series of the same indicator. This figure is very close to the KRW 2 795 000 value for the "average monthly wage" of a regular salaried worker in Korea in August 2016, based on the *Economically Active Population Survey* (Statistics Korea, 2017[5]) (KOSIS table ID: DT_1DE7082). Korea's unemployment insurance benefit range refers to the respective floor and ceiling amounts of KRW 46 584 and KRW 50 000 per day, defined under EI as of April 2017. Korea's unemployment assistance benefit amount refers to the maximum transfer of KRW 400 000 per month participants can currently receive at stage 2 of ESPP.

12. A minimum-wage employee in Korea earns KRW 6 470 per hour, as of January 2017. Under Korea's labour laws, full-time employees work for around 173 hours per month (calculated as 40 x 52 ÷ 12); discounting any overtime; but actually get paid for 209 hours (due to Korea's statutory "paid weekly holiday"), amounting to a minimum wage of KRW 1 352 230 per month (6 470 x 209). By comparison, an EI claimant can receive no less than 90% of the daily minimum wage for each day they are entitled to benefits, amounting to a minimum benefit of KRW 1 413 048 per month (6 470 x 8 x 0.9 x 7 x 52 ÷ 12). This amount represents 104.5% of the monthly minimum wage. The explicit benefit ceiling under EI is currently KRW 50 000 per day, amounting to a maximum benefit of KRW 1 516 667 per month (50 000 x 7 x 52 ÷ 12). This amount represents 112.2% of the monthly minimum wage.

13. Korea's average wage in 1995 was KRW 13 720 964 per year (OECD, 2017[39]) – equivalent to KRW 37 695 per day (calculated as 13 720 964 ÷ 52 ÷ 7). The formula replacement rate of 50% therefore amounted to an average benefit of KRW 18 848 per day (37 695 x 0.5). The explicit floor amount for EI benefits was set at 70% of the daily minimum wage and, therefore, equal to KRW 6 748 per day (1 550 x 8 x 0.7). The original ceiling amount was fixed at KRW 30 000 per day.

14. In 2014, for example, Korea's average wage was KRW 32 428 968 per year (OECD, 2017[39]) – equivalent to KRW 89 091 per day (calculated as 32 428 968 ÷ 52 ÷ 7). The formula replacement rate thus amounted to an average benefit of KRW 44 545 per day (89 091 x 0.5). The EI floor amount was smaller at KRW 37 512 per day (5 210 x 8 x 0.9). The ceiling amount was also smaller at KRW 40 000 per day.

15. Korea's nominal average wage grew at a compound rate of 1.7% per year, on average, during 2011-16 (OECD, 2017[39]). Assuming a constant trajectory, Korea's average wage could reach an estimated KRW 99 200 per day by 2020. The explicit floor amount of EI; at 90% of a minimum wage of KRW 10 000 per hour; would equal KRW 72 000 per day by 2020 (calculated as 10 000 x 8 x 0.9) – equivalent to 72.6% of the average wage, which is considerably higher than the formula replacement rate of 50% of gross earnings. Given that the EI floor takes precedence over the ceiling in deciding the benefit amount, the ceiling would also effectively be pushed up to this amount (or adjusted to something higher).

16. At 50-55% of the average wage, this would be the highest-value flat-rate unemployment benefit in the OECD. Such a high amount, however, might be coherent with the relatively short average duration of unemployment in Korea and almost non-existent long-term unemployment (see Figure 3.3).

17. In practice, some employers in Korea do provide legitimate protections for their workers through their own internal policies, under collective agreements or on a case-by-case basis.

Nevertheless, many of them (and smaller firms in particular) offer no such commitments nor security to workers. In any case, Korean labour laws oblige none to provide any such support.

18. Note that some countries provide additional benefits in kind under such circumstances covering, for example, the costs of hospital treatments, out-patient care and medicines. Such support is left out of the present discussion insofar as Korea's national health system already provides adequate care that is free at the point of delivery. Cash parental benefits plus protection from work-related injury or illness also apply to more specific forms of temporary work incapacity in a majority of countries. Such measures are likewise left out of the present discussion insofar as both are adequately addressed in Korea: income support for temporary work incapacity among women during pregnancy is addressed through social insurance and employers' liability for maternity; statutory paid parental leave extends to women and men alike following childbirth as well as (since 2010) adoption; income support for temporary work incapacity arising from a specifically work-related ailment has existed since 1953 (for short-term paid sick leave) and 1963 (insurance for compensation in case of industrial accidents) while today's laws automatically cover all salaried employees and enable voluntary affiliation for own-account workers (SSA and ISSA, 2017[42]).

19. The United Kingdom offers a somewhat unique example, where employers pay their workers a fixed-rate amount during a period of absence lasting up to 28 weeks, regardless of usual earnings. Flat rate protections of this kind may be good for limiting the overall cost of liability for employers while providing relatively long lasting and equitable support for employees.

20. Note that employers' mutual insurance funds in Luxembourg are likewise accessible to self-employed persons: those contributing to a mutual insurance fund can reimburse 80% of their earnings in case of sickness during a period of 77 days, beyond which cash sickness benefits can start (for which they are covered on a compulsory basis).

21. During this period, employers in the Netherlands are obliged to make concrete efforts to restore the worker's capacity, reintegrate them into work or secure for them another position (either internally or elsewhere). Failure in this may result in an additional year of liability for the employer.

22. Note that the rehabilitation chain in Sweden is applied somewhat less rigidly under certain circumstances. Some workers, for example, can continue their claim beyond 180 days if a full recovery is expected within the first year of sickness. Highly-specialised and older workers may claim it is unreasonable to accept any job from any formal employer and limit their search accordingly. Self-employed persons are assessed against their original work during the first 180 days but must consider any available work (whether salaried or non-salaried) beyond that point. Finally, workers unsure about their work capacity may take leave from their employer in order to try out another job before committing to it and, thus, end their entitlement.

23. Another form of in-work benefit may come about if an unemployment benefit measure continues to provide a degree of income support to low-income beneficiaries for a period of time after their return to work. So-called "transitional unemployment benefits", "into work benefits" or "activation allowances" of this kind apply in a number of OECD countries including Canada, Japan and Norway. Korea's EI has such a mechanism in terms of its Early Re-employment Allowance, while ESPP has it in its Employment Success Allowance. While such benefits can be a worthwhile tool for combating benefit traps among jobseekers, it is unclear how effective they really are at promoting more rapid returns to work or higher job retention. In any case, such benefits offer only transitional support, at best, and are not elaborated upon further in the present chapter.

24. Note that under this set-up the gap between total income (represented, in each figure, by the tip of the stacked bars in each column) and net income (represented, in each figure, by the black dot in each column) thus represents the total amount of income taxes and social contributions deducted from each household.

25. In some of these countries, as in Korea, social assistance benefits typically only apply to households earning at or below the full-time minimum wage. In others, however – such as France, Germany, Japan and Luxembourg – social assistance benefits apply also to earnings above the minimum wage level.

26. Data on individual "topics" in Google Trends are derived using Google's internal algorithms to group together key search expressions relating to a particular theme, regardless of the language used in the original search. Key expressions thus grouped under the basic income topic include the English-language "basic income" and "universal income"; the French-language "revenu universel"; the German-language "grundeinkommen" and "bedingungslose grundeinkommen"; the Italian-language "reddito di cittadinanza"; the Japanese-language "ベーシック インカム"; the Korean-language "기본 소득"; and the Spanish-language "renta basica", among other such equivalent expressions in other languages.

References

Albert, F. and R. Gal (2017), *ESPN Thematic Report on Access to Social Protection for People Working on Non-Standard Contracts and as Self-Employed: Hungary*, European Commission, Brussels, http://ec.europa.eu/social/keyDocuments.jsp?pager.offset=10&&langId=en&mode=advancedSubmit&year=0&country=0&type=0&advSearchKey=ESPNsensw (accessed on 10 October 2017). [32]

Bäcker, G. (2017), *ESPN Thematic Report on Access to Social Protection for People Working on Non-Standard Contracts and as Self-Employed: Germany*, European Commission, Brussels, http://ec.europa.eu/social/keyDocuments.jsp?pager.offset=10&&langId=en&mode=advancedSubmit&year=0&country=0&type=0&advSearchKey=ESPNsensw (accessed on 09 October 2017). [7]

BIEN (2017), *About basic income*, Basic Income Earth Network (BIEN), http://basicincome.org/basic-income/ (accessed on 04 August 2017). [49]

Chłoń-Domińczak, A., A. Sowa and I. Topińska (2017), *ESPN Thematic Report on Access to Social Protection for People Working on Non-Standard Contracts and as Self-Employed: Poland*, European Commission, Brussels, http://ec.europa.eu/social/keyDocuments.jsp?pager.offset=20&&langId=en&mode=advancedSubmit&year=0&country=0&type=0&advSearchKey=ESPNsensw (accessed on 10 October 2017). [33]

Davies, R. (2013), "Self-employment and social security: effects on innovation and economic growth", http://www.europarl.europa.eu/RegData/bibliotheque/briefing/2013/130646/LDM_BRI(2013)130646_REV1_EN.pdf (accessed on 10 May 2017). [34]

Dervis, K. (1994), *Slovakia: Restructuring for recovery*, World Bank, https://books.google.fr/books?id=8WvIhn1MtAcC&pg=PA80&lpg=PA80&dq=introduced+unemployment+insurance+for+self-employed+new&source=bl&ots=xWdGlm60Nb&sig=JbdwuwWhUk5flyYhB9KA8jFTEvQ&hl=en&sa=X&ved=0ahUKEwjilrOR4tbWAhXE5xoKHZuvDk04ChDoAQhoMAc#v=onepage&q=intr (accessed on 04 October 2017). [13]

Di Maggio, M. and A. Kermani (2016), "The Importance of Unemployment Insurance as an Automatic Stabilizer", *Columbia Business School Research Paper* 15-31, http://dx.doi.org/10.2139/ssrn.2575434. [3]

European Commission (2011), *Adapting Unemployment Benefit Systems to the Economic Cycle*, European Commission, Brussels. [10]

Fleckenstein, T. and S. Lee (2017), "Democratization, post-industrialization, and East Asian welfare capitalism: the politics of welfare state reform in Japan, South Korea, and Taiwan", *Journal of International and Comparative Social Policy*, Vol. 33/1, pp. 36-54, http://dx.doi.org/10.1080/21699763.2017.1288158. [46]

Fondeville, N. et al. (2015), "Recent changes in self-employment and entrepreneurship across the EU", *European Commission Research Note* 6/2015, http://www.euro.centre.org/data/1466590158_15885.pdf (accessed on 10 May 2017). [11]

Försäkringskassan (2016), *Sickness benefit [Sjukpenning]*, Försäkringskassan, Stockholm, https://www.forsakringskassan.se/wps/wcm/connect/b6ec6788-05a7-49b4-a365-559c316a9a54/4086_sjukpenning_FK_Fa_enGB.pdf?MOD=AJPERES (accessed on 31 July 2017). [45]

Gerbery, D. and R. Bednárik (2017), *ESPN Thematic Report on Access to Social Protection for People Working on Non-Standard Contracts and as Self-Employed: Slovakia*, European Commission, Brussels, http://ec.europa.eu/social/keyDocuments.jsp?pager.offset=20&&langId=en&mode=advancedSubmit&year=0&country=0&type=0&advSearchKey=ESPNsensw (accessed on 10 October 2017). [25]

Google (2017), *Google Trends*, https://trends.google.com/trends/ (accessed on 28 April 2017). [51]

Hombert, J. et al. (2017), "Can Unemployment Insurance Spur Entrepreneurial Activity? Evidence from France", http://appli8.hec.fr/hombert/Hombert_Schoar_Sraer_Thesmar.pdf (accessed on 04 October 2017). [35]

Ignjatović, M. (2013), *Slovenia: Social partners involvement in unemployment benefit regimes*, European Observatory of Working Life (EurWORK), Brussels, https://www.eurofound.europa.eu/observatories/eurwork/comparative-information/national-contributions/slovenia/slovenia-social-partners-involvement-in-unemployment-benefit-regimes (accessed on 05 October 2017). [15]

ILO (2013), *Comparative review of unemployment and employment insurance experiences in Asia and worldwide*, International Labour Organization (ILO), http://www.ilo.org/asia/publications/WCMS_229985/lang--en/index.htm (accessed on 17 May 2017). [8]

Iudicone, F. and A. Arca Sedda (2015), *Italy: Reforms to system of unemployment benefits | Eurofound*, Eurofound, https://www.eurofound.europa.eu/observatories/eurwork/articles/industrial-relations-law-and-regulation/italy-reforms-to-system-of-unemployment-benefits (accessed on 16 May 2017). [20]

Jessoula, M., E. Pavolini and F. Strati (2017), *ESPN Thematic Report on Access to Social Protection for People Working on Non-Standard Contracts and as Self-Employed: Italy*, European Commission, Brussels, http://ec.europa.eu/social/keyDocuments.jsp?pager.offset=10&&langId=en&mode=advancedSubmit&year=0&country=0&type=0&advSearchKey=ESPNsensw (accessed on 13 October 2017). [21]

Kalliomaa-Puha, L. and O. Kangas (2017), *ESPN Thematic Report on Access to Social Protection for People Working on Non-Standard Contracts and as Self-Employed: Finland*, European Commission, Brussels, http://ec.europa.eu/social/keyDocuments.jsp?pager.offset=0&&langId=en&mode=advancedSubmit&year=0&country=0&type=0&advSearchKey=ESPNsensw (accessed on 10 October 2017). [12]

KPMG (2017), *Icelandic Tax Facts 2017: In-depth Information on the Icelandic Tax System*, KPMG Iceland, Reykjavik, https://assets.kpmg.com/content/dam/kpmg/is/pdf/2017/01/KPMG-TaxFacts2017.pdf (accessed on 04 October 2017). [30]

Langenbucher, K. (2015), "How demanding are eligibility criteria for unemployment benefits, quantitative indicators for OECD and EU countries", *OECD Social, Employment and Migration Working Papers*, No. 166, OECD Publishing, Paris, http://dx.doi.org/10.1787/5jrxtk1zw8f2-en. [37]

Lee, B. et al. (2016), "Social Protection for the Self-Employed", *Korea Labor Institute Research Series*, https://www.kli.re.kr/kli_eng/engRsrchReprtView.do?key=382&pblctListNo=8813 (accessed on 31 July 2017), p. 185. [9]

MISSOC (2013), *Overview of means testing in MISSOC countries*, European Commission, Brussels, http://www.missoc.org/INFORMATIONBASE/OTHEROUTPUTS/ANALYSIS/2013/MISSOC%20Analysis%202013_1%20EN.pdf (accessed on 30 October 2017). [47]

MISSOC (2017), *Social protection of the self-employed*, Mutual Information System on Social Protection (MISSOC), Brussels, http://www.missoc.org/INFORMATIONBASE/COUNTRYSPECIFICDESCS/SELFEMPLOYED/socialProtectionSelfEmployed2017.htm (accessed on 26 July 2017). [6]

MISSOC (2017), *MISSOC Comparative Tables Database*, http://www.missoc.org/INFORMATIONBASE/informationBase.jsp (accessed on 30 October 2017). [48]

Nelson, K. et al. (2017), *ESPN Thematic Report on Access to social protection for people working on non-standard contracts and as self-employed: Sweden*, European Commission, Brussels, http://ec.europa.eu/social/keyDocuments.jsp?pager.offset=30&&langId=en&mode=advancedSubmit&year=0&country=0&type=0&advSearchKey=ESPNsensw (accessed on 06 October 2017). [27]

OECD (2008), "Pension Country Profile: Iceland", in OECD (ed.), *OECD Private Pensions Outlook 2008*, OECD Publishing, http://dx.doi.org/10.1787/517137382748. [14]

OECD (2008), "Declaring Work or Staying Underground: Informal Employment in Seven OECD Countries", in *OECD Employment Outlook 2008*, OECD Publishing, Paris, http://dx.doi.org/10.1787/empl_outlook-2008-4-en. [36]

OECD (2011), "Earnings Volatility: Causes and Consequences", in *OECD Employment Outlook 2011*, OECD Publishing, Paris, http://dx.doi.org/10.1787/empl_outlook-2011-5-en. [2]

OECD (2013), *OECD Economic Surveys: Greece 2013*, OECD Publishing, Paris, http://dx.doi.org/10.1787/eco_surveys-grc-2013-en. [16]

OECD (2014), *Mental Health and Work: Switzerland*, Mental Health and Work, OECD Publishing, Paris, http://dx.doi.org/10.1787/9789264204973-en. [41]

OECD (2014), "Non-regular employment, job security and the labour market divide", in *OECD Employment Outlook*, Organisation for Economic Cooperation and Development (OECD), http://dx.doi.org/10.1787/empl_outlook-2014-7-en. [43]

OECD (2016), *Connecting People with Jobs: The Labour Market, Activation Policies and Disadvantaged Workers in Slovenia*, OECD Publishing, Paris, http://dx.doi.org/10.1787/9789264265349-en. [38]

OECD (2017), *Employment database*, http://www.oecd.org/employment/emp/employmentdatabase-employment.htm (accessed on 04 May 2017). [39]

OECD (2017), "Basic Income as a Policy Option: Can it add up?", *Policy Brief on the Future of Work*, http://www.oecd.org/employment/future-of-work.htm (accessed on 28 July 2017). [50]

OECD (2017), *Benefits and Wages: Country specific information*, http://www.oecd.org/els/soc/benefits-and-wages-country-specific-information.htm (accessed on 28 April 2017). [52]

Ólafsson, S. (2017), *ESPN Thematic Report on Access to Social Protection for People Working on Non-Standard Contracts and as Self-Employed: Iceland*, European Commission, Brussels, http://ec.europa.eu/social/keyDocuments.jsp?pager.offset=10&&langId=en&mode=advancedSubmit&year=0&country=0&type=0&advSearchKey=ESPNsensw (accessed on 10 October 2017). [29]

Oostveen, A. et al. (2013), *Self-employed or not self-employed? Working conditions of 'economically dependent workers' - Background paper*, Eurofound, Dublin, https://www.eurofound.europa.eu/publications/customised-report/2013/working-conditions-labour-market/self-employed-or-not-self-employed-working-conditions-of-economically-dependent-workers-background (accessed on 13 October 2017). [22]

Pacolet, J. and L. Op de Beeck (2017), *ESPN Thematic Report on Access to Social Protection for People Working on Non-Standard Contracts and as Self-Employed: Luxembourg*, European Commission, Brussels, http://ec.europa.eu/social/keyDocuments.jsp?pager.offset=20&&langId=en&mode=advancedSubmit&year=0&country=0&type=0&advSearchKey=ESPNsensw (accessed on 10 October 2017). [26]

Perista, P. and I. Baptista (2017), *ESPN Thematic Report on Access to Social Protection for People Working on Non-Standard Contracts and as Self-Employed: Portugal*, European Commission, Brussels, http://ec.europa.eu/social/keyDocuments.jsp?pager.offset=20&&langId=en&mode=advancedSubmit&year=0&country=0&type=0&advSearchKey=ESPNsensw (accessed on 04 October 2017). [18]

Rejda, G. (1966), "Unemployment Insurance as an Automatic Stabilizer", *The Journal of Risk and Insurance*, Vol. 33/2, p. 195, http://dx.doi.org/10.2307/251032. [1]

Ríkisskattstjóri (2017), *Reiknað endurgjald 2017*, https://www.rsk.is/atvinnurekstur/stadgreidsla-og-reiknad-endurgjald/reiknad-endurgjald/2017#tab1 (accessed on 10 October 2017). [28]

Rodríguez-Cabrero, G. et al. (2017), *ESPN Thematic Report on Access to Social Protection for People Working on Non-Standard Contracts and as Self-Employed: Spain*, European Commission, Brussels, http://ec.europa.eu/social/keyDocuments.jsp?pager.offset=30&&langId=en&mode=advancedSubmit&year=0&country=0&type=0&advSearchKey=ESPNsensw (accessed on 06 October 2017). [19]

Sirovátka, T., R. Jahoda and I. Malý (2017), *ESPN Thematic Report on Access to Social Protection for People Working on Non-Standard Contracts and as Self-Employed: Czech Republic*, European Commission, Brussels, http://ec.europa.eu/social/keyDocuments.jsp?pager.offset=0&&langId=en&mode=advancedSubmit&year=0&country=0&type=0&advSearchKey=ESPNsensw (accessed on 09 October 2017). [24]

Spasova, S., D. Bouget and B. Vanhercke (2016), *Sick pay and sickness benefit schemes in the European Union: Background report for the Social Protection Committee's in-depth review of sickness benefits*, European Commission, http://bookshop.europa.eu/is-bin/INTERSHOP.enfinity/WFS/EU-Bookshop-Site/en_GB/-/EUR/ViewPublication-Start?PublicationKey=KE0217045 (accessed on 28 April 2017). [40]

SSA and ISSA (2016), *Social Security Programs Throughout the World: Europe, 2016*, https://www.ssa.gov/policy/docs/progdesc/ssptw/2016-2017/europe/ssptw16europe.pdf (accessed on 27 April 2017). [31]

SSA and ISSA (2016), *Social Security Programs Throughout the World: The Americas, 2015*, Social Security Administration (SSA) and International Social Security Association (ISSA), https://www.ssa.gov/policy/docs/progdesc/ssptw/2014-2015/americas/ssptw15americas.pdf (accessed on 27 April 2017). [44]

SSA and ISSA (2017), *Social Security Programs Throughout the World: Asia and the Pacific, 2016*, https://www.ssa.gov/policy/docs/progdesc/ssptw/2016-2017/asia/ssptw16asia.pdf (accessed on 27 April 2017). [42]

Statistics Korea (2017), *Korean Statistical Information Service (KOSIS)*, http://kosis.kr/eng/ (accessed on 15 June 2017). [5]

Stropnik, N., B. Majcen and V. Prevolnik Rupel (2017), *ESPN Thematic Report on Access to Social Protection for People Working on Non-Standard Contracts and as Self-Employed: Slovenia*, European Commission, Brussels, http://ec.europa.eu/social/keyDocuments.jsp?pager.offset=20&&langId=en&mode=advancedSubmit&year=0&country=0&type=0&advSearchKey=ESPNsensw (accessed on 10 October 2017). [23]

Theodoroulakis, M., I. Sakellis and D. Ziomas (2017), *ESPN Thematic Report on Access to Social Protection for People Working on Non-Standard Contracts and as Self-Employed: Greece*, European Commission, Brussels, http://ec.europa.eu/social/keyDocuments.jsp?pager.offset=10&&langId=en&mode=advancedSubmit&year=0&country=0&type=0&advSearchKey=ESPNsensw (accessed on 05 October 2017). [17]

Yoo, G. (2013), "Institutional Blind Spots in the South Korean Employment Safety Net and Policy Solutions", *KDI Focus* 28, https://www.kdi.re.kr/kdi_eng/publication/publication_view.jsp?pub_no=13273 (accessed on 01 August 2017). [4]

Chapter 4. Policy solutions for a broader and fairer safety net in Korea

This chapter discusses various policy solutions Korea can implement towards achieving more complete social protection coverage and better labour market outcomes. Drawing from the experiences of other OECD countries, Korea has managed to put in place an effective legislative framework with a strong focus on activation and employment. Nevertheless, various steps can be taken to broaden and improve Korea's existing social protection measures. First, Korea can achieve considerable improvements through more rigorous enforcement of current policies and legislation. Second, Korea can enhance each of its existing social protection measures to further narrow down their remaining coverage gaps. Third, Korea should urgently introduce more far-reaching changes to support workers encountering temporary work incapacity due to poor health.

The current progress on social protection

Korea has taken remarkable initiative over the past 25 years to develop and expand a welfare state with sound activation features oriented towards positive labour market outcomes. Since 1995, Korea's Employment Insurance (EI) measure has provided insurance-based support for millions of workers encountering involuntary unemployment. Since 2000, the Basic Livelihood Security Programme (BLSP) has guaranteed a minimum floor of income support for Korea's poorest families. Since 2008-09, the Employment Success Package Programme (ESPP) and Earned Income Tax Credit (EITC) provide additional employment support and in-work benefits for vulnerable participants and struggling households.

Nevertheless, important debates linger around the considerable blind spots that remain around coverage under each of these social protection measures – which groups to encompass and who to exclude as the system continues to mature. Blind spots are the combined result of eligibility and entitlement rules that explicitly exclude some workers (*institutional* blind spots) and a labour market that either hinders or neglects others who, by all rights, should be covered (*effective* blind spots). The result is that many Koreans who lose or change their jobs do not receive any income or employment support. This is problematic for at least the following reasons:

- *First*, it creates considerable discrepancies between jobseekers who are covered and those who are not, with the latter struggling more to re-enter work or more readily settling for a poor-quality, low-paid job or for work in the informal sector.
- *Second*, it poses a considerable risk for many jobseekers of poverty, social exclusion and disengagement from the labour market. Especially in an economic downturn effective income support acts as an important economic stabiliser.
- *Third*, a lack of effective employment support for often disadvantaged workers leads to poorer matching in the labour market and thus poorer job outcomes overall and, consequently, less inclusive economic growth.

Policy makers in Korea are aware of these measures' weaknesses and the imperfect outcomes coverage gaps produce. Successive governments have introduced incremental policy reforms to gradually broaden out the coverage of social protection measures and enhance the support they deliver. Gradual reform of this kind is very common in social and labour market policy-making given how any new change can distort finely-tuned institutions and behavioural norms in unpredictable ways (and often be tricky to reverse after the policy is implemented). Irrespective of how rapidly any reform might take place in Korea, the changes introduced over the past ten years have had too little impact: while they have succeeded in broadening coverage at the margins, they have largely failed to capture the bulkiest groups of disadvantaged workers. Labour market dualities present ongoing problems, in particular, consistently demonstrating their resistance to change.

Korea is thus at a crossroads. Public spending on social and labour market programmes is still relatively low in Korea – only half the level of the OECD average, relative to GDP, and just one-third of that in most European countries. Providing better services for more people cannot be achieved without additional investments which in turn will require some increase in taxes or social contributions. The government should decide how much more it is willing to spend in order to provide better services and realise its social and labour market objectives.

Bolder decisions are necessary to finally tackle Korea's ongoing coverage gaps; to ensure that considerably more people can benefit from statutory income and employment support; and to promote high-quality employment for more workers. Successful policy action will require at least three key elements:

1. Considerably stricter and more consistent enforcement of legislation already in place to ensure affiliation to social insurance measures for all workers who ought to be covered.
2. Continuation on the current reform path of expanding social protection measures to those not currently covered and increasing support for those in need.
3. Introducing a degree of statutory support for workers experiencing health problems and temporary work incapacity – an issue whose neglect currently leads to much strife among individuals and weakens labour market outcomes.

Enforcing existing legislation

Korea's four main social protection programmes – EI, ESPP, BLSP and EITC – entail strong support mechanisms that neatly complement one another. Sequential reforms have continuously improved each measure. Moreover, each measure has proven effective for those it covers at delivering income support, improving jobseeker's employability, encouraging activation and making work more rewarding.

All four measures, nevertheless, suffer the same drawback in terms of coverage levels that fall far below the potential in each case. While policy-level reforms could improve the situation somewhat, potentially more could be achieved by simply enforcing each measure's existing rules more strictly and consistently.

Stricter implementation could especially benefit EI. Recent estimates from Korea's *Economically Active Population Survey* reveal that as many as 4.0 million workers were not enrolled in EI during 2016 out of a total group of 16.6 million salaried workers eligible for the measure. These estimates imply that EI's effective blind spot encompasses almost a quarter of all eligible workers, especially workers employed in micro-businesses, signifying a significant shortcoming on the implementation side.

Much of this discrepancy inevitably arises from illicit practices among employers (sometimes in collusion with workers) who evade their formal obligation to register workers for social insurance and pay the necessary contributions. Enforcement of EI obligations currently happens relatively rarely: Korea's labour inspectorate lacks the resources necessary to monitor EI registration systematically while penalties for wrongdoers are far too low to be a real deterrent (currently just KRW 300 000 per worker under EI's arbitration process). Meanwhile, insufficient use is currently made of existing taxation and social insurance records whose databases could be linked together to pinpoint irregularities – after all, most of those people not insured by EI are covered by IACI and many of them are registered for tax purposes.

Enforcing EI legislation will require political will and leadership. Employers that renege on social insurance obligations could be treated with less discretion; be monitored with more scrutiny; and fined with higher penalties. A broader mandate for Korea's labour inspectorate to monitor compliance could be part of a possible solution. Retrospective payment of EI contributions by way of EI's existing arbitration process could also play a stronger role alongside stronger sanctions for offenders. In turn, more could be done to raise workers' awareness of their labour rights and encourage more to secure affiliation in the first place or, failing that, complete the arbitration procedure upon dismissal. The short lifespan of many businesses in Korea cannot be a reason for inaction. In most European countries, every single day of employment has to be reported to the corresponding insurance authority. Having a single, unified registration in place for all social insurance branches would simplify matters and generate more consistent compliance with existing rules.

More can also be done to raise the effective coverage of Korea's other main social protection measures, including by more systematic, proactive outreach and by making claims and participation sufficiently attractive to ensure high take-up on a voluntary basis.

- To raise EITC participation, tax authorities could play a more proactive role in raising awareness by reaching out to low-income workers who should be entitled. Existing tax records should contain all of the information needed to identify such individuals and families.
- To raise BLSP participation, a targeted outreach programme could also increase claims and take-up to boost not only households' income but also the employment outcomes of potential (conditional) recipients. Take-up of last-resort income support measures like BLSP is stigmatised in all OECD countries and therefore often lower than it should be.
- To raise ESPP participation, better incentives could be provided for Job Centres and private services suppliers to reaching out to potential clients and those in need of employability support. The financial support provided to participants themselves could also be increased.

Improving existing social protection measures

Legislative changes will be needed to boost social protection coverage and participation under Korea's main social protection measures. Coordinated reforms to EI, BLSP, ESPP and EITC should ensure a robust safety net that supports all jobseekers, workers and low-income households in need.

Employment insurance for the entire workforce

While much of EI's low coverage can be addressed through stronger enforcement, its institutional blind spots will require new entitlement conditions for some groups of the workforce. Since 2012, self-employed persons in Korea have had the opportunity to opt in for EI coverage on a voluntary basis. In practice, however, extremely few of them do. This may be unsatisfactory and potentially unsustainable in view of the very large number of self-employed persons in Korea who (together with contributing family workers) make up one quarter of total employment.

The blurring of boundaries between employment and self-employment – in the form of "dependent self-employment" – has led many countries to question their social protection measures and explore ways of extending unemployment insurance to all or most self-employed people. Like Korea, several OECD countries including Germany have introduced voluntary affiliation for self-employed persons over the past few years. Greece and Slovenia have recently introduced mandatory affiliation, as has Portugal for employers and for most dependent self-employed persons.

Policy makers in Korea should also consider mandatory EI affiliation for some groups of self-employed persons, building upon the existing rules for voluntary affiliation. Such a policy could ensure that effective employment services benefit a much bigger base within the workforce to help previously self-employed jobseekers move into better jobs (whether salaried or non-salaried). Such a policy would manage the risk of unemployment more broadly within society, thus insuring against it more effectively. Such a measure could also be further expanded to include contributing family workers plus workers in situations of dependent self-employment.

Policy makers in Korea should also explore ways of relaxing EI's entitlement conditions, which currently disqualify all jobseekers who left their jobs on a voluntary basis. Most OECD countries penalise such jobseekers through benefit sanctions or suspensions lasting for a few weeks or up to several months instead of disqualifying them from EI entitlements altogether. A similar approach could be implemented gradually under EI also in Korea, possibly starting with a somewhat severe penalty that policy makers can then relax in steps once the relevant implementation channels are established and any undesired behavioural effects (including moral hazards) are contained.

Restoring the link between earnings and EI benefits

The way income support is structured under EI has gradually changed over time. When EI was first introduced in 1995, it generally replaced 50% of beneficiaries' usual earnings between benefit floor and ceiling amounts set at roughly 20% and 80% of Korea's average monthly wage. By 2017, the floor and ceiling amounts have converged so much that EI is in actual fact a flat-rate benefit of KRW 46 584-50 000 per day. Moreover, Korea's EI floor has become the highest unemployment benefit minimum in the entire OECD which might be an unsustainable situation. From January 2018, both amounts will be pushed up to KRW 54 216 per day by Korea's rising minimum wage.

This gradual shift over time has effectively eroded the original link between EI benefits and jobseekers' regular earnings. Low and high earners may pay different EI premiums although they ultimately receive virtually the same amount of income support under EI. Given such a significant policy drift over time, policy makers might benefit from going back to the drawing board to decide what type of structure would be best for EI benefits:

- Whether delivered as a genuine flat-rate benefit for all beneficiaries regardless of their previous earnings and, if so, at what value.
- Whether delivered as a genuinely variable-rate benefit, the value of which is bound within a broader range and linked more closely to beneficiaries' previous earnings or insurance contributions.

Whatever the ultimate choice, the EI benefit floor and ceiling amounts should entail an adjustment mechanism that preserves its basic structure more coherently over time. This may require pegging *both* the benefit floor and ceiling amounts to the minimum wage or an alternative variable like the national average wage. Any such adjustment in the benefit structure might also require the premium structure and levels to be adjusted, accordingly.

EI also has two specific features that are ineffective and carry large deadweight losses: the *Social Insurance Subsidy Programme* and the *Early Re-employment Allowance*.

The *Duru Nuri Social Insurance Subsidy Programme* subsidises part of the EI premium for low-paid workers and their employers in enterprises with fewer than 10 workers to help ensure compliance with EI affiliation rules. This incentive scheme could find a valuable complement in tighter EI enforcement if financial support could be coupled with stricter penalties for those who continuously fail to comply by their EI obligations. The scheme could also reduce its current large deadweight costs if its support was gradually phased-out for individual workers after a given period of time.

EI's *Early Re-employment Allowance* offers a lump-sum payment to jobseekers finding work before they exhaust their EI claim period. The measure carries large deadweight costs, especially in view of Korea's relatively short average duration of unemployment of only three months (in 2016). It would be more effective to abolish this allowance altogether and invest the funds in something else, such as improving EI compliance.

Social assistance for people in need

BLSP is Korea's last resort social assistance payment and the primary source of income support for jobseekers after EI. Recent reforms have done away with many of BLSP's previous weaknesses. The different payments provided under BLSP are now better customised to individual needs and work incentives have improved as the various payments are no longer phased out simultaneously. The reform has also increased the number of claims, especially for the payment that supports young people's education.

There are still relatively few claims, however, from individuals classified as *conditional* recipients who are capable of working and gain activation support through either BLSP's *Self-Reliance Programme* or a referral to ESPP. Ways should be sought to bring bigger numbers of low-income jobseekers capable of working who receive no other statutory income support under BLSP and into these activation programmes. Participation could be made more accessible for low-income jobless families while at the same time becoming more conditional on labour market participation and job search in harmony with the behavioural requirements applied to EI participants.

Further easing and, eventually, phasing out BLSP's "family support obligation" would help to increase the number of BLSP recipients and spread its benefits more fairly (even though such change would probably affect older claimants more than those of working age). The strictly applied family support obligation implies that the income of parents and children of any BLSP applicant is taken into account in determining BLSP entitlement, irrespective of whether the applicant receives any support from close relatives.

Many BLSP recipients encounter a range of labour market barriers, ranging from physical and mental health problems to broader social and skills deficiencies or financial insolvency. Korea has made important steps towards addressing such multiple obstacles by co-locating various support and counselling services under one roof within the Job Centres. Such services could be improved further by bringing them under the responsibility of a single provider offering a truly integrated service. The current dispatching of social workers from local government authorities, for example, offers an imperfect solution since end-users are ultimately made to identify and seek out the right services by themselves. This does not guarantee that multiple problems are systematically identified and addressed, back-to-back with other employment barriers.

Korean-style unemployment assistance

There was much debate in Korea about expanding ESPP into a broader "Korean-style" unemployment assistance measure. This might offer a logical step insofar as ESPP seeks to fill the gap between EI and BLSP by targeting jobseekers not eligible for either of the two programmes. An expanded ESPP could potentially bridge a significant gap in

Korea's social protection system. One tangible proposal recommended to policy makers a few years ago was to broaden ESPP's eligibility criteria by alleviating the low-income threshold in such a way as to double the current number of participants. The proposal would have raised the income support component of ESPP to around 20% of Korea's average wage, payable on a monthly basis for periods of up to 12 months.

Under its latest five-year plan, the current government has announced it will move in this direction, earmarking new funding for a higher participation grant during stage 3 of ESPP, initially only for youth but from 2020 on encompassing low-income jobseekers as well. The revised payment will amount to KRW 300 000 per month for up to three months in 2018 and KRW 500 000 per month for up to six months from 2019.

These changes offer a positive policy direction for ESPP, although they could be disappointingly small in terms of fulfilling ESPP's full potential. ESPP has shown to deliver strong employment outcomes for all types of participants, especially among low-income households. Data reveal that outcomes have improved over time for both the programme's reach and for participants' immediate and medium-term employment outcomes. Such results should prompt policy makers to broaden ESPP access further.

The proposed benefit increase is not particularly high, though the amount is roughly comparable to unemployment assistance benefits in other OECD countries. Nevertheless, the increased payment appears very low relative to the EI benefit floor of 90% of the minimum wage (which will rise to KRW 60 240 per day from January 2018) – amounting to a minimum benefit of KRW 1.6 million per month in 2018. Such a large discrepancy between these benefit amounts may be difficult to justify under a two-tier system.

International comparisons offer limited lessons regarding how far ESPP coverage could or should be expanded. The purpose and target groups of unemployment assistance measures can differ massively from country to country. In view of the limited income support alternatives jobseekers in Korea have, ESPP should be accessible for all low-income groups – perhaps even all those earning below the median wage – and encompass (as it currently does) new labour market entrants, those who have exhausted their EI entitlement and those who have never been entitled to any public income support (irrespective of their previous employment type and status).

However large the expansion of ESPP might be, there is no reason to rebrand it as an unemployment assistance measure. ESPP's current design nicely reflects the central aims unemployment assistance measures have in common anyway, delivering effective employability support and employment services to people in need of them.

Managing the expansion of ESPP

The rapid expansion of ESPP over the past five years was a challenge to administer. In particular, it proved difficult to increase the number of ESPP counsellors sufficiently enough, as a result of which the average caseload per counsellor increased to 120 customers (and 100 in the public Job Centres). Such caseloads could endanger ESPP's consistently strong employment outcomes. The average caseload per counsellor should be changed back nearer to what it used to be when introduced to ensure quality standards, though this might not be possible under a rapidly increasing ESPP caseload.

To maintain and further improve ESPP results, policy makers have already taken steps to ensure the quality of services delivered by the many (often new) private employment service providers. Outsourcing and subcontracting ESPP services in this way has generally been a success. Nevertheless, it will be important that only effective private providers delivering the highest-quality services stay in business – which may come as a key challenge at a time of expanding the programme's capacity. A stronger quality assurance framework could be implemented – potentially following the example of Australia's start rating system – and the contracts of underperforming private providers discontinued more decisively and perhaps more frequently. In exchange, it will be necessary to offer contracts lasting longer than the current one-year timeframe to encourage private providers to develop more specialised competencies.

Improving performance measurement should also be a priority for public Job Centres. First, their performance could be audited more systematically and steps taken to improve practices among under-performing ones – perhaps including through more transparent sharing of performance data, as other countries have done. Second, some variation could be introduced into the way Job Centres are currently funded and to the sorts of performance targets they have to take better account of the differences between different types of jobseekers and how difficult some might be to manage than others. Such variable funding might equally benefit private employment service providers.

Moving forward, the chosen split of responsibilities between private and public providers and the efficiency of the current choice could also be reconsidered. Publicly-run Job Centres currently serve all low-income and disadvantaged clients, while all others plus youth are dealt with by private employment service providers. Evidence from other countries suggests that there is no real justification for keeping the provision of services for the most disadvantaged jobseekers under public control – a robust legal framework should enable private providers to deliver equally good outcomes. Further expansion of ESPP among low-income jobseekers could thus in large part be stemmed by private providers. Australia and the United Kingdom offer a useful benchmark for policy makers in Korea to consider: both countries outsource and subcontract employment service provision for all clients, irrespective of their level of disadvantage, while concentrating public Job Centres' efforts on monitoring both employment outcomes among jobseekers and the quality of services among providers.

Addressing in-work poverty

In-work poverty represents a key problem for Korea, where roughly one in every six workers earns the minimum wage or lower.

Korea currently addresses in-work poverty through EITC – an in-work benefit measure that provides tax breaks for low-income families and, since recently, single-member households and, very recently, self-employed individuals. The number of EITC recipients is currently about 1.4 million, which represents only around one-fifth of the 7 million individuals with low earnings in Korea. Despite continuous expansion, EITC thus remains a relatively marginal programme affecting too few households.

EITC provides a relatively low level of income support, currently amounting to only around 2% of the average wage per year for an average beneficiary. EITC was modelled after a similar programme in the United States. One major feature EITC adopted is to initially increase the value of its support in line with working hours before gradually phasing it out at higher income levels (though the phase out happens at much lower levels of incomes in Korea than it does under the United States' measure). What limited evidence is available suggests that EITC improves incomes and raises employment in the income range where the benefit increases.

To tackle in-work poverty more decisively, additional steps will be necessary. These could include an expansion of EITC through a later and longer phase-out and, possibly, less stringent asset tests in line with BLSP, to increase the number of households eligible while maximising their work incentives. EITC could also increase the value of the tax credit it provides.

Korea's current government is strongly advocating for further policy changes that will improve conditions for low-earners. One such initiative is to increase the statutory minimum wage, from its current KRW 51 760 per day to a target of KRW 80 000 per day by 2020 – setting in place a nominal increase of 15.6% per year over the next three years. This will bring a rapid pay rise to many formal low-wage workers – as 2020's minimum wage converges close to 2016's average wage – entailing likely knock-on effects for informal low-wage workers. All the same, a minimum wage increase of such magnitude will have larger effects on the economy and on social protection measures further down the line – not the least because the EI floor is currently pegged explicitly to the minimum wage. It will therefore be important to carefully evaluate the wider impacts of the planned minimum wage increase and its interactions with other labour market institutions.

BLSP could also play a stronger role around in-work poverty. In most OECD countries, it is common for social assistance benefits to support workers and self-employed persons with low incomes. This is effectively not the case in Korea, given that BLSP has a considerably low number of recipients who are working (only 7% of the caseload are in the labour force and most of them are unemployed) – despite the fact that reforms made in 2015 made it easier for families with earnings at or below the minimum wage to qualify for BLSP support. More could be done to promote BLSP among such groups, while ensuring and enforcing a strong activation approach.

Some OECD countries provide large in-work benefits – often related to family status, such as Ireland's Family Income Supplement – or family benefits capable of addressing in-work poverty issues. If a much expanded EITC, the promotion of BLSP top-ups for working families and a higher minimum wage fail to sufficiently address Korea's issues around in-work poverty, such approach to help poor families might also be needed in Korea. Korea's Child Tax Credit falls in this category but again, beneficiary numbers and the actual credit provided (KRW 500 000 per child per year) are small.

Introducing a much-needed safety net for sick workers

Workers encountering acute or chronic health problems and resulting temporary work incapacity receive very little attention under Korea's current social protection policies. Most OECD countries have measures in place to provide income support for workers during a period of ill-health. Such measures virtually always put mechanisms in place to ensure that workers' sickness does not result in their job loss and that all those who regain their work capacity receive help in making a timely return to work – a process known as "rehabilitation". Korea currently has neither a statutory income support measure in place to address the needs of sick workers, nor any given strategy to ensure their rehabilitation.

Despite the veritable progress Korea has made in recent decades around developing a contemporary welfare state, the apparent policy vacuum in this area represents its biggest remaining gap. Inaction on workers' rehabilitation simultaneously leads to significant wasted opportunities for the labour market and the economy, as workers recovering from sickness gain no support for re-entering the labour market – prolonging unemployment for most while leading others to disengage from economic activity altogether.

Some collective agreements in Korea may contain allowances for paid sick leave and define protocols for workers' subsequent rehabilitation. Nevertheless, most workers encountering temporary work incapacity in Korea are treated according to their employer's discretion and many are promptly dismissed.

Two relevant regulations within the framework of EI touch upon this issue, though neither goes nearly far enough:

- When *jobseekers* falls ill while receiving EI benefits, they may seek relief from EI's behavioural conditions (availability and active search for work) until they regain their health or, alternatively, until the end of the regular maximum EI entitlement period (lasting between 90 and 240 days, in any case). In 2015, 8 250 people benefited from this rule.
- Alternatively, when *workers* fall ill and relinquish their job as a result, EI allows them to postpone the start of their benefit claim for a period of up to four years or until they are well enough to look for work (ordinary jobseekers may also choose to postpone the start of their EI claim period but only for up to one year). Under such circumstances, entitlement to support necessitates a worker to sever their employment relationship – which can significantly hamper their rehabilitation. Such workers gain no income support during the time of their actual sickness but only once they are well enough to abide by EI's behavioural rules and begin their formal EI claim period. Those experiencing sickness for longer than four years effectively lose their EI entitlement altogether. In 2013, 9 810 people received EI benefits following a delay of this sort.

Among EI's roughly 1.3 million beneficiaries per year, fewer than 20 000 generally benefit from either of the two regulations. On the other hand, sick workers who are not entitled to EI fail to benefit even from these very limited options.

Korea's limited statutory support for workers undergoing sickness is particularly problematic for workers' rehabilitation. Research unequivocally shows that workers recovering from sickness find it significantly easier to return to the *own* job or stay with the *same* employer than to gain alternative work. Social protection measures should therefore ensure every effort is made to help sick people return quickly to work and to prevent long periods of inactivity. Otherwise, many such workers – especially those suffering from chronic illness – can easily enter a path into unstable employment and, eventually, permanent labour market exit.

Typically, OECD countries have a dual system in place to ensure both income support and rehabilitation for workers undergoing sickness:

- Most OECD countries legislate for employers to face a liability for their workers' absences in case of sickness over a given period of time. Employers' liability typically obliges them to continue paying all or part of their absent worker's wage during a stated period – the length of which varies from several days in some countries to a matter of years in others (roughly three weeks or a month is the mode in most OECD countries). In most countries workers cannot be dismissed during this period and in many countries employers and workers have specified obligations to facilitate rehabilitation and return to work.
- Most OECD countries complement statutory employers' liability with statutory cash sickness benefit measures. Entitlement for such benefits commonly begins immediately after the employers' liability period expires. Cash sickness benefits

are usually insurance-based and replace a fraction of the workers' usual earnings (typically 50-80%) over a longer period of time. The maximum duration of claims may differ among countries but tends to last for around 6-12 months. Benefits of this kind always entail assertive rehabilitation strategies, combining a number of policy tools to ensure that workers transition back into their jobs (or to another opportunity) as soon as they are able.

Countries administer cash sickness benefit measures in various different ways. Virtually all such measures, however, are insurance-based and financed from employer and employee contributions. Most either form part of a broader health insurance measure (like in Japan); part of a broader employment insurance measure (like in Canada); or exist as stand-alone social insurance measures, operating their own insurance funds.

For Korea, cash sickness benefits could emerge directly from a modified EI measure, making use of the existing EI infrastructure to manage benefit administration and premium collection. Workers in Korea would thus gain income support over a given duration of time when sickness prevented them from working. Upon recovery, those who regained their full work capacity could return to their original jobs without ever having had to sever their employment relationship. Workers regaining only part of their work capacity could undertake an alternative role for the same employer or seek out alternative opportunities through employment services specifically tailored towards rehabilitation.

How much such benefits could be worth and how long they would last are matters for political deliberation. Cash sickness benefits in Canada form part of the country's broader EI measure, delivering income support equivalent to unemployment benefits in terms of both their value and their maximum duration. Canada's example could be a worthwhile starting point for Korea for cash sickness benefits under an expanded EI measure.

Complementing social sickness insurance with legislation on employers' liability for their workers' sickness would be advantageous. It would enable workers not entitled to social insurance to retain their jobs, nevertheless, and benefit from a period of income support – if at least for a certain period. Such protection could encompass regular and non-regular workers alike. Finally, a degree of employers' liability would take some of the cost burden off from statutory sickness insurance, enabling them to charge smaller premiums. This might offer a more equitable solution for Korea – where individual workers currently take on the entire burden of their sickness.

Any effective cash sickness benefit measure requires a robust rehabilitation strategy and return-to-work focus – the counterparts of a strong activation strategy under any unemployment benefit measure. Any such new measure in Korea should therefore ensure it has rigorous channels in place to assess and regularly reassess beneficiaries' work capacity; that it has tools in place to help them return to work (including on a gradual basis, if necessary); and that it puts protocols in place to define the various rights and obligations sick workers, their employers, their doctors and the insurance authorities should have under different circumstances.

The combined effect of the proposed reforms

The reform proposals outlined in this report will help Korea to: i) reach more individuals within the existing support framework, closing the large blind spots that there currently are; ii) achieve fairer outcomes across the board – especially for workers who encounter sickness; and iii) realise higher employment and higher incomes for the poorest and most disadvantaged families.

Figure 4.1 illustrates social protection coverage in Korea under the current status quo (Panel A), comparing it with a stylised illustration of what a reformed social protection system could look like, based on this report's recommendations (Panel B). The figure indicates situations under which coverage conditions might involve means-testing (indicated by an "M"), voluntary affiliation (indicated by a "V") and additional employers' liability (indicated by an "L").

Broadly speaking, Korea's social protection system currently provides sound support in case of unemployment for some but not for others; virtually no statutory support in case of sickness; and relatively comprehensive support against poverty regarding coverage (though not necessarily in terms of its value) (Figure 4.1, Panel A):

- EI benefits cover only just over half of the workforce as they exclude several categories of non-regular workers; contributing family workers; jobseekers in voluntary unemployment and jobseekers with insufficient contributions; and effectively fail to cover most self-employed persons and many workers working in micro-businesses. ESPP provides a degree of support for some of those groups, including low-income jobseekers ineligible for EI; those who have exhausted their EI entitlement; and new labour market entrants.
- Income support for workers and jobseekers experiencing sickness is non-existent. Under limited circumstances, support can continue for those who become sick when they are already claiming EI benefits. All other sick employed individuals and sick jobseekers not entitled to EI gain no income and return-to-work support.
- BLSP benefits tackling out-of-work poverty cover all poor families, pending a means test, but exclude those who have potential family support (whether or not such support is actually provided) under Korea's unique family support obligation rules. EITC benefits tackling in-work poverty cover virtually all low-wage salaried employees and self-employed individuals, even though effective take-up is relatively low, but with only indirect support for contributing family workers.

The recommendations outlined in this report could be applied to close virtually all of the remaining coverage gaps within Korea's social protection system (Figure 4.1, Panel B).

- Much of the additional coverage would result from an expanded EI measure. Several categories of workers currently excluded from EI benefits could come under the measure's protection if affiliation became mandatory for self-employed persons; if voluntary affiliation encompassed contributing family workers; and if jobseekers in voluntarily unemployment were not disqualified from EI altogether but penalised, instead, through a benefit sanction of some duration.
- Millions of workers ever year who experience sickness would also gain income support if EI (or another social insurance measure altogether) could provide cash sickness benefits. This new protection could cover the entire workforce and be complemented for salaried workers through employers' liability. BLSP could provide a secondary tier of (means-tested) income support for those ineligible for cash sickness benefits or who have exhausted their entitlement.
- Finally, the remaining coverage gaps for poor households could be addressed via better support opportunities for contributing family workers under EITC and by gradually phasing out of BLSP's family support obligation alongside efforts to improve the actual take-up of EITC and BLSP.

Figure 4.1. Stylised social protection coverage in Korea – status quo and potential

A. Social protection coverage of the working-age population in Korea today

		Social protection in case of unemployment	Social protection for work absence due to sickness	Social protection against poverty
Employed	Regular salaried employees			M
	Non-regular salaried employees	(only some*)		M
	Self-employed persons	V		M
	Contributing family workers			
Unemployed	With adequate UI contributions			M
	- Of which are voluntarily unemployed	(disqualification)		M
	With inadequate/exhausted UI entitlement	M^		M
	- Of which have potential family support	M^		
	New labour market entrants	M^		M

B. Social protection coverage of the working-age population in Korea after implementation of all reforms

		Social protection in case of unemployment	Social protection for work absence due to sickness	Social protection against poverty
Employed	Regular salaried employees		L	M
	Non-regular salaried employees		L	M
	Self-employed persons			M
	Contributing family workers	V	V	M
Unemployed	With adequate UI contributions			M
	- Of which are voluntarily unemployed	(with sanction)		M
	With inadequate/exhausted UI entitlement	M^	M	M
	- Of which have potential family support	M^	M	M
	New labour market entrants	M^	M	M

Legend:
- ● Employment insurance (EI)
- ● Employment Success Package Programme (ESPP)
- ● Basic Livelihood Support Payment (BLSP)
- ● Earned Income Tax Credit (EITC)

"M" indicates coverage is conditional on a means test. "V" indicates coverage is available but only on a voluntary basis. "L" indicates employers' liability protections are also in place.

Note: Information assumes local nationality status (i.e. excludes non-national workers). *: Some non-regular salaried workers are excluded from EI coverage, such as dependent self-employed workers, seasonal workers and domestic workers, among others. ^: Two broad groups are exempted from a means test under ESPP – certain "vulnerable groups" under type-1 programmes and jobseekers aged 18-34 under type-2 programmes.
Source: Authors' own compilation.

The combined effect of such changes would be a more comprehensive social protection system with significantly broadened coverage. A large part of income support would be means-tested, except for a temporary period of unemployment and sickness that would be covered through insurance benefits. All participants would be subjected to a robust activation and rehabilitation framework.

Conclusion

Korea faces a challenging task to close the many blind spots in the coverage of its social protection measures while delivering income and employment support to a greater number of vulnerable jobseekers and low-income workers. In a labour market replete with non-regular and informal work arrangements, self-employment and a dominance of micro-businesses, the path to success is not straightforward.

Korea's incredible economic development now gives policy makers the fiscal space to upgrade existing social protection measures and expand the system still further. The opportunity is also there for streamlining the system, as a whole, and finally addressing its remaining enforcement gaps. Any further reform will have a stronger impact if policy makers further address Korea's widespread labour market dualities and eliminate the incentives for employers to hire workers on a non-regular basis.

The characteristics of Korea's labour market place it in a somewhat unique position. Providing adequate income and employment support may be more difficult but, potentially, enhanced social protection measures will bring about a brighter situation for workers and their families. It is unclear what shape Korea's labour market will take in the future but labour markets in most OECD countries are changing, with developments characterised by a growth in new forms of non-regular work (such as "gig economy" or "platform-based" work) often similar in nature to self-employment. Addressing Korea's current social protection deficits can therefore go a long way towards preparing its institutions for the future. Many countries are currently struggling to provide social protection coverage for the newly-arising forms of work, putting social protection reform squarely back on the agenda. Not too long from now, other OECD countries might well turn to Korea to learn how to manage a more fragmented labour market. When that time comes, Korea's institutions should show that they are fit for purpose.

ORGANISATION FOR ECONOMIC CO-OPERATION AND DEVELOPMENT

The OECD is a unique forum where governments work together to address the economic, social and environmental challenges of globalisation. The OECD is also at the forefront of efforts to understand and to help governments respond to new developments and concerns, such as corporate governance, the information economy and the challenges of an ageing population. The Organisation provides a setting where governments can compare policy experiences, seek answers to common problems, identify good practice and work to co-ordinate domestic and international policies.

The OECD member countries are: Australia, Austria, Belgium, Canada, Chile, the Czech Republic, Denmark, Estonia, Finland, France, Germany, Greece, Hungary, Iceland, Ireland, Israel, Italy, Japan, Korea, Latvia, Luxembourg, Mexico, the Netherlands, New Zealand, Norway, Poland, Portugal, the Slovak Republic, Slovenia, Spain, Sweden, Switzerland, Turkey, the United Kingdom and the United States. The European Union takes part in the work of the OECD.

OECD Publishing disseminates widely the results of the Organisation's statistics gathering and research on economic, social and environmental issues, as well as the conventions, guidelines and standards agreed by its members.

OECD PUBLISHING, 2, rue André-Pascal, 75775 PARIS CEDEX 16
(81 2018 01 1 P) ISBN 978-92-64-28824-9 – 2018

www.ingramcontent.com/pod-product-compliance
Ingram Content Group UK Ltd.
Pitfield, Milton Keynes, MK11 3LW, UK
UKHW051503290926
15471UKWH00008B/1387

9 789264 288249